Why Do You Need this New Edition?

If you're wondering why you should buy this new edition of *Writing Places*, take a look at the new readings that explore the questions below.

Where Are We From?

- **Mobility:** Kathryn Carey, a University of Michigan undergraduate, describes her attempts to negotiate the cultural differences between the Upper and Lower Peninsulas in Michigan ("Say yah to da U.P., eh?").

- **Questioning Mobility:** "The Most Radical Thing You Can Do" by Rebecca Solnit explores the radical concept of staying put, and how and why that isn't an option for many groups of people.

Where Are We?

- **Food Politics:** Student writer Alayne Brown's essay "The Effects of Fast Food Restaurants on the Caribbean People" explores her Caribbean heritage and examines the dramatic shifts taking place in the diets of Caribbean people influenced by Western food supplies.

- **Shifting Populations:** "Refugees Find Hostility and Hope on Soccer Field," a **New York Times** feature by Warren St. John, explores the racial and community struggles facing foreign war refugees in Clarkston, Georgia.

Where Are We Going?

- **Natural Disasters:** "Apocalypse: What Disasters Reveal" by Pulitzer Prize winner Junot Diaz explores the social causes and reverberations of Haiti's devastating earthquake and provokes readers to become apocalyptic thinkers.

- **Social Media:** In "Social Movements in the Age of Social Media: Participatory Politics in Egypt," S. Craig Watkins writes about the evolving role of Twitter, Facebook, and other media in global politics and our sense of place.

- **Evolving Cities and Towns:** In his essay, "Borderland/Borderama/Detroit," Jerry Herron explores the past, present, and future of a struggling city. In Jonathan Lerner's "How Urban Planning Can Improve Public Health," he urges planners to (re)create cities that promote healthy and sustainable living. In "Elm City," student writer Kevin Savage explores his family's role in a small central-Illinois town, as his family and the town itself have changed over the years.

- The newly revised **Tools for Getting Places** chapter has several new "Tools for Exploring," including Mobile Apps, Networked Scavenger Hunts, Hyperlocal News and Blogging, Citizen Science, and Maps and Geographic Data.

PEARSON

Writing Places

Other readers featured in the "Longman Topics" series include:

Writing Places

SECOND EDITION

PAULA MATHIEU
Boston College

GEORGE GRATTAN
Earthwatch Institute

TIM LINDGREN
Boston College

STACI SHULTZ
St. Thomas Aquinas College

PEARSON

Boston   Columbus   Indianapolis   New York   San Francisco   Upper Saddle River
Amsterdam   Cape Town   Dubai   London   Madrid   Milan   Munich   Paris   Montreal   Toronto
Delhi   Mexico City   Sao Paulo   Sydney   Hong Kong   Seoul   Singapore   Taipei   Tokyo

Executive Editor: Katharine Glynn
Executive Marketing Manager: Sandra McGuire
Production Manager: S.S. Kulig
Project Coordination, Text Design, and Electronic
    Page Makeup: S4Carlisle Publishing Services
Cover Design Manager: Wendy Ann Fredericks
Cover Image: Tim Lindgren
Senior Manufacturing Buyer: Dennis Para
Printer/Binder: Edwards Brothers
Cover Printer: Demand Production Center

Credits and acknowledgments borrowed from other sources and
reproduced, with permission, in this textbook appear on the
appropriate page within text [or on page 235].

Library of Congress Cataloging-in-Publication Data
Writing places / edited by Paula Mathieu . . . [et al.].
    p. cm.—(A Longman topics reader)
    Includes bibliographical references.
    ISBN 978-0-321-84548-1—ISBN 0-321-84548-X 1. Readers—
Geography. 2. Geography—Problems, exercises, etc. 3. English
language—Rhetoric—Problems, exercises, etc. 4. Report writing—
Problems, exercises, etc. 5. College readers. I. Mathieu, Paula.
    PE1127.G4W76 2012
    808'.0427—dc23
                                                2012025171

10 9 8 7 6 5 4 3 2 1—EDW—16 15 14 13 12

www.pearsonhighered.com

ISBN 10:   0-321-84548-X
ISBN 13: 978-0-321-84548-1

This anthology is dedicated to all the threatened places on this planet and to all the people—writers, students, *flâneurs*, activists, and others—working to understand, portray, and protect them.

*New for this edition.

Food Production and Consumption

Commuting and Transportation

Work and Workplace Conditions

The Natural World and the Built World

Travel, Leisure, and Exploration

Technology and Place

WHY DOES PLACE MATTER?

Writing Places invites students to develop writing skills through an inquiry into places from their past, present, and future. The act of *place writing* involves researching and writing about both familiar and new locales via a range of inquiry methods and writing genres. This anthology combines an eclectic range of place-based essays written by professional writers, community members, and college students whose work spans geographic areas across the United States and beyond—from Colorado to Egypt, Massachusetts to Haiti, North Dakota to the Caribbean. We feel the range of writers from professional to student is important, not as a model/anti-model approach, but because it presents place writing from people of different literal and metaphorical ages and locations, at different places in their own lives and in their development as writers. All of the essays were chosen as powerful examples of writers seeking to engage places important to them. Taken together, the essays showcase a variety of methods for inquiring into and researching places—from observation, interviewing, and memoir to library and web-based research. For each reading, *Writing Places* offers questions and activities to encourage students' own explorations of places. The book concludes with a toolkit of skills and exercises geared to helping students observe, remember, explore, record, research, and write.

WHAT'S NEW IN THE SECOND EDITION . . .

Writing Places continues to strike a unique balance among professional, student, and community writers who explore a variety of places from unique perspectives. But in this edition, we have added several new essays from professional authors—such as Pulitzer Prize winner Junot Diaz and media specialist Craig S. Watkins—and introduce exciting new student essays. Our new content includes the following:

Where Are We From?

- *Mobility:* Kathryn Carey, a University of Michigan undergraduate, describes in her essay her attempts to negotiate the cultural differences between the Upper and Lower Peninsulas in Michigan ("Say yah to da U.P., eh?").
- *Questioning Mobility:* "The Most Radical Thing You Can Do" by Rebecca Solnit explores the radical concept of staying put, and how and why that isn't an option for many groups of people.

Where Are We?

- *Food Politics:* "The Effects of Fast Food Restaurants on the Caribbean People" by Alayne Brown explores this student writer's Caribbean heritage and examines the dramatic shifts taking place in the diets of Caribbean people influenced by Western food supplies.
- *Shifting Populations:* "Refugees Find Hostility and Hope on Soccer Field," a *New York Times* feature by Warren St. John, explores the racial and community struggles facing foreign war refugees in Clarkston, Georgia.

Where Are We Going?

- *Natural Disasters:* "Apocalypse: What Disasters Reveal" by Junot Diaz explores the social causes and reverberations of Haiti's devastating earthquake and provokes readers to become apocalyptic thinkers.
- *Social Media:* In "Social Movements in the Age of Social Media: Participatory Politics in Egypt," S. Craig Watkins writes about the evolving role of Twitter, Facebook, and other media in global politics and our sense of place.
- *Evolving Cities and Towns:* In his essay "Borderland/Borderama/Detroit," Jerry Herron explores the past, present, and future of a struggling city. In Jonathan Lerner's "How Urban Planning Can Improve Public Health," he urges planners to (re)create cities that promote healthy and sustainable living. In "Elm City," student writer Kevin Savage explores his family's role in a small central-Illinois town, as his family and the town itself have changed over the years.

Our updates allow readers and writers to explore new places and to bring new questions to the places we all explore.

Our unique Tools for Getting Places chapter includes several new "Tools for Exploring" that reflect explosive shifts in the number and type of online and mobile tools in the past five years: Mobile Apps, Networked Scavenger Hunts, Hyperlocal News and Blogging, Citizen Science, and Maps and Geographic Data. We hope this new edition illustrates our continued commitment to evolving conversations about places as fruitful topics of inquiry and the ways in which these conversations can inform composition classrooms.

WRITING PLACES . . .

allows students to learn important writing and academic skills . . .

Asking students to examine and write about a place—whether a favorite haunt or a new locale on a campus, in a city, or in the wild—invokes questions and issues that are simultaneously personal, social, and academic. How students initially remember or respond to a given place depends on their individual experiences; that impression can also be formed, changed, or challenged by the broader social and environmental contexts of the place itself, its history and changing dynamics. Observing, listening, interviewing, researching the past and present, and placing oneself within larger social structures and ongoing debates are all skills gained from encountering places as a writing student. As students become attentive observers and participants in a variety of places, they also practice the writing skills critical to academic success.

in ways that provoke innovative and engaging essays . . .

In any writing classroom, the simple question "Where are you from?" can evoke an amazingly rich variety of locales, stories, and histories in response. As a teacher, when you encourage students to write about places, you will likely receive essays on topics that are wide-ranging, specific, and, best of all, interesting to read. Place writing allows students to bring their personal histories and experience to bear while encountering new places and developing new academic skills. When asking students to write about and attend to places, you can teach skills important to academic success—including careful observation, critical thinking, and accurate recording—while encouraging students to explore questions important to the places from their pasts, the changing places around them today, and their individual and collective future places in the world.

in a spirit of personal, cultural, and academic inquiry . . .

Writing Places assumes that students learn writing most organically when engaged in relevant, intellectual inquiries. Working from that assumption, we have organized this collection around three simple, yet essential questions: Where Are We From? Where Are We? Where Are We Going? Learning from our pasts, attending to present places, and imagining and working toward specific futures are all hallmarks of conscientious students and mindful citizens. *Writing Place* underscores the role writing can play in thinking through and debating issues of personal and social importance. Additional possibilities for inquiry—centered on topics such as technology, food production, the environment, and globalization—are offered in our alternative table of contents.

in a small, inexpensive book that can be used flexibly, in a variety of courses, in a variety of ways.

We, the four editors of this collection, each come to the topic of *place writing* from different geographic starting points and different intellectual motivations—including cultural studies, environmental studies, technological concerns, and pedagogical interests—and as such, we do not teach the same writing classes in the same way. (In fact, some of us no longer teach writing in traditional classroom settings at all, and are instead engaged in writing and thinking about place in different arenas such as education technology and curriculum development, and place-based volunteering efforts.) Additionally, none of us has ever liked to ask students to buy large, expensive readers for one short semester. Our goal has been to offer a collection that is concise but flexible. *Writing Places* compiles a range of student and professional essays that can be used in a variety of classes with various inquiries from which to choose and design your own place-writing course. Because the needs of writing instructors and students differ, we also include "Tools for Getting Places," a collection of exercises and resources for helping students learn to observe, interview, and research places.

ACKNOWLEDGMENTS

The creation of *Writing Places* involved collaborations that extended well beyond the four authors and our editor, and we wish to give our thanks to all those who helped us.

We wish to thank the faculty, students, and volunteers from our respective academic and professional institutions—Boston College, University of Michigan, Wesleyan College, St. Thomas Aquinas College, College of the Holy Cross, and Earthwatch—who continue to generate such dynamic discussions of place-based writing and who have provided support and inspiration in a variety of ways. We particularly thank our former and current students, and especially the student authors included in this volume: Alayne Brown, Kathryn Carey, Andrea Casassa, Robin Dunn, Sonny Fabbri, Kevin Savage, and Kimberly Wheaton. These writers earned our considerable appreciation and respect for their diligence and goodwill during the editing process.

Thank you to our editor, Katharine Glynn, for encouraging the second edition of this project and for her ongoing patience and support. Thanks also to our assistant editor, Rebecca Gilpin, for helping us keep track of all the details involved in preparing the second edition.

Thanks to the writers and editors at the *Journal of Ordinary Thought* for presenting such important, ongoing examples of "ordinary" people writing about the places around them. Thank you as well to the contributors to *Orion Magazine*; *Places: Forum of Design for the Public Realm;* the *New York Times*; *Transformative Works and Cultures*; Beacon Broadside; and *Boston Review* who allowed us to reprint their work in this collection.

Derek Owens, your work in place-based and sustainable composition continues to inspire us; we thank you for opening the door into this world and for supplying such wonderful examples.

Finally, thanks to all our friends and family who generously shared their own thoughts on place and identity and who continue to know more about place-based studies than they ever thought they would.

ORIENTING TO A PLACE

At most colleges and universities, orientation introduces students like you to a new campus. This introduction may involve dry lectures from administrators about financial aid and course registration, stacks of brightly colored handouts describing all the services and activities on campus, and enthusiastic orientation leaders organizing social events to ease the awkwardness of meeting new people.

While orientation is designed to introduce you to a new place, the actual process of orienting yourself occurs over a much longer period as you take classes, build friendships, and learn to work and study in this new environment. Knowledge of places, however, comes not only through time spent *in* them but also through attention paid *to* them. When we talk about attending to place, we refer to the meanings that we create in spaces ("place [equals] space [plus] meaning" is one common description of this dynamic), what we sometimes refer to as one's "sense of place." We believe that mindfulness about places—critical thinking, close observation, and personal reflection—can help us better understand ourselves and our environment while we also hone the very skills necessary for academic success.

WRITING ONE'S PLACE

Now that we have introduced the topic of academic success, you may be wondering what the concept of place has to do with writing. Writing can help create a sense of place because writing is a fundamental way of making meaning, not just a way of getting a grade for a class or "expressing" innermost feelings. Because we often do not know what we think until we write it down, writing plays an important role in constructing a sense of place. At the same time, as we explore places, we learn to attend to details and value the complexity and dynamic nature of the everyday—skills important for any writer. Put simply, writing helps us understand places, and paying attention to places helps us become better writers.

For this reason, this book is organized around three guiding questions: Where are we from? Where are we? Where are we going? These may seem like simple questions, but in fact figuring out our relationships to various places is a lifelong process.

When writing in academic settings, we are often encouraged to think critically about how our identities are shaped by racial backgrounds, social classes, and gender and sexual identities. But *place* is often overlooked as a useful category for exploring who we are and what shapes us. Places are so fundamental—we cannot imagine life without them—yet we often take them for granted so that they recede into the background, like the scenery in a play. We focus on the actors, not on the set.

When we turn our attention to place, however, it can become a central character and we learn to relate to it on a deeper level. This increased attention may occur because the places we know well undergo change, because we encounter new places, or because we simply decide to be more mindful of places in general.

Writing makes sense only when it is put in meaningful context; taking a quote out of context often leads to misinterpretation or confusion. Similarly, our lives only make sense when we understand our sense of place in a broader context: both the physical make-up of that place—including things like buildings, trees, roads, size, weather, animals, concrete—and the shared social meanings associated with that place before we ever get there.

But it is not necessary to be a geography, environmental studies, or engineering major in order to explore both cultural and physical contexts; every discipline has something to contribute to the conversation, and in fact, we cannot fully understand where we are unless we can draw on diverse areas of knowledge. As you can tell by the Topical Table of Contents, there are numerous directions from which you can approach the topic of place, regardless of whether your major is business or biology, political science or computer science, art or agriculture.

Cultivating a critical sense of place does matter. If you are not able to do this, there is a good chance someone else will do it for you—advertisers who want you to buy their products or stay in their hotels, developers who want to change the neighborhood around you whether or not you agree to it, or companies that want to dump toxic waste near you despite its impact on your health. For this reason, the writers in this collection tend to ask hard questions about place: Who has the power to change places? Whose interests do these changes serve? How do places affect our health? How does our use of places affect their non-human inhabitants? How do the choices we make in local places affect the health of those in other countries? When does a place become unjust?

In addition to reading about these writers' places and considering some of their questions, you will also go out and explore some places from *your* past, present, and possible futures. In doing so, you will develop important writing and research skills that will serve you through your academic career and beyond. And by research, we mean many things: surfing the Internet and properly citing books and articles from the library are important forms of *secondary research*, but you will also practice skills of *primary research*—for instance, conducting your own interviews or carefully recording observations.

Writing in a college or university setting is a way to start some important conversations that you will continue, whether you return to the neighborhood you grew up in or move to another continent. In this book, you will encounter a group of writers engaged in this process at various stages of their lives, and their essays invite you to join in the conversation with your own writing. Whether written by other students your age or by professional writers with more experience, these essays offer positive examples of different approaches to exploring your sense of place, approaches that will vary widely based on your geographic location, your stage in school, and your unique life experiences. As you start writing about place, we hope you will find you are more interested in these topics than in traditional writing assignments and that the writing you produce matters more to you and the audiences for whom you write.

PAULA MATHIEU
GEORGE GRATTAN
TIM LINDGREN
STACI SHULTZ

Where Are We From?

Where are you from? It is a question you have likely asked—and answered—a thousand times, especially when meeting new people or traveling to unfamiliar places. We all rely on this seemingly simple question because it reveals crucial information about other people's histories and identities. But how often do you pose this question to yourself? How thoughtfully do you regard the places of your past? If who you are is bound up with the places you are from, it seems worthwhile to investigate those places of your past and how they have helped define you.

Pausing to consider where you're from seems particularly relevant when journeying from one place to another. For instance, you have likely begun considering the places you are from, even unconsciously, during your transition to college, whether you're coming from high school, military service, time in the workforce, traveling, or some other pursuit. Here are a few questions for you to answer as you begin to more deeply reflect on where you are from:

- Would you describe your hometown as urban, suburban, or rural?
- Would you describe it as rapidly changing or relatively stable?
- Were you raised in the same state or country where you were born? What meaning does your home state or country have for you?
- Does your family still live in the same house/apartment where you grew up? What is the first place that comes to mind when you think of "home"?
- How many cities, states, or countries have you lived in? Which ones, if any, feel like "home"?

- How would you describe the street on which you grew up? What would a visitor notice first?
- What places beyond your home were regular and important to you (a grandparent's house, a neighborhood gathering place, a wilderness area, a secret spot for you and your friends)?
- What public or semi-public spaces in your hometown or neighborhood were important to you or seemed to define the place (a park, store, school, church, community center)?
- Was there a place that was important to you (a park, meadow, open beach, store, or vacant lot) that is no longer there today and is now something else? How do you feel about the new place?
- Did your family travel, move around much, or vacation in certain places regularly?
- What are, or what were, the most noticeable or important features of the natural environment in the place you consider home or another place that's very important to you? Is it near the ocean? A river? A swamp? A forest? Mountains? Prairie or grassland? Does it have any particularly well-known animal populations, such as salmon, deer, or birds of any kind? What about any predominant crops, such as wheat, tobacco, or corn? Or any prominent wildflowers or grasses?
- What was the population of your hometown twenty years ago? What is it now?
- What are the most important or most noticeable aspects of the weather (or the climate in general) in the place you think of as home? Do you feel like these have changed in the last ten, fifteen, or twenty years?
- How might you describe the street where you grew up in terms of economics, traffic patterns, and neighbor relations? Did people take public transportation or drive to work? Did people hang out on the sidewalks and talk or have gated yards? How was your street different from others in your town, city, or state?

The contributing authors in this chapter have addressed many of these questions. Their essays vary in their style and purpose: some are persuasive, some are celebratory, and some are critical as they examine the traditions, families, communities, and landscapes that have helped shape their identities. What becomes clear is that the authors share a similar goal: discovering the often complex and symbolic meanings attached to the notion of place. For example, Kathryn Carey describes in her essay her attempts to negotiate the cultural differences between the Upper and Lower Peninsulas in Michigan ("Say yah to da U.P., eh?"), and Tim Lindgren argues against Hollywood's depiction of Fargo, North Dakota, while struggling to determine his own relationship to the city ("On Being from *Fargo*"). Whether writing about specific physical landmarks or more general cultural landscapes, the reflections of the writers in this section often fluctuate—from pride to despair to joy to all the other sentiments the places of our past can invoke.

To write about place means to write about yourself, which means tapping into your emotions to ultimately generate writing that is meaningful to you. Writing about place can serve as a vehicle for you to describe, research, narrate, and understand topics that are important to you, and to inform, entertain, move, and persuade readers. Working with topics that are inherently interesting to you, such as many of the issues that get raised when thinking and writing about the places you are from, will likely make your audience interested in them as well.

Like the authors in this chapter, you might find that your emotions and memories complicate how you understand yourself and the places you have encountered, which in turn makes answering the question of where you are from rather difficult. Your answer might be nuanced: "Well, I was born here but raised there," or "I am a native of there but a transplant to here," or "I consider several different places home." How you define home varies according to individual needs and associations. For instance, "home" could mean the place where you vacation every year, the coffee shop where you worked during high school, another country in which you spent a brief but significant time, the wilderness camp where you get to be by yourself, or wherever you are surrounded by friends or family. Chances are that none of your answers to the questions on the list are simple.

For some of us, our home is far from where we are now; home can mean that place to which we return occasionally, only to leave again. Because we live in an increasingly mobile culture, it is possible to consider more than one place home. On the one hand, this mobility offers the freedom to pursue opportunities in other places. Each new place represents a move from the past to the present to the future. On the other hand, this freedom can compromise our sense of stability, our rootedness in one place. No wonder, then, that our attachment to "home" seems tenuous, that just as we move from place to place, the places of our past seem to change in profound ways—or perhaps *we* are the ones who change.

But it is not just the changes in ourselves that we should consider. The places of our past have pasts as well, and as we reflect, research, and write about these places we should also think about how much they, too, change over time as well. Questions about the changes in population and traffic flow of a hometown or neighborhood attempt to get at the change that is almost inevitable everywhere we go. Whether we define this change as progress or destruction depends on our attachment to and understanding of a particular place. Over the next few years, the place you call home might undergo tremendous change, whether it be to the physical landscape or socioeconomic climate. Do such changes reflect changes on a national or even global level? How will these changes affect you? How will they affect your understanding of the places you inhabit now, such as your university?

All college students share at least one place in common: their campus. The university setting can bring together students from various parts of a city, state, country, or even the world. But this migration to one common place can disrupt connections to home places and destabilize an ingrained sense of identity. The authors in this chapter recall places as disparate as Washington State's Grand Coulee Dam and a coffee shop in suburban Hopkinton, Massachusetts, and reflect on their transitions from one place to another and the disruptions that accompany their journeys. As a group, they contribute to a national and intergenerational experience of past places.

Where we are from colors our present and future experiences: It helps shape our political views, our responses to environmental concerns, and our positions on social issues. The places of our past inform our present and future sense of place, community, and self. Throughout this book, we ask you to examine the places that shape who you are—and how you shape them. In this chapter, we will ask you to think specifically about where you are from and to reflect on the interplay of the physical and socioeconomic landscapes and your perceptions, memories, and identities of those places.

Mom and the Kitchen
KIMBERLY WHEATON

Kimberly Wheaton attended Phillips Exeter Academy in New Hampshire and is a 2005 graduate of Boston College. This essay comes from Wheaton's Lodge, *a longer nonfiction narrative that she wrote for a first-year writing seminar.* "Mom and the Kitchen" *illustrates Wheaton's personal connection to her family's fishing lodge in Maine where she was born and raised.*

———————— ✦ ————————

She looks back at me, dishcloth in one hand, spatula in the other, and finishes her sentence, " . . . but these women deserve a raise every year. I'm just worried that if we keep on going at this rate your father and I will be in debt by the time we retire!" She scratches her nose with her wrist—the only part of her forearm free of turkey grease.

"I know it's hard, Mom," I reply empathetically, "but if you ask me, I don't think they'd take another job for the world. They tell me that they appreciate everything you do for them while they clean the cabins. I mean, what other boss buys each employee a fifty-dollar gift at the end of the working season? I don't think they would even question your decision to deny them *another* raise . . . at this point in their careers, they've probably forgotten how much they earn anyway!"

Mom considers my response but conscientiously returns to her original thought, "Oh I know, but it's a matter of being fair, and if I were in their position I would expect a larger paycheck. They are certainly worth it! I'm just getting tired," she says, as if to scold herself for dwelling on the issue of money. "It's that time of the season again."

The calendar hanging above the dinner table indicates Mom's point. It *is* that time of the season: September ninth, less than a month left until closing time. It is filled with colorful scenes drawn by guides and kitchen women who collectively agree that a countdown for the end of the season is in order. Each day a worker digs into the basket of my old markers and crayons, and carefully sketches something in his or her designated square. The traditional calendar countdown helps us all maintain optimism and a sense of humor during a time when most workers (including my parents) become frustrated with the business and its necessity for constant attention. The first drawing is made when there is one month left of work—one month until "the end of the year party" that is held in the dining room to celebrate another great season. The latest drawing is signed by Mitchell, an old fishing guide who used to hand me butterscotch candies when Mom and Dad weren't looking. His artwork exhibits a guest (whom he hopes will catch a glimpse of his clever idea) fishing, but on the end of the guest's line are the feces of the fish on his own line. I remember hearing him chuckle as he drew this after a long day out on the lake.

5   Mom continues to talk as soon as I look back from the calendar, "Mr. Gwirtzman came up from his camp last night because his father keeled over in chest pains. We called an ambulance and luckily the old fella got back on his feet by the time it got here, thank goodness. It's ridiculous how long it takes the Houlton ambulance to get all the way out here to Forest City—almost an hour! I would just hate to think about what'd happen if old Mr. Gwirtzman's pain had continued. All I can say is it's been a long day following a long night." She begins to saw through the clean turkey with a loud electric knife, but pauses after three slices. "So, what's on the docket for the day, Kimbo?" she inquires, hoping to free her mind of the morning trifles involved in serving breakfast, and the wages of the kitchen crew.

My ambitions hardly compare to hers but I reply, "I might try the new kayaks out." Actually, my agenda only involves getting back to this very table to taste the buttermilk squash, stuffed turkey, and sugar snapped peas on the menu for tonight.

She moves from counter to counter in the large but orderly kitchen, with no more haste than brushing her teeth. While watching these mechanical movements, I ask, "Don't you get sick of this, day in and day out?" but realize immediately that my harsh reaction contradicts her daily optimism.

"I don't have time to get sick of it," she says with a smirk. "The good thing about this job is that as there is a beginning, there is also an end—but even the end wasn't as promising back when your father and I started out. I can remember going to bed with a Betty Crocker book every night, trying to learn recipes so it didn't take me five times to boil an egg. Believe me, I was probably more clueless back then than you would be if you took this place over now. It took some time to get used to the cooking, the desk-work, the cleaning . . . and everything else that goes along with the job, especially when you and your sister were first born. God bless you, but I got so little sleep that I started having panic attacks! Your dad would be exhausted from guiding fisherman out in the sun all day, and so it took us every bit of strength to get up with you in the middle of the night.

"But as far as that goes, I wouldn't have missed having you girls for the world. In fact, when you started getting older, I would set aside about two hours every night to read to you—even when we had guests who wanted to talk with us in the lobby. I figured that your father could handle that part of the business on his own. I knew that if I didn't get my time in with you while I still could, it would come back to haunt me later on. That was the best part of my day, reading to you girls. I could get off my feet and away from the chaos of this place, spending time with the greatest kids in the world." She winks at me, puts the electric knife down since she has finished dressing the turkey, and washes her hands. I am always amazed at the amount of cooking she does, separately from our two cooks. She rarely sits down, unless it is at the desk to fill out fishing licenses for guests or to book reservations from phone conversations. She momentarily breaks from the action, however, when she returns to the topic of the kitchen women.

"They were so helpful when you girls were young. First of all, you were a lot easier to handle than your sister. It's a wonder we even decided to have another child after the way she used to cry. But you, oh you were great. During dinner, while we all sat eating around the table, you would sleep peacefully in the center. The women may not be the most educated crew, but they sure know how to handle a baby. It was and still is great having them work here since they're like an extended family." She pauses for a moment, and I can sense her new train of thought. "But sometimes our closeness has repercussions. As you know, I'm already uncomfortable in the position of 'boss,' so it's hard to voice my mind when something needs to be done differently in the dining room or during cleaning. When a guest is unhappy, it's essential that I inform the women of what needs to be done, and I just hate instructing people who I consider to be my equals—especially those equals who helped raise my own two children! Granted, they do the job just as precisely as I would most of the time, so there is no need for excessive criticism."

I chuckle to show that I'm still listening, and she carries on. "Your father has an easier time directing the guides. If something

10

they do is not correct, or isn't done efficiently, he will tell them straight out. Men are very different than women when it comes to constructive advice. Your father doesn't understand why I can't treat the kitchen crew like the guides, but I tell him that if I did, we wouldn't *have* a kitchen crew!

Mom's tone becomes edgy as she speaks of Dad. I remember her telling me about how hard the fishing lodge is on a marriage. "It is a stressful job, and all of that stress falls on the little time I share with your dad." Despite hard times, though, they have managed to stay together, and now both Mom and Dad speak comically about being "too damn tired to split up."

In the summer, when the guests are taken care of, Mom is usually thinking about whether the lodge meets the guests' expectations. If the topic of business improvement arises, she will fully exhaust every possibility for change, until she cannot think aloud anymore. Usually these bursts of brainstorming end with: " . . . overall I think we do a pretty good job of keeping the customers happy. And the guests love the Maine culture—even if the accents and hard nature of the kitchen women. It all seems to come together from season to season, and that's why we keep coming back to work hard." Mom is in the middle of this contemplation as she washes her hands in the sink.

For a moment, I forget that I am in the kitchen with her. I revisit moments within the last week in which several guests have come up to me and complimented the lodge, the fishing, the meals, and the hospitality of the business. I reply to each comment with a "thank you," but cannot begin to take responsibility for the work behind such praise.

Guiding Questions

1. How would you describe Wheaton's mom? Why does Wheaton choose the kitchen as the backdrop for this essay?
2. How would you describe Wheaton's relationship with her mom? What moments in this narrative offer insight into their relationship?
3. What physical and/or sensory details does Wheaton focus on to give you a sense of the day-to-day realities of her mother's experience?
4. Can you imagine how the kitchen or the lodge in general might be described from the point of view of someone else Wheaton mentions in the essay, such as the women who work at the lodge, the fishing guides, her father, or a guest? What factors shape different people's experiences of the same place in this essay?

Paths for Further Exploration

1. Write a character sketch of a friend or relative. What place do you associate with that person?
2. Have you ever lived in the same place (or near) where you worked? Write about that experience if you have, or write about what you imagine that would be like if you have not.
3. Try writing about a place you know well from a point of view you don't. For example, if you've worked at a fast food restaurant, try describing it from the manager's or customers' point of view. Or if you're a field hockey or lacrosse player, write about the field from the point of view of a referee or coach.

A History in Concrete
BLAINE HARDEN

Blaine Harden has been a national correspondent for The New York Times *since April 2001 and a writer for the* Sunday New York Times Magazine *since January 1999. He is the author of* Africa: Dispatches from a Fragile Continent *and* A River Lost: The Life and Death of the Columbia. *In "A History in Concrete," Harden recalls his—and his father's—relationship to Washington's Grand Coulee Dam, a place that sustained father and son in different ways. The essay was first published in* Preservation *magazine. It also appears in the collection* A Certain Somewhere: Writers on the Places They Remember, *edited by Robert Wilson.*

--------------------- ✦ ---------------------

D own in the bowels of Grand Coulee Dam, you can feel the industrial-strength menace of the Columbia. The river, as it pounds through turbines, causes an unnerving trembling at the core of the largest chunk of concrete on the continent. Vibration jolts up from the steel flooring, through shoes and up legs, and lodges at the base of the spine, igniting a hot little flame of panic. The gurgle of water creeping through seams in the dam doesn't help.

Grand Coulee Dam won't hold still. And it does leak. Water sluices noisily through drainage galleries that line the fourteen miles of tunnels and walkways inside the dam. Engineers say all dams leak, they all tremble. It is absolutely harmless, completely normal, nothing to worry about. I don't trust engineers.

This gray monstrosity gives me the creeps. It has ever since I was ten, when my uncle Chester took me on a dam tour, fed me extra-hot horseradish at a scenic restaurant, and laughed until he cried when I spat out my burger. Ever since I learned from my father at the dinner table that this mile-wide monolith was the rock upon which our middle-class prosperity was built. Ever since I worked here in college and got myself fired.

The dam sits out in the middle of nowhere—the tumble-weed coulee country of north-central Washington, a wind-swept landscape of basalt cliffs and grayish soil. Seattle is a 240-mile drive west across the Cascade Mountains, which scrape moisture from the sky and leave the country around the dam in a rain-shadow desert. When construction began, *Collier's* magazine described the dam site as so hell-like that "even snakes and lizards shun it." For as long as I can remember, I have kept coming back to this unhandsome land to feel the addictive tingle of being near an object that is intimidating and essential and big beyond imagining.

5 And it is big. The Bureau of Reclamation, which built Grand Coulee in the 1930s in its crusade to turn every major Western river into a chain of puddles between concrete plugs, loves to talk bigness. The dam is so big, the bureau said, that its concrete could pour a sixteen-foot-wide highway from New York City to Seattle to Los Angeles and back to New York. So big that if it were a cube of concrete standing on a street in Manhattan, it would be two and a half times taller than the Empire State Building. As Franklin D. Roosevelt, who ordered the dam built, boasted, "Superlatives do not count for anything because it is so much bigger than anything ever tried before."

It was a tonic for the Great Depression and a club to whip Hitler, a first to smash the private utilities monopolies and a fountainhead for irrigated agriculture. The dam was a gloriously mixed metaphor validating the notion that God made the West so Americans could conquer it. Grand Coulee's turbines came online just as the United States entered World War II. It sated an unprecedented national appetite for electricity—to make, for example, aluminum for B-17 Flying Fortress aircraft at Boeing's Seattle plant and plutonium at the top-secret Hanford Atomic Works downriver. Without the dam, said Roosevelt's successor, Harry S. Truman, "it would have been almost impossible to win this war."

My hometown, Moses Lake, about an hour's drive south of the dam, owed its existence to Grand Coulee. Before the dam, the town was notable for its large jackrabbits and frequent sand-storms. It was a hard-luck town, where farmers worked until they wore themselves out, went broke, and moved away without regrets. Even the town fathers had admitted, before the dam, that Moses Lake had a certain pointlessness about it. As one chamber of commerce brochure put it, "Out of the desert a city was built. Some of the earliest homesteaders and settlers would ask, 'Why?' " When I grew up, the answer to that question was obvious. Everyone knew that life itself—at least life as lived in our prosperous farm community, with subsidized irrigation and the nation's cheapest electricity—would be impossible without the dam.

My father, the out-of-work eldest son of a failed Montana dirt farmer, joined four thousand men who were building the dam in early 1936. Arno Harden was a broom-and-bucket man, working in the gut of the construction site. Dams rise from the bedrock of a river in a series of rectangular pours stacked like dominoes, and before each pour, laborers must tidy up, hose down, and sand-blast every surface. Otherwise new concrete will not adhere, and cracks and structural weaknesses could cause the dam to fail. For fifty cents an hour, eight hours a day, six days a week, my father scooped up loose rocks and bits of wire and ensured that Grand Coulee would stand for generations.

He hated it, of course, but he did it until he had saved enough money to go to trade school and learn to be a first-class union welder. He then spent most of his working life building dams and welding at other federal projects along the Columbia. Because of the dams, my family was something other than poor, and I grew up in a handsome lakefront house with a bedroom for me and one for each of my three siblings, a new car in the driveway, and money in the bank for a private college.

The dam, though, meant far more than money to my father. 10
It had been the great adventure of his life. He lived at the construction site during six wild years when it was gluey mud in the winter, choking dust in the summer, and live music all night long. He and his brother frequented an unpainted, false-fronted saloon on B Street—a dirt road thick with cardsharps, moonshiners, pool hustlers, pickpockets, piano players, and a few women who, like everybody else, had come to town for money. An ex-con named Whitey Shannon employed fifteen dime-a-dance girls at the Silver Dollar, where the bartender, Big Jack, tossed out men who got too friendly with the ladies. A sweet-voiced crooner named Curly sang like Gene Autry, and between numbers a skinny kid shoveled dirt from the muddy boots off the dance floor. Mary Oaks, the dam's

telephone operator, took calls from B Street nearly every night: "The owners would say, 'We got a dead man over here and would you call the police.' If they weren't dead, of course, they would want a doctor."

As my father explained it at the kitchen table, Grand Coulee was an undiluted good. It may have killed more salmon than any dam in history and destroyed the lives of the Colville Indians, who centered their existence around the fish. It may have launched a dam-building craze that turned America's most powerful rivers into adjustable electricity machines. But that was not what I learned at home. I once asked my father if he thought it might have been a mistake to kill all those fish, dispossess all those Indians, and throttle the river. He did not understand the question.

My first real job was at the dam. Grand Coulee was expanding in the early 1970s, and my father used his connections to get me a summer job as a union laborer. It paid the then princely sum of five dollars an hour. My labor crew cleaned up bits of wire, half-eaten pickles, wads of spat-out chewing tobacco, and whatever else might be left behind by craftsmen higher up on the wage scale. This was the same job that my father had hated in the thirties.

I was nineteen, a rising sophomore at Gonzaga University in nearby Spokane, and very impressed with myself. I told my crew how boring our jobs were and how I could not wait to get back to school. Many of the laborers were middle-aged Indians with families. They kept their mouths shut and their eyes averted from me.

Federal inspectors nosed around after our work, spotting un-picked-up wire and other crimes. They complained to a superintendent, who complained to some other boss, who complained to an unhappy man named Tex, our foreman, who then yelled at me, the loudmouthed college boy. Tex wasn't much of a talker. When he did speak, he had an almost incomprehensible west Texas twang. *Wire* came out as *war.*

15 "Git off yer ass, pick up that war," he would instruct me after complaints about our cleanup job had trickled down the chain of command. We worked swing shift, four to midnight, near the spillway. The river, swollen in the summer of 1971 with heavy snowmelt from the Canadian Rockies, rioted over the dam twenty-four hours a day in a cascade eight times the volume of Niagara Falls and twice as high. The dam's base was a bedlam of whitewater and deep-throated noise, and when Tex shouted *"war"* in my face, I could never hear him. Along with the racket, cold spray geysered up, slathering the construction site in a slippery haze slashed at

night by hundreds of spotlights. The entire dam site—wrapped in the spray and yowl of the river—struck me as a death trap. At weekly safety meetings, I filled out lengthy reports on what I considered to be hazardous work practices.

By my fourth week at the dam, Tex had had enough. He told me at the end of the shift not to come back. He mumbled something about *war* and how I spent too much time on my butt when bosses were around. I slunk away from the river, driving home to Moses Lake after midnight. I barely managed not to cry. My father had paid for the Volvo I was driving, paid the eight-hundred-dollar initiation fee that got me into the Laborers' Union, and paid for a big slice of my college education. He had been shrewd enough to work much of his life for men like Tex without getting canned.

When I got home at 2 A.M., I left a note on the kitchen table. My father would be getting up in three hours to drive back up to Grand Coulee, where he was still a welder. The note said I was sorry for letting him down, which was true. What I did not say was that I was relieved to be away from that dam.

Twenty-three years later, I invited my eighty-two-year-old father to ride with me up to Grand Coulee. I would buy him lunch, and he would tell me everything he could remember about the dam. Like most father-son transactions, the deal favored me. But my father welcomed any excuse to look at the dam.

It was an abnormally hot Saturday in May. Snow in the mountains was melting, and water in the reservoir behind the dam was rising faster than the turbines could swallow. The river had to be spilled, a spectacle that only occurs once every few years. We had no idea this was happening until we drove down into the canyon that cradles the dam. Before we could see anything, we heard the dull thunder of falling water and rushed to the railed sidewalk overlooking the dam's spillway.

The river exploded as it fell, and the dam trembled beneath   20 our feet. We had to shout to talk. At the base of the spillway, three hundred feet below us, the Columbia seethed, boiling up a milky spray in the warm wind and turning a marbled green as it scuffled downstream. The din from the falling river and the vibration from the dam made my father smile. For him, it was a song from the thirties, a snatch of dance-hall music from B Street.

Neither of us had ever said a word over the years about that morning when I left him the note on the kitchen table, and it didn't come up that day, either. He had come into my bedroom before leaving for work and woken me up. He had told me it wasn't my fault that I got fired, although he must have known it was. He had said I was a good son.

Instead, as we stood together on that trembling dam, I told my father that the noise, the vibration, and the height scared me. He said it did not scare him, that it had never scared him.

Guiding Questions

1. What techniques does Harden use to create a character out of Grand Coulee Dam?
2. How would you describe the narrator's relationship to the dam?
3. Through Harden's descriptions of the dam, what do we learn about Moses Lake? About his connections to the town?
4. Harden ends his essay by noting the difference in his and his father's attitudes toward the dam. What does the last line reflect about Harden's relationship to his father?
5. Harden and Kimberly Wheaton, in her essay "Mom and the Kitchen," connect certain places with their parents. How do these places connect the generations, or do they? How do these two essays compare in terms of the authors' treatment of parents and places?

Paths for Further Exploration

1. Write a researched narrative about your hometown. Is there a specific place (building, park, monument, highway, or other major piece of public infrastructure) around which you might focus your narrative? What is the significance of that place?
2. Harden claims, "For as long as I can remember, I have kept coming back to this unhandsome land to feel the addictive tingle of being near an object that is intimidating and essential and big beyond imagining." Is there a place that inspires a similarly complicated response from you?
3. Explore a place in your hometown that has a different meaning for you than it does for someone in an older generation, and try to explain—through researching, interviewing, and writing—what accounts for those differences.
4. Research dams and their effects on the places where they are built. You might want to focus on large projects such as historic dams in the United States, such as the Grand Coulee or the Hoover Dam, or look at the many dam projects going on in China and some South American countries. Consider the environmental, economic, and social impacts of dams. If you have a dam in a place you know well, take a stand on whether it should be decommissioned (torn down), as many dams in New England, the Northwest, and elsewhere have been.

On Being from *Fargo*
TIM LINDGREN

Tim Lindgren is an instructional designer at Boston College. While completing his doctoral work in English, Tim focused his dissertation research on blogging and how writers use new media to help foster a deeper sense of place (www.placeblogging.com). His ongoing interests include social media, usability, open-source software, and mobile technologies.

———————————— ✦ ————————————

Where are you from?

It's an unsettling feeling to realize that you're no longer from where you thought you were from. I remember where I was when it happened, at a party where someone asked me where I was from. It marked a familiar turn in conversation, the moment when I would shift from new acquaintance to momentary novelty. "North Dakota," I answered, and when her eyes widened, I added, "Fargo." "Oh my God," she responded, looking up and turning away slightly to the left. Facing me again, she slowly said, "Oh . . . my God. No, really? You are from Fargo." A little taken aback by her enthusiasm, all I could muster was, "Yep, Fargo."

When she motioned to a friend and exclaimed, "He's from Fargo!" I realized something I probably had known unconsciously for quite some time. Most of my life I had been from Fargo, North Dakota. Now, however, this new acquaintance made it clear that I was from *Fargo*—the Coen brothers' 1996 film – and I would just have to get used to it.

Fargo, North Dakota

Since leaving home to attend college in Chicago, I've been having conversations about where I am from. For a long time, they usually took a similar form: "Where are you from?"– "Fargo, North Dakota." – "Really? I think you're the first person I've met who's from North Dakota." Before the Coen brothers' film, saying "North Dakota" meant I could look in my interlocutor's eyes and find a blank space on their mental maps just above South Dakota and below Canada, a tabula rasa of ignorance as pure white as the winter fields I encountered anew when home for the holidays recently.

As I drove on county highways north of Fargo, blowing snow blended the horizon into the clouds, erasing any sign of boundary to the white expanse of fields. In front of me snow flowed across the road, at one moment a stream of smoky white and the next moment a flock of wisps that tore and regrouped in flight, as if someone left their smoke machine on in Montana and a momentous wind was blowing it low across the plains. I passed a massive pile of decaying sugar beets with steam rolling off it in thick billows that faded just as they reached the road. This pervasive whiteness became the canvas for a late afternoon sundog, a winter rainbow made by airborne ice crystals that forms a nearly complete circle, except where its bottom edge dips just below the horizon.

5   A white blankness of the mind appeared each time someone ventured to me, "North Dakota, isn't that where Mount Rushmore is?" It was a friendly form of ignorance that I usually found empowering. By the time I gently let them know, "No, that's South Dakota," they had already commissioned me their myth-maker, letting me shatter their misconceptions if they had them or, if they did not, create a fresh portrait of Fargo they could call their own. Show me someone from Malibu or Manhattan, and I will show you a clean canvas prepared for the brush.

It was always difficult for my new myths not to start off sounding flat. Difficult because Fargo lies in one of the flattest spots in North America, in what was 9,000 years ago the bottom of a glacial lake. To grow up in Fargo is to see the world lying down, a horizontal life with no overlooks and all sky, with no vistas but the Twelfth Street overpass or the bird's-eye view when flying into Hector International Airport. Our only mountains were the thunderheads rolling in over the plains that I watched when working in the fields on college summer breaks, the dark gray Rockies that we could watch until the gust-front winds blew the first drops ahead and sent us running for the pickup.

To live in Fargo is to learn to walk backwards. Someone once said that in the Chinese view of time we back into the future, facing our past as we move into the unknown of what is to come. I often backed my way through the winters of my childhood, trudging with my front side shielded from the certainty of the North wind. In places where winters are rainy and wet, the cold will seep into your bones as you stand waiting for the train. But in Fargo, when it's 15 below with a brisk wind, the cold crashes in around you within seconds of walking out doors and drenches you within a minute. As you crunch and creak across the partially shoveled sidewalks, bodily fluids begin changing state—hair and eyelashes get crispy, snot begins to congeal. But this is only true of some days, and of only one season, and if you learn to walk backwards, keeping warm means you forget less quickly where you have been. So Fargo is flat and cold. The unspoken question I often face is "Why does anyone live there?" Believe it or not, I will often answer that Fargo was once rated the most desirable city in the nation, based on factors like cost of living, pollution, education, unemployment, and crime rate. Somehow the poll politely evaded the issue of the weather, but there is no doubt for me that Fargo was a fine place to grow up for all the reasons the ratings noticed. It is safe and clean, the schools are good, and the people are friendly. It's a college town with 25,000 students and a lively economy, and the winter weather is nothing you can't get used to.

Have you seen the movie?

There was a time when talking about where I was from gave me opportunity to act as advocate for my hometown, to save it from the East Coast cultured despisers or the West Coast cosmopolitans. However, after 1996 that blank gaze of ignorance I once relished became a look glazed over by a thick film called *Fargo*. For more than three years after the movie hit the box office, I lacked a convincing answer for why I had failed to see the movie. Usually I claimed to dislike violent movies, but in reality, I was simply unwilling to admit that I had a rival in representing where I'm from.

I had become comfortable having license to create people's   10 myth of Fargo, and now there was a movie out that usurped that role, that caricatured the natives of Minnesota and North Dakota, and did so under the title of my hometown. I have never been much of a movie critic, but since the movie *Fargo* came out, talking about where I am from has become a movie review.

So what did you think?

Once I finally saw the film, I was willing to admit that I liked it, though I hoped conversations would last long enough for me to voice a few modest criticisms. Normally I wouldn't have bothered, but this particular movie made things personal. Since the Coen brothers chose to call their film *Fargo* (where *I* grew up) even though the movie really takes place in Minneapolis and Brainerd, MN (near where *they* grew up), their attempt to represent their hometown impinged on my effort to figure out what it means to be from mine.

In the movie *Fargo*, Jerry Lundegaard, a car salesman from Minneapolis, hatches a scheme to deal with his mounting financial problems by hiring two thugs to abduct his wife so they can demand a ransom of $80,000 from his father-in-law to be split between him and the kidnappers. A series of murders ensues at the hands of the men Jerry has hired, and it falls to Marge Gunderson, a pregnant policewomen from Brainerd, MN, to investigate the increasingly violent consequences of Jerry's inept machinations.

The danger for the Coen brothers, like anyone who has moved away to one (often self-appointed) cultural power center or another, is that in representing their hometown they too often land at one of two extremes—idealization or disparagement. We usually idealize when we stand to benefit from associating ourselves with something that, in hindsight, appears superior to where we now live. We malign our hometown when we have more to gain by severing any associations with what seems to be a provincial, benighted past. Avoiding either extreme is the more difficult task.

As one *Washington Post* reviewer (originally from Fargo) put it, the problems with *Fargo* can be stated simply: too much violence, too much accent, too little Fargo. If I fault the Coen brothers for anything in *Fargo*, it is for what I see as a loss of nerve. When faced with a stark white landscape populated by simpleminded yokels, they couldn't resist the urge to splatter it with blood, as if violence was their preferred antidote against the risks of an unremarkable setting. As environmental activist, author, and cultural critic Wes Jackson once put it, "Any fool can appreciate California; it takes real character to appreciate Kansas."

Moreover, the caricatures of the Minnesota accent at moments sound like the graceless humor of someone who has been away too long, one who knows enough to do hilarious impersonations of Minnesotans at New York parties but has lost the ability to sustain nuanced humor through an entire movie. Minnesotans do not mind being made fun of—Garrison Keillor does it every Saturday night with his inimitable *A Prairie Home Companion* public radio show—but they have a right to expect that someone from Minnesota will avoid letting good-natured ribbing slip into body checking.

I liked it

Despite my initial frustrations with the film, I developed a fond-   15
ness for it by learning to adopt a Marge-centric perspective.
Marge is intelligent, acutely observant, and shrewdly witty. She
is tough-minded in doing her job but also deeply compassionate
in a brilliantly understated Minnesota way. She deals with crime
when it comes her way, but her robust affirmation of the everyday makes it clear that the "malfeasance" she investigates in no
way defines her life. Marge is not only the redemptive element in
an otherwise bleak story, but she also compensates for the Coen
brothers' loss of imaginative nerve in other aspects of the film.
The excessive violence may have seemed an artistic risk, but it was
not nearly as risky as having a heroine more brilliantly and tri-
umphantly ordinary than most of us were prepared to appreciate.

I like to imagine that Marge occasionally appears in the Coen
brothers' dreams, the voice of their repressed consciences, making them regret for just a moment that in representing where they
were from, they may have overdone a few things. Echoing her
lines at the end of the movie, she might say, "So I hear ya made
a movie about a string of murders up there in Minnesota then.
Even put a guy in a wood chipper. Ya, that sure was different.
Well I suppose when you've lived out East a while ya gotta throw a
guy in wood chipper once in while to make the old home country
seem a little more interesting. (Pause) Well, there's more ta making movies than being violent and ironic, ya know. (Pause) Don't
ya know that?"

In the end, I would like to believe that at some level the Coen
brothers, like me, were trying to answer the question, Where
are you from? If Marge was their best attempt to represent their
hometown, to tread a middle path between idealization and disparagement, I would say they did a pretty good job.

I have to admit I am still a bit sore that the movie broke up
a perfectly good monopoly on representation, making my job of
portraying Fargo a bit more challenging than it was before. But
I suppose a little competition never hurts. If the movie does not
literally represent where I am from, I am more willing to admit,
now, that the pictures I draw of Fargo also bear the marks of my
own idiosyncrasies and shortcomings. While I am originally from
the geographical place called Fargo, a place with a particular
landscape and a particular culture that has shaped me, the reality is that I no longer live there and I am shaped as much by the
story I am writing about *being from* Fargo as by physically being

there. If answering the question of where I am from has made me a movie critic, it also has made me more conscious of the myths I have created since leaving home.

20   "A lot can happen in the middle of nowhere" is the advertising catchphrase on the DVD rental box for *Fargo*, but the more I try to talk about where I am from, the more I have to believe that in fact quite a lot happened in Fargo before the movie came out, if for no other reason than because I grew up there and my family still lives there. And if it ever becomes "the middle of nowhere" in my imagination and in the stories I tell of it, if I ever become content either to malign or idealize it, then leaving there—being from there—has done me little good.

Guiding Questions

1. Lindgren writes, "By the time I gently let them know, 'No, that's South Dakota,' they had already commissioned me their myth-maker, letting me shatter their misconceptions if they had them or, if they did not, create a fresh portrait of Fargo they could call their own." How and why do we create myths about places? How would Lindgren respond to this question?
2. Examine Lindgren's rhetorical style. Is his initial organization around a conversation at a party effective?
3. What physical and environmental details does Lindgren use in his attempt to represent Fargo to you as a reader? Are they effective? Why or why not?
4. What is at stake for Lindgren in the inaccuracies depicted in the film version of the place where he is from? Do these inaccuracies complicate his sense of identity?

Paths for Further Exploration

1. What kinds of responses do you get when you tell people where you are from? What do they assume they know about that place, and why do they assume it? Script a conversation at a party between you and a new acquaintance in which you describe where you are from. What kinds of questions might the image of your hometown elicit from outsiders? What kind of myths would you have to dismantle?
2. What does it mean to represent a place? What are the various ways in which you represent your hometown? What kind of media do you use: oral storytelling and conversation? Writing? Photos? Videos? Hanging mementos on your wall? Wearing clothes with logos? Do these different media affect how you are able to represent a place?

3. "While it is true that I am from the geographical place called Fargo, a place with a particular landscape and a particular culture that has shaped me, it also true that now I no longer live there and I am shaped as much by the story I am writing about *being from* Fargo as by physically being there. If answering the question where I am from has made me a movie critic, it has also made me more conscious of the myths I have created since leaving home." What myths have you created about where you are from? What does it mean for you to participate in this myth-making process?
4. What factors authorize people to create the "definitive" stories about places? Who gets to say what New York City is like, or what it means for people to be from Kansas, or how it feels to have lived in both Florida and Paris?

The Ship-Shape
DAVID SEDARIS

David Sedaris's account of the summer his family considered the merits and pitfalls of owning a summer home first appeared in The New Yorker *in 2003. He is recognized for his humorous critique of the American family, and in this essay he notes the chronic pressure families experience when it comes to owning a house— or two. Sedaris has been featured on Public Radio International's* This American Life *and is the author of several plays as well as collections of essays and short stories, including* Naked, Me Talk Pretty One Day, Dress Your Family in Corduroy and Denim, *and, most recently,* Squirrel Seeks Chipmunk: A Modest Bestiary.

———————— ✦ ————————

My mother and I were at the dry cleaner's, standing behind a woman we had never seen. "A nice-looking woman," my mother would later say. "Well put together. Classy." The woman was dressed for the season in a light cotton shift patterned with oversize daisies. Her shoes matched the petals and her purse, which was black-and-yellow striped, hung over her shoulder, buzzing the flowers like a lazy bumblebee. She handed in her claim check, accepted her garments, and then expressed gratitude for what she considered to be fast and efficient service. "You know," she said, "people talk about Raleigh but it isn't really true, is it?"

The Korean man nodded, the way you do when you're a foreigner and understand that someone has finished a sentence. He wasn't the owner, just a helper who'd stepped in from the back, and it was clear he had no idea what she was saying.

"My sister and I are visiting from out of town," the woman said, a little louder now, and again the man nodded. "I'd love to stay awhile longer and explore, but my home, well, one of my homes is on the garden tour, so I've got to get back to Williamsburg."

I was eleven years old, yet still the statement seemed strange to me. If she'd hoped to impress the Korean, the woman had obviously wasted her breath, so who was this information for?

5   "My home, well, one of my homes"; by the end of the day my mother and I had repeated this line no less than fifty times. The garden tour was unimportant, but the first part of her sentence brought us great pleasure. There was, as indicated by the comma, a pause between the words "home" and "well," a brief moment in which she'd decided, Oh, why not? The following word—"one"—had blown from her mouth as if propelled by a gentle breeze, and this was the difficult part. You had to get it just right or else the sentence lost its power. Falling somewhere between a self-conscious laugh and a sigh of happy confusion, the "one" afforded her statement a double meaning. To her peers it meant, "Look at me, I catch myself coming and going!" and to the less fortunate it was a way of saying, "Don't kid yourself, it's a lot of work having more than one house."

The first dozen times we tried it our voices sounded pinched and snobbish, but by midafternoon they had softened. We wanted what this woman had. Mocking her made it seem hopelessly unobtainable, and so we reverted to our natural selves.

"My home, well, one of my homes . . . " My mother said it in a rush, as if she were under pressure to be more specific. It was the same way she said, "My daughter, well, one of my daughters," but a second home was more prestigious than a second daughter, and so it didn't really work. I went in the opposite direction, exaggerating the word "one" in a way that was guaranteed to alienate my listener.

"Say it like that and people are going to be jealous," my mother said.

"Well, isn't that what we want?"

10   "Sort of," she said. "But mainly we want them to be happy for us."

"But why should you be happy for someone who has more than you do?"

"I guess it all depends on the person," she said. "Anyway, I suppose it doesn't matter. We'll get it right eventually. When the day arrives I'm sure it'll just come to us."

And so we waited.

At some point in the mid- to late nineteen-sixties, North Carolina began referring to itself as "Variety Vacationland." The words were stamped onto license plates, and a series of television commercials reminded us that, unlike certain of our neighbors, we had both the beach and the mountains. There were those who bounced back and forth between one and the other, but most people tended to choose a landscape and stick to it. We ourselves were Beach People, Emerald Isle People, but that was mainly my mother's doing. I don't think our father would have cared whether he took a vacation or not. Being away from home left him anxious and crabby, but our mother loved the ocean. She couldn't swim, but enjoyed standing at the water's edge with a pole in her hand. It wasn't exactly what you'd call fishing, as she caught nothing and expressed neither hope nor disappointment in regard to her efforts. What she thought about while looking at the waves was a complete mystery, yet you could tell that these thoughts pleased her, and that she liked herself better while thinking them.

One year our father waited too late to make our reservations, and we were forced to take something on the sound. It wasn't a cottage but a run-down house, the sort of place where poor people lived. The yard was enclosed by a chain-link fence and the air was thick with the flies and mosquitoes normally blown away by the ocean breezes. Midway through the vacation a hideous woolly caterpillar fell from a tree and bit my sister Amy on the cheek. Her face swelled and discolored, and within an hour, were it not for her arms and legs, it would have been difficult to recognize her as a human. My mother drove her to the hospital, and when they returned she employed my sister as Exhibit A, pointing as if this were not her daughter but some ugly stranger forced to share our quarters. "This is what you get for waiting until the last minute," she said to our father. "No dunes, no waves, just this."

From that year on, our mother handled the reservations. We went to Emerald Isle for a week every September and were always oceanfront, a word that suggested a certain degree of entitlement. The oceanfront cottages were on stilts, which made them appear if not large, then at least imposing. Some were painted, some were sided, "Cape Cod style," with wooden shingles, and all of them had names, the cleverest being "Loafer's Paradise." The owners had cut their sign in the shape of two moccasins resting side by side. The shoes were realistically painted and the letters were bloated and listless, loitering like drunks against the soft faux leather.

15

"Now that's a sign," our father would say, and we would agree. There was The Skinny Dipper, Pelican's Perch, Lazy Daze, The Scotch Bonnet, Loony Dunes, the name of each house followed by the name and home town of the owner. "The Duncan Clan—Charlotte," "The Graftons—Rocky Mount," "Hal and Jean Starling of Pinehurst": signs that essentially said, "My home, well, one of my homes."

While at the beach, we sensed more than ever that our lives were governed by luck. When we had it—when it was sunny—my sisters and I felt as if we were somehow personally responsible. We were a fortunate family, and therefore everyone around us was allowed to swim and dig in the sand. When it rained, we were unlucky, and stayed indoors to search our souls. "It'll clear after lunch," our mother would say, and we would eat carefully, using the placemats that had brought us luck in the past. When that failed, we would move on to Plan B. "Oh, Mother, you work too hard," we'd say. "Let us do the dishes. Let us sweep sand off the floor." We spoke like children in a fairy tale, hoping our goodness might lure the sun from its hiding place. "You and Father have been so kind to us. Here, let us massage your shoulders."

If by late afternoon it still hadn't cleared, my sisters and I would drop the act and turn on one another, searching for the spoiler who had brought us this misfortune. Which of us seemed the least dissatisfied? Who had curled up on a mildewed bed with a book and a glass of chocolate milk, behaving as though the rain were not such a bad thing after all? We would find this person, most often my sister Gretchen, and then we would beat her.

20 The summer I was twelve, a tropical storm moved up the coast, leaving a sky the same mottled pewter as Gretchen's subsequent bruises, but the following year we started with luck. My father found a golf course that suited him, and for the first time in memory even he seemed to enjoy himself. Relaxing on the deck with a gin-and-tonic, surrounded by his toast-colored wife and children, he admitted that this really wasn't so bad. "I've been thinking, to hell with these rental cottages," he said. "What do you say we skip the middleman and just buy a place?"

He spoke in the same tone he used when promising ice cream. "Who's up for something sweet?" he'd ask, and we'd pile into the car, passing the Tastee-Freez and driving to the grocery store, where he'd buy a block of pus-colored ice milk reduced for quick sale. Experience had taught us not to trust him, but we wanted a beach house so badly it was impossible not to get caught up in the excitement. Even our mother fell for it.

"Do you really mean this?" she asked.

"Absolutely," he said.

The next day, they made an appointment with a real-estate agent in Morehead City. "We'll just be discussing the possibility," my mother said. "It's just a meeting, nothing more." We wanted to join them but they took only Paul, who was two years old and unfit to be left in our company. The morning meeting led to half a dozen viewings, and when they returned my mother's face was so impassive it seemed almost paralyzed. "It-was-fine," she said. "The-real-estate-agent-was-very-nice." We got the idea that she was under oath to keep something to herself, and the effort was causing her actual physical pain.

"It's all right," my father said. "You can tell them."   25

"Well, we saw this one place in particular," she told us. "Now, it's nothing to get worked up about, but . . ."

"But it's perfect," my father said. "A real beauty, just like your mother here." He came from behind and pinched her on the bottom. She laughed and swatted him with a towel and we witnessed what we would later come to recognize as the rejuvenating power of real estate. It's what fortunate couples turn to when their sex life has faded and they're too pious for affairs. A second car might bring people together for a week or two, but a second home can revitalize a marriage for up to nine months after the closing.

"Oh, Lou," my mother said. "What am I going to do with you?"

"Whatever you want, Baby," he said. "Whatever you want."

It was queer when people repeated their sentences, but we   30
were willing to overlook it in exchange for a beach house. My mother was too excited to cook that night, and so we ate dinner at the Sanitary Fish Market, in Morehead City. On taking our seats I expected my father to mention inadequate insulation or corroded pipes, the dark undersides of home ownership, but instead he discussed only the positive aspects. "I don't see why we couldn't spend our Thanksgivings here. Hell, we could even come for Christmas. Hang a few lights, get some ornaments, what do you think?"

A waitress passed the table and, without saying please, I demanded another Coke. She went to fetch it and I settled back in my chair, drunk with the power of a second home. When school began my classmates would court me, hoping I might invite them for a weekend, and I would make a game of pitting them against one another. This was what a person did when people liked him for all the wrong reasons, and I would grow to be very good at it.

"What do you think, David?" my father asked. I hadn't heard the question but said that it sounded good to me. "I like it," I said. "I like it."

The following afternoon our parents took us to see the house. "Now, I don't want you to get your hopes up too high," my mother said, but it was too late for that. It was a fifteen-minute drive from one end of the island to the other, and along the way we proposed names for what we had come to think of as our cottage. I'd already given it a good deal of thought but waited a few minutes before offering my suggestion. "Are you ready?" I said. "Our sign will be the silhouette of a ship."

Nobody said anything.

"Get it?" I said. "The shape of a ship. Our house will be called The Ship Shape."

"Well, you'd have to write that on the sign," my father said. "Otherwise nobody will get it."

"But if you write out the words you'll ruin the joke."

"What about The Nut Hut?" Amy said.

"Hey," my father said. "Now, there's an idea." He laughed, not realizing, I guess, that there already was a Nut Hut. We'd passed it a thousand times.

"How about something with the word 'sandpiper' in it?" my mother said. "Everybody likes sandpipers, right?"

Normally I would have hated them for not recognizing my suggestion as the best, but this was clearly a special time and I didn't want to ruin it with brooding. Each of us wanted to be the one who came up with the name, and inspiration could be hiding anywhere. When the interior of the car had been exhausted of ideas, we looked out the windows and searched the passing landscape.

Two thin girls braced themselves before crossing the busy road, hopping from foot to foot on the scalding pavement. "The Tar Heel," Lisa called out. "No, The Wait 'n' Sea. Get it? S-E-A."

A car trailing a motorboat pulled up to a gas pump. "The Shell Station!" Gretchen shouted.

Everything we saw was offered as a possible name, and the resulting list of nominees confirmed that, once you left the shoreline, Emerald Isle was sorely lacking in natural beauty. "The TV Antenna," my sister Tiffany said. "The Telephone Pole." "The Toothless Black Man Selling Shrimp from the Back of His Van."

"The Cement Mixer." "The Overturned Grocery Cart." "Gulls on a Garbage Can." My mother inspired "The Cigarette Butt Thrown Out the Window" and suggested we look for ideas on the beach rather than on the highway. "I mean, my God, how depressing can you get?" She acted annoyed, but we could tell she was really enjoying it. "Give me something that suits us," she said. "Give me something that will last."

What would ultimately last were these fifteen minutes on the coastal highway, but we didn't know that then. When older, even the crankiest of us would accept them as proof that we were once a happy family: our mother young and healthy, our father the man who could snap his fingers and give us everything we wanted, the whole lot of us competing to name our good fortune.

The house was, as our parents had promised, perfect. This was an older cottage with pine-panelled walls that gave each room the thoughtful quality of a den. Light fell in strips from the louvred shutters and the furniture, which was included in the sale, reflected the tastes of a distinguished sea captain. Once we'd claimed bedrooms and laid awake all night, mentally rearranging the furniture, it would be our father who'd say, "Now hold on a minute, it's not ours yet." By the next afternoon, he had decided that the golf course wasn't so great after all. Then it rained for two straight days, and he announced that it might be wiser to buy some land, wait a few years, and think about building a place of our own. "I mean, let's be practical." Our mother put on her raincoat. She tied a plastic bag over her head and stood at the water's edge, and for the first time in our lives we knew exactly what she was thinking.

By our final day of vacation our father had decided that instead of building a place on Emerald Isle we should improve the home we already had. "Maybe add a pool," he said. "What do you kids think about that?" Nobody answered.

By the time he finished wheedling it down, the house at the beach had become a bar in the basement. It looked just like a real bar, with tall stools and nooks for wine. There was a sink for washing glasses and an assortment of cartoon napkins illustrating the lighter side of alcoholism. For a week or two my sisters and I tottered at the counter, pretending to be drunks, but then the novelty wore off and we forgot all about it.

On subsequent vacations, both with and without our parents, we would drive by the cottage we had once thought of as our own. Each of us referred to it by a different name, and over time qualifiers became necessary. ("You know, our house.") The summer after we didn't buy it, the new owners, or "those people," as we liked to call them, painted The Ship Shape yellow. In the late seventies, Amy noted that The Nut Hut had extended the carport and paved the driveway. Lisa was relieved when the Wait 'n' Sea returned to its original color and Tiffany was incensed when The Toothless Black Man Selling Shrimp from the Back of His Van sported a sign endorsing Jesse Helms in the 1984 senatorial campaign. Five years later my mother called to report that The Sandpiper had been badly damaged by Hurricane Hugo. "It's still there," she said, "but barely." Shortly thereafter, according to Gretchen, The Shell Station was torn down and sold as a vacant lot.

I know that such a story does not quite work to inspire sympathy. ("My home, well, one of my homes fell through.") We had no legitimate claim to self-pity, were ineligible even to hold a grudge, but that didn't stop us from complaining.

In the coming years, our father would continue to promise what he couldn't deliver, and in time we grew to think of him as an actor auditioning for the role of a benevolent millionaire. He'd never get the part but liked the way that the words felt in his mouth. "What do you say to a new car?" he'd ask. "Who's up for a cruise to the Greek isles?" In response he expected us to play the part of an enthusiastic family, but we were unwilling to resume our old roles. As if carried by a tide, our mother drifted further and further away, first to twin beds and then down the hall to a room decorated with seascapes and baskets of sun-bleached sand dollars. It would have been nice, a place at the beach, but we already had a home. A home with a bar. Besides, had things worked out you wouldn't have been happy for us. We're not that kind of people.

Guiding Questions

1. What does it mean to live in one place and then vacation in another? How might your identity change in each place?
2. How does Sedaris capture the tension between his mother and father? How does he use humor to explore certain aspects of this tension, and of his family's relationship to their vacation place?
3. What does it mean that people own multiple "homes"? What emotions do owning property, to belonging to more than one place, evoke in those who do? In those who do not?

Paths for Further Exploration

1. Did your family take vacations? Were there certain places that you visited regularly? Did you have another "home" to which you journeyed? What did this place mean to you? To your family? How did it differ from your other "homes"?

2. Vacation places often create subcultures that are temporary. Describe a subculture that you have observed, documenting the ways people relate to each other and to the places in which they find themselves.
3. Many people live year-round in places that are vacation destinations for others. If this is your experience, write an essay that describes the relationship between "locals" and "outsiders" created in a community where tourism plays an important role in the economy.
4. How do the ways people name and decorate their homes (try to) say something about their sense of themselves to a larger community? What factors affect the "rules" for naming vacation homes, or aspiring to a certain public style centered on a place? Do things like class, race, and religion play a part?

The Coffee Shop
ANDREA CASASSA

Andrea Casassa is from Hopkinton, Massachusetts, and graduated from Boston College in 2005. She attended law school at the University of Connecticut and currently works as a tax lawyer in Boston. This essay is excerpted from a longer nonfiction narrative written throughout the semester of a first-year writing seminar, centered on her hometown's coffee house. In it, Casassa explores various aspects of the coffee house, from the locals who inhabit this place to the issues plaguing the coffee industry.

———————— ✦ ————————

I. Tips

"Good coffee is like friendship: rich, warm, and strong."

—PAN-AMERICAN COFFEE BUREAU

6:00 A.M.

Brisk New England winds tumble into the coffee shop as I open the back door. The warm aura of cranberry scones and dark roast beans confronts the frigid air. Mary, already hunched over a mixing bowl of poppy seed muffin mix, greets me. Quietly rattling, the old oven readily accepts the bowl's gooey inhabitants for baking. Newly delivered newspapers slouch patiently against the wall waiting to reveal their stories, or to become drenched with spilled cappuccinos. I fold a green apron around the waistband of my jeans; after three years as an employee at the Hopkinton Gourmet, I know too well the hazards and stains capable from steaming coffee. With a warm cup of tea, my six A.M. lethargy transforms into a more roused familiarity; the day begins.

Each community needs a coffee shop, not only for the obvious reasons like caffeine addictions but also for sanity. Some may love Starbucks with their caramel coffee concoctions or the ubiquitous pink and orange signs of Dunkin' Donuts, but quickly fading are the small town hubs like the Gourmet that specialize not in fancy Frappuccinos but in customers. Articles from the local newspaper, *The Hopkinton Crier*, decorate the yellow walls of the shop. From five-year-old Little League players to varsity field hockey stars, town athletes frequent the store to beam at their pictures displayed for the community to see. PTA mothers hang up flyers to promote their newest fundraisers. Fathers clad in Dockers and polo shirts discuss new business and sports.

From the road, the store appears comfortably nestled between two Victorian townhouses peering onto the main street below it. Two flower boxes wrap around the small white building; a golden pineapple separates the "Hopkinton" from the "Gourmet" on the large sign. Flapping in the wind, a sewn flag with a blue mug of steaming coffee welcomes the store's visitors. Upon entering, one immediately notices the bright yellow walls hiding behind the coffee bean jars spanning across the left of the store and the baskets of bagels in the back center. A few feet forward, the pastry counter and register leave barely enough room for the two employees to maneuver around their workspace. The coffee-grinding machine rests inches away from the sink and the shiny steel brewers crowd the neatly stacked supply of cups. One small table is positioned next to a window on the right side of the store and seven more stools squeeze into the corners, making popular window seats and practically violating fire codes. Although small, the Gourmet always seems full and, consequently, very intimate. When an actual crowd does emerge, lines spill onto the outdoor steps.

Monday through Friday, our quaint shop cranks out gallons of java and offers a plentiful array of bagels, muffins, and biscotti to the community. Groggy high school students fill their mugs and astute businessmen awaken with a shot of espresso. Cars frequently pull in and out of the three spots directly in front of the store; their drivers leave them running because their quick orders do not warrant a long stay. A small but growing town located in western Massachusetts, Hopkinton is now bursting with an abundance of kindergarten classes, Friday night football games, and eager "townies" that take pride in their community.

Once a year, these traditional New Englanders awaken to witness the start of the Boston Marathon. The town common's green transforms into a labyrinth of wide-eyed spectators, zealous newscasters, and vendors sending off almost 100,000 runners into the 26-mile stretch into the city. On typical weekend mornings, however, the town really stretches its legs and reflects on the week's disappointments and small victories.

7:00 A.M.

The early morning customers always seem crazy to me. Maybe I'm just jealous that I cannot muster up enough enthusiasm to match their unfailing chipper moods. Nevertheless, the "earlys" start off our day, always to get the freshest bagels, the first cup of coffee, or just to claim their rightful seats. Today Dennis, like a grand marshal leading the parade, approaches the counter first. "Fill it right to the rim," he always gently instructs, *"with just a little bit of milk. Just a little bit, dear."* About 5 foot 6 Dennis stands just a bit taller than me. Gray hair encircles his small ears and his chin always tilts upward a little, making it seem that he is smelling the air around him. Perched with his newspaper in the corner of the shop he oversees at least the first two hours of the day's business, taking note of all the customers, conversing with some, smiling at others, and always inquiring about my college plans. By now, I know his favorites from my list and a thoughtful nod tells me he approves of my progress.

I relate more to another early bunch, mostly construction workers but also other Saturday morning employees, with their last minute attempts to awaken for the day with a jolt of coffee. I admit quite readily that some arrive at our store only for the pure, stimulating power of caffeine, but they still make up our Saturday morning routine and the day would seem empty without them. Paul, with a scruffy beard and mustache, slaps three dollars on the counter for his large cup, leaving an extra dollar for my tip. He tells me to wake up and grins. *Coffee, mostly black, maybe a little cream and sugar. If time allows, a lightly toasted cinnamon raison bagel smothered with butter in a bag.*

9:00 A.M.

A line wraps around the store. Pinging the floor, coffee beans from a nearby canister scatter like little Mexican jumping beans because of a clumsy patron's fumbling. Chatter buzzes, people swarm the sugar and cocoa station. I start to get dizzy from the noise. The hot toaster singes my hands and my head begins to throb. Among the pandemonium, I see Martha in the crowd and I prepare her order before she reaches the counter. Her wide frame jiggles as she chuckles at another customer's joke. A retired mother, she now religiously attends Mass and the Gourmet. Her blond bushy eyebrows rise with approval as I place a chocolate biscotti and lid-free cup of flavored coffee before her.

Many times before, Martha's countenance shrank in discontent if I forgot her order. *Small cup, one cream, one sugar, little "drop" of water, ice if you have it.* Now, I earnestly aim for perfection and she accepts me into her inner circle. Her daughter left for Israel yesterday, she relays to me with a sullen look. "If you study abroad, take your mother with you," she instructs. Traipsing towards Dennis, she engages in tête-à-tête with him about the construction of the new high school.

11:00 A.M.

10　Baby carriages and soccer moms disrupt the ebb and flow of a more demure clientele. The end of Saturday morning cartoons brings a new tide of coffee goers. *Iced coffees, blueberry muffins warmed, chocolate milks, lots of napkins.* An occasional tantrum sends mothers fuming back out to their cars. Toys decorated with cream cheese drop to the floor by the end of the hour. The colorfully striped coffee cookies are popular commodities for this rowdy bunch, and small hands force their way into the jars lining the counter. Tottering, little Jack peers through the pastry glass at his reflection, and his fingerprints smear the surface. I cut up sesame seed bagels into bite-sized pieces as Sharon, Jack's mother, tells me about her baby shower and lets him place a handful of quarters in my tip jar. Someone grabs a handful of napkins to clean the puddle of cappuccinos just spilled on to the floor.

Managing to find stools among the makeshift playgroups, Charlie and Morgan, two "regular" patriarchs of Hopkinton, sit among the children examining the activity outside the store. The former town moderator, Charlie sits with an aura of authority. Morgan's silver hair seems to glisten as the outside sun shines on the two. Young contrasts with old, wisdom competes with naivety, the past converges with the future.

12:00 P.M.
Cell phones ring, "Yeah, I'm at the Gourm'. What's going on tonight?" A group of my friends gather in the corner. Escaping the teenage gossip, parents usually leave the shop as students brag about their accomplishments or mishaps the night before. I drop a container of cream cheese while trying to hear the nearby conversations; I start cleaning all over again. *Three iced coffees, five croissants, lots of honey mustard with turkey and sprouts.*

1:30 P.M.
The lines stop, coffee lays stagnant, and my back aches with exhaustion. I hear the faint lull of the radio, Magic 106.7, over the sink's sputtering as I wash dishes. I sigh at the dirt smudged into the black and white tile floor and grab a mop. Predictable but distinct, another day passes. *One last bagel, a few sandwiches, a latte with skim milk, make it large.* I wipe off the green bubbled letters decorating the community bulletin board, "Fishing derby today at noon," "Soccer car wash, $5," "Polyarts festival next weekend."

I empty the jar and fold forty-six dollars in my back pocket. I wonder if Starbucks employees receive tips like I do.

Hectic, exhausting, comfortable, familiar . . . just right.   15

II. Regulars

"Coffee is one of the special things I have, instead of a social life."

—JOEL ACHENBACH

I've been away at college for a few months now. Today, I come back to the Hopkinton Gourmet to visit some of its regulars. A few photographs of customers have been added to the growing collection on the wall since the last time I was here. Ted, the owner, insists on sneaking pictures of customers as they sip their java. Still, newspapers are stacked neatly, the small tub of Equal packets rests perfectly against the sugar, and the bagels are toasted, leaving traces of blueberry, garlic, and cinnamon in the air. In the wake of September 11th, a flag flaps in the wind and the town newspaper articles of the tragedy are neatly taped to the door.

Since the Hopkinton Gourmet opened its doors in 1992, certain customers appear at the shop day after day, week after week. These "regulars" define this small coffee shop and create a sense of family not often found in the commercialized chains. When one expected patron fails to visit, the equilibrium of the store wavers, not dramatically but noticeably. So, to learn about such a place, one must start at the center, the customers, to appreciate the dynamics of the coffee shop.

I almost laugh as Dennis, an old Hopkinton resident, swings open the door at exactly 8:00, right after church and right on schedule. After filling his mug with dark roast, I invite him to join me at a table, in his favorite seat for an interview. I start our chat by asking him why he comes to the Gourmet. He chuckles. "Well, the camaraderie, of course." Pulling something out of the pocket of his Eddie Bauer plaid shirt, he shows me a picture of Martha, his coffee shop companion, beaming above a birthday cake. "We bought her this last weekend for her birthday," he says proudly, slightly parting his thinning gray hair as he runs his hand through his scalp. The group in the photograph encircles the table where I now sit, leaning over a grinning Martha. A mother and Gourmet matron, she sits complacently and comfortably in the picture, with, of course, her cup of coffee.

When I ask him about the service at the shop, he comments on how the employees, "just know you, and they are always waiting for you with your order ready." I inquire about how this atmosphere differs from a Starbucks or Dunkin' Donuts and Dennis replies that "it's not the building, but the coffee and the people" that make him return every day. He doesn't find that at the chain stores.

20   Walmarts and Starbucks replacing mom and pop stores is a reality, I say. Could those sweeping changes ever affect the Gourmet? "Definitely not," he says without hesitation. "There exists a certain ritualism here. Everyone has their own little niche."

I take note of how true his comment really is. I turn to watch the rituals of the shop. A football coach enters the store before practice, as usual. He buys a copy of the *Herald* and the *Globe* and drinks his medium regular at a corner stool. Creatures of habit, different customers enter, drinking a specific coffee, sitting at their usual spot, living rhythmic lives.

Guiding Questions

1. Casassa claims, "Every community needs a coffee shop, not only for the obvious reasons like caffeine addictions but also for its sanity." What does this place do for Casassa? What does it do for the community?
2. What do locally owned coffee shops do for communities that national chains cannot? Conversely, what advantages do the national chains have over locally owned shops? What evidence does Casassa give to

support her claim that locally owned shops "keep us connected to each other"?

3. Hopkinton assumes a personality through Casassa's use of metaphors. List some of the metaphors she uses to describe the town and the coffee shop. What other rhetorical methods does she employ to convey the character of this place?

4. How does she use the coffee shop to tell us about herself? What does her choice of details reveal about her personality?

Paths for Further Exploration

1. Is there a place in your hometown where the community gathers? Describe its physical appearance and discuss how it functions within the community.

2. Are there places in your community that are being threatened? What argument can you make for why the places should be preserved? Alternatively, if you cannot identify any threatened places in your community, consider what allows a place or places to continue to exist for a long period of time despite other changes in the area.

3. Conduct an interview with a "regular" at a place you frequent. Decide what you hope to learn about the place through this interview and design questions accordingly.

Say yah to da U.P., eh?
KATHRYN CAREY

Kathryn Carey is from Iron Mountain, in Michigan's Upper Peninsula. She graduated from the University of Michigan, located in the Lower Peninsula, in 2011 with a B.A. in mathematics, a minor in psychology, and a secondary teaching certificate. In this essay, she describes how she negotiates these two different places and two different cultures. She currently lives in Eagle River, Wisconsin, and teaches math at Northland Pines Middle/High School.

———————————— ✦ ————————————

I sink into the chair that I pulled up to the bonfire. The night is crystal clear, and only my dad and I are left outside. The S'mores material is still on the picnic table, so I grab the stick that I had cut off a tree and shaved to a sharp point earlier that evening and roast myself another marshmallow. If I listen carefully I can hear the waves lapping gently on the beach over the crackling of the fire. A log rolls deeper into the flames sending a dancing shower of orange, yellow, and green sparks into the air. It's prettier than fireworks on the Fourth of July.

Dad and I are quiet; neither of us feels like talking when the fire is so mesmerizing. I tip my head back to look at the stars, drinking in the sight that I know I won't be able to see when I return to Ann Arbor. As much as I love the bustling city life I find in Ann Arbor, I feel sorry for the residents who've never seen more than the three or four stars that are bright enough to be seen over the lights of the city. Once the light from the fire has faded from my eyes, I can see more stars than I could ever count. I wonder if this is what infinity looks like. I lean farther back so that I can't see anything but sky. Without trees for reference points, I no longer have depth perception. The stars seem to press on my face. I reach my hand up to touch one, knowing that I couldn't possibly do so but trying anyway. Growing up under these stars is why I consider myself a Yooper.

A Different State . . . of Mind

Michigan's Upper Peninsula (the U.P.) has a culture of its own. In fact, the cultural differences between it and Michigan's Lower Peninsula are so prominent that there have been multiple proposals—some as recently as the mid '70s—for the U.P. to become its own state: the State of Superior. But though it makes up an entire quarter of the total landmass of Michigan, it holds a mere three percent of its population. This lack of inhabitants, combined with the amount of monetary support received from the Lower Peninsula, has kept the area from reaching its goal of becoming independent.

When people in the Lower Peninsula ask me where I'm from, I regularly get surprised responses, as if I'm from another country entirely. I've even had people say, "I didn't know people actually lived up there!" or "Do you have running water?" Others don't realize that the U.P. is not a part of Canada. Such stereotypes are not helped by the way Yoopers[1] are portrayed in movies and

---

[1] Yooper is a term for people who live in the Upper Peninsula of Michigan. It stems from the fact that the Upper Peninsula is commonly referred to as "The U.P." so the people that live there are called U.P.-ers, or Yoopers.

books such as *Escanaba in da Moonlight* and *The Sweater Letter*, or the fact that the U.P. is often left off of maps or included as part of Wisconsin. While I'll admit that we do have some of our own quirks, the U.P. is your basic Small Town, America.

A Constant Connection

Growing up in such an atmosphere is equally fun and exasperating. For instance, it's normal to withdraw money from your bank account without being asked for identification or a signature. On the other hand, going to the store is as much a social outing as it is a milk-run.

"Katie! It's so good to see you. How have you been?"

I turn from the dairy department in the local grocery store, where I had been trying to decide if I wanted blueberry or strawberry-banana yogurt, to find Mr. Irish approaching me – his own shopping cart preceding him down the aisle.

"I've been great, Mr. Irish. How are you and Mrs. Irish?" I reply.

"Oh we're just fine. We've been working a lot in the garden lately. You tell your mom that we have some extra tomato plants we'd like to give her, eh?"

"Ok, I'll be sure to let her know."

"Thanks, Katie. By the way, Bob tells me that your grandma said you've decided to go to the University of Michigan!" I nod my head. "That's great. We're all so proud of you. You be sure not to come back a snobby Troll, though," he commands, his eyebrows pinched in warning. "You keep a good hold on your small-town morals. Don't be coming back a crazy liberal!"

I thank him for the warning and ask him to say hello to Mrs. Irish for me, and then roll my eyes as I walk away.

I've become accustomed to warnings such as these. Many Yoopers, especially the older generation, assume Trolls[2] are snooty. This is based simply on the fact that they see the Lower Peninsula as an area of big cities, and according to them, nothing good can come of a big city. I'm often informed that such practices as "just being friendly" (waving to people you pass when you're in the car, whether or not you know them) don't exist in bigger cities, and that doing so "could get you shot." Since these

---

[2] A term for people from the Lower Peninsula–taken from the fact that they lived under the Mackinac Bridge, like the troll in the Norwegian Fairy Tale, "Three Billy Goats Gruff," that lives under a bridge.

older Yoopers rarely spend time in the Lower Peninsula,[3] the only encounters they have with Trolls are when the Trolls travel north to hunt or vacation. And, like locals of any tourist area, they are too annoyed by the presence of these aliens to give them a chance. I'm annoyed by my small town because people like Mr. Irish hear through the grapevine about what's going on in your life and feel free to give unsolicited comments or advice. But I love my small town because everyone cares about everyone. People like Mr. Irish express their pride in your accomplishments in the middle of the dairy aisle. Invitations to weddings are posted in grocery stores so that no one is left out of the celebration. Funerals are attended whether or not you know the deceased—you go to comfort those left behind. The U.P. provides a built-in support system. A constant connection.

Are We Cousins?

My hometown only has a population of 8,154, but it is the fifth largest city in the Upper Peninsula. I am surprised to find out that there are over 8,000 people who live in my hometown, because it's one of those places where you can walk up to someone and determine exactly how you are related—one of your cousins married one of their cousins, or your mother's grandfather is their uncle's father-in-law. It's a place where a town hall meeting also serves as a family reunion.

I grew up playing with my second cousins, though I never made any distinction between them and my first cousins—if you're not sure exactly how you're related, which is often the case, you improvise. For instance, I call one of my father's cousins "Uncle Kim" and the other "Cousin Pat."[4] The lack of distinction makes it especially difficult to draw a family tree for the eighth-grade genealogy unit. Unlike my classmates whose families haven't been born and raised in the area, my family tree project took up multiple poster boards. I was proud to show how many cousins I had and demonstrate that I could trace my heritage back to the Native Americans who lived in the area, but embarrassed to explain to my classmates how I knew that you could, in fact, marry your

---

[3] Because it's easier to get to Wisconsin, Minnesota, or Canada than it is to get to the Lower Peninsula.

[4] This distinction depends on their age: if they are as old as or older than my dad, I usually call them "uncle"; otherwise they're my "cousin."

second cousin—all you had to do was sign a piece of paper that said you would never have children.

Would You Like That with or without Rutabeggies?

I once visited a friend's house near Detroit, and we decided to have a Popsicle after lunch. I opened her freezer, and was momentarily confused by what I saw. Frozen pizzas and microwavable dinners were stacked in neat rows. There was no fresh venison[5] packaged in white parchment paper, no ice cream containers filled with homemade spaghetti sauce, and no mason jars holding chicken stock. But what most surprised me was that there were no homemade frozen pasties ready to be thrown in the oven for a quick dinner. Of course I knew that pasties weren't normal cuisine in the Lower Peninsula, but it still surprised me. It's like opening a fridge and not seeing the milk: you just expect it to be there. In the U.P., seeing a pasty[6] shop is as common, maybe even more common, as seeing a McDonald's or Burger King. When you pull up to these little road-side shops, instead of having an angsty teenager ask if you'd like pickles on your burger, there's a little old woman in the window asking if you'd like your pasty with or without "rutabeggies."[7]

When we stay home for a meal, we cook with our home-grown vegetables or the meat my father and brothers had shot the previous fall. Hunting and gardening are not recreational activities; they are always for the purpose of providing food. People who hunt for sport are looked down upon; people who kill more animals than necessary are scolded, and then directed to the local food pantry where they could drop off the extra meat. Hunting is such an important part of the Yooper culture that students are given the opening day of Deer Season—November 15th—off of school.

One of my favorite annual activities is to spend a late fall afternoon crowded into my grandparents' basement with all of my uncles, aunts, and cousins to make potato sausage. We work

---

[5] The meat from a deer.
[6] Pronounced "pass-tee" . . . Pie crust stuffed with meat and potatoes, and then folded in half with the edges pinched together. They were brought to the U.P. by Cornish miners. The miners found them doubly useful, as they were able to put the hot pasties in their pockets in the morning to keep their hands warm, and then reheat them on their shovels over a candle and eat them with their hands.
[7] The local way of pronouncing "rutabaga"—a type of vegetable.

in an assembly line worthy of a Ford plant, with every member of the family pitching in. My aunts and mom sit upstairs cleaning the freshly killed venison, which is then hauled downstairs to my grandfather, who is in charge of putting it through the meat grinder. We laugh at my uncles as they cry while slicing onions and potatoes, which they pass off to my oldest cousins who are in charge of running the sausage stuffer. Grandma hovers over everyone, sticking her fingers in the mixture to ensure no one added too much salt or left out the pepper. Those cousins who aren't old enough to help with the sausage are put to work taking care of the youngest cousins. On any other afternoon, the damp heat of the basement would have been something we avoided, but on sausage-making day, it is the most exciting room in the house.

Among The Trees

I learned how to drive long before I turned sixteen. In the lower state of Michigan, teenagers learn how to drive just before age sixteen. Usually, the drivers' education classes offered by the city or by the school are a student's first time being behind the wheel. In the U.P., however, children learn how to drive as soon as they can reach the wheel. I remember sitting on my grandfathers', uncles', and father's laps to steer the truck as they worked the gas and brake pedals. As soon as I was tall enough to see over the steering wheel *and* reach the pedals, I was allowed to practice driving through the woods. We still had to abide by state laws because, unfortunately, the road police did not think that twelve-year-olds should be driving. However, as soon as we got off a main road and onto a side road, which was usually dirt or gravel, we'd pull over and switch drivers. The Department of Natural Resources officers, who are essentially the police of the woods, were much more lenient. In fact, we would often pass them on these dirt roads, and they would do nothing but smile and wave.

On cool afternoons in late spring or early fall,[8] my family—grandparents, aunts, uncles, and cousins included—would pile into our SUVs and head out into the woods to look for wild mushrooms, berries, or asparagus, or to find new cricks[9] to fish

---

[8] Summer is considered the week in mid-July when the temperature reach above 80 degrees. Everything else is considered spring or fall.

[9] The local way of pronouncing "creeks," or small streams of water running through the woods.

in. The young cousins would take turns driving, and the aunts would lay down all the seats in the back of the car and create a picnic area. We could've sat on the ground outside, but sitting in one place in the woods is not advisable, as doing so gives little Lyme-disease-carrying bugs called wood ticks the opportunity to climb onto us. During these outings, our uncles would lead everyone on explorations through the woods. They'd show us which plants were edible, and teach us the names of trees and animals. They stressed the importance of "walking like Indians"[10] while they pointed out animal prints and markings. We were often asked, "If you were to get stuck right here, how would you survive? What could you use for food, shelter, and warmth?" My cousins and I saw this as a fun game we played in the woods. Our uncles were never trying to scare us, but rather ensuring that we would always be able to survive in our surroundings.

City Life

When I describe my Yooper life to people I meet in Ann Arbor, especially those who have never had the pleasure of spending time in the Upper Peninsula, I show how I am a typical Yooper: I seem to know everyone in my hometown, and am related to nearly all of them; I prefer trees to sky scrapers, and two-rut roads to eight-lane freeways; I can tell the difference between a silver maple and a birch tree; I know how to hunt, fish, and determine if a mushroom is edible or poisonous. I had to train myself to lock my car and house doors when I'm in big cities. I have seen the Northern Lights, and have experienced that sensation of having the stars press on my face. According to the people of Ann Arbor, I'm your basic small town girl.

But when I am in my hometown, I am considered a city girl. Even before moving to Ann Arbor, I wasn't included in the group of true Yoopers for one major reason: I don't have the Yooper accent. Walking into the old corner café around 10:00 A.M., you wouldn't be able to understand what was being talked about by

---

[10] Walking stealthily through the woods so as to not alert animals to our presence. Also, older Yoopers, my uncles included, are not aware that it's no longer politically correct to refer to Native Americans as "Indians."

the group of regulars—old men in to reminisce about "the good ol' times." Their conversations would sound something like:

"D'ya 'member da time Chum's tird boy fell on da stove in da saouwnah, eh?"

"Ya, ya, ya. He had dat down state gal home w'him, eh? Poor chump had t'get tirty stitches in his tigh! I bet dat gal neva' came back."

"I heard da gal screamed da whole way 'cross da Bridge on der way Nort'. Poor kid didn' know what i'takes t'get inter God's Country."[11]

The combination of their thick accent and the sheer rapidity with which they deliver each sentence is mind boggling (the above conversation would have taken just seconds). I even find myself having to read their lips as they talk, and I've grown up hearing the accent! Growing up, my parents refused to let my brothers and me acquire a Yooper accent. They thought it would make us sound less intelligent. But try as I may to keep out the accent, I still slip into it when I get upset or excited: My "o" vowel becomes unnecessarily elongated; "eh"s appear at the end of my questions (pronouncing our question marks, we call it); my "th"s get replaced with a "d" so that the word "that" becomes "dat." I end my sentences with prepositions, and start referring to "crossing The Bridge," or "taking saunas"[12] without remembering that I may have to explain these terms.

But the part-time accent doesn't count. I was raised in the fifth biggest town in the Upper Peninsula—the closest thing to a true city for hundreds of miles. I didn't ride my snowmobile to school in the winter. I didn't wake up at 4:00 in the morning to trek out to a deer blind to go hunting. I drove a car that didn't have four-wheel drive, and had real neighbors who lived across a lawn, not across a potato field. According to the "true Yoopers," I wasn't anything more than a city-girl.

---

[11] Translation: "Do you remember the time Chum's third boy fell on the stove in the sauna?" / "Yes. He had that girl from [the Lower Peninsula] home with him, right? Poor chump had to get thirty stitches in his thigh! I'll bet that girl never came back." / "I heard the girl screamed the whole way across the [Mackinac] Bridge on their way North. Poor kid didn't know what it takes to get into [the Upper Peninsula]."

[12] "The Bridge" refers to the Mackinac Bridge: the only way to get between the Lower and Upper Peninsulas. "Saunas" are Finnish steam rooms.

At home I'm a city girl; in Ann Arbor, some think of me as from a different country entirely. I've learned not to care what others consider me, but to be proud of my unique position. I get to embody both distinctions depending on my location. But when I stare at the skies of Ann Arbor, longing to see a million stars when all I can find are two, I know I'm a Yooper at heart.

Guiding Questions

1. Compare Carey's essay with Tim Lindgren's essay, "On Being from *Fargo.*" Do they share similar concerns about how outsiders perceive them and about how outsiders perceive their hometowns?
2. Examine Carey's rhetorical style. Is her use of subtitles and her movement between the U.P. and Ann Arbor effective?

Paths for Further Exploration

1. Look at a dialect map that divides North America according to dialect regions. (For example, see www.aschmann.net/AmEng.) According to the map, in what dialect region do you live? What are the features of that dialect? Write an essay in which you examine your dialect region and describe the dialect. Do you feel like you belong to this particular dialect region, or does your dialect diverge in some way? What assumptions or prejudices do people have about you when they hear your accent? Likewise, what assumptions do you make about others when you hear them speak?
2. What aspects of the natural environment seem to set the Upper Peninsula—and the Yoopers who live there—apart from the Lower Peninsula? How does Carey communicate these features in an essay that's primarily focused on other issues, such as dialect and culture?

Where I'm From
FELICIA MADLOCK

Felicia Madlock received her Master's in social work from Loyola University–Chicago and is a medical social worker for a trauma hospital in Chicago. She has published her work in several publications, and her novel, Sins of the Father, *like much of her work, centers on the issues confronting urban families living in Chicago. The following poem originally appeared in the* Journal of Ordinary

Thought, a Chicago publication that sponsors writing workshops free and open to all Chicago residents. The publication's motto is "Every Person Is a Philosopher." For more writing from this journal, see www.jot.org.

———————— ✦ ————————

I am from
Malcolm X memories and Martin Luther King's dreams
I am from hands that toiled cotton, steel, and paper
And red bone women with neck snapping charisma

I am from family that stretches along the mud paths of
5   the Mississippi
Grazing the greenery of Georgia
And reciting folktales in Tennessee

I am from hope that crept north in the darkness
Dodging demons on their quest for freedom
10   I am from dreams deferred

For I, too, am America
And life for me hasn't been no crystal stairs
I am from Langston Hughes' lyrical poetry
Frost's indecisiveness in his cross roads
15   Emily's sheltered world
And Zora's silent voice

I am from Double Dutch days
When Mary Mack was dressed in Black
And Jack be Nimble changed to Jack be Quick
20   I am from the dying days of Disco
When Funk was the fever
And House was planted in the streets of Chicago

I am from Saturday morning shopping
And Sunday School sermons
25   I am from corporal punishment capitalists
Who never believed that "Whipping " was abuse

I am from Michael Jackson mania
Prince's Purple Passion
And Boy George girly gears "garments"
I am from pigtails to perms   30
From cornrows to French-rows
From straight to kinky and somewhere in between

I am from the façade of Jane Byrne's reign
To Harold Washington's historical victory
I am from heroes being reduced to humans   35
Presidents lying to stay in the White House
And unfit leaders lying to get in the White House

I am from the Engle of the Woods
The center of Chatham
And the migration to the Rose of the Land   40

I am from BB King's Blues
Motown's memories
Al Green's Transformation
And Marvin Gaye's moments

I am from lust that disguised itself as love   45
From hearts ripped open from lies and deception
I am from dreams forgotten
In blue puddles of passion
Poison with procrastination

I am from hope that has been revived   50
Passion found
And dreams that fight to live
I am from life lessons
Moments that transfix into memories at the blink of
    an eye

I am from poetry   55
My most pleasing passion
I am from Joy's jovial sound on a July's afternoon

I am from eyes that seek truth
And decipher wisdom

60 I am from lover's goodbyes
And acquaintances fleeing passing
I am from friends who have written their initials in my
  heart forever
I am from heaven and hell
And Earth's ecstasy
65 I am from . . . .

Guiding Questions

1. How does Madlock use culture to define the places where she is from? What does it mean that she invokes these mass-culture experiences to define her individual sense of where she is from?
2. What role does her use of repetition play in providing structure to her piece? What role does sensory detail play? What does the absence of concrete place descriptions do to her ability to convey a sense of place?
3. Can you imagine how Madlock's sense of place linked to mass cultural movements and moments might be conveyed by a more traditional prose approach? What does she gain (or lose?) by using a poetic approach? Does the concept of "place" mean different things to you in poems and in prose?

Paths for Further Exploration

1. What parts of mass culture and shared history create specific places in *your* life? Do you "come from" the culture of Facebook, reality TV, hip-hop music, sports, Harry Potter or other novel series, religion, YouTube, movies and TV, video games, academics, comic books, the collective culture around September 11th, political movements, or some other cultural heritage? Describe your relationship to this group or cultural phenomenon and how it functions for you as a kind of place that you're from.
2. What allows an individual to "claim" a particular cultural space, moment, or movement as his or her own? Can people trespass into others' cultural places of origin? Can they be invited in?

The Most Radical Thing You Can Do
REBECCA SOLNIT

Rebecca Solnit is an art critic, activist, museum curator, and the author of Motion Studies: Time, Space and Eadweard Muybridge, Wanderlust: A History of Walking, *and* Hollow City: The Siege of San Francisco and the Crisis of American Urbanism. *Solnit's central concerns as a writer and thinker involve the ways our sense of place is affected by—and sometimes obliterated by—the rapid pace of technology and global development. In this essay, she considers the "radical" concept of staying home and the impact doing so can have on the environment.*

———————— ✦ ————————

1 Long ago the poet and bioregionalist Gary Snyder said, "The most radical thing you can do is stay home," a phrase that has itself stayed with me for the many years since I first heard it. Some or all of its meaning was present then, in the bioregional 1970s, when going back to the land and consuming less was how the task was framed. The task has only become more urgent as climate change in particular underscores that we need to consume a lot less. It's curious, in the chaos of conversations about what we ought to do to save the world, how seldom sheer modesty comes up—living smaller, staying closer, having less—especially for us in the ranks of the privileged. Not just having a fuel-efficient car, but maybe leaving it parked and taking the bus, or living a lot closer to work in the first place, or not having a car at all. A third of carbon-dioxide emissions nationwide are from the restless movements of goods and people.

2 We are going to have to stay home a lot more in the future. For us that's about giving things up. But the situation looks quite different from the other side of all our divides. The indigenous central Mexicans who are driven by poverty to migrate have begun to insist that among the human rights that matter is the right to stay home. So reports David Bacon, who through photographs and words has become one of the great chroniclers of the plight of migrant labor in our time. "Today the right to travel to seek work is a matter of survival," he writes. "But this June in Juxtlahuaca, in the heart of Oaxaca's Mixteca region, dozens of farmers left their fields, and women weavers their looms, to talk about another right, the right to stay home. . . . In Spanish, Mixteco, and Triqui, people

repeated one phrase over and over: the derecho de no migrar—the right to not migrate. Asserting this right challenges not just inequality and exploitation facing migrants, but the very reasons why people have to migrate to begin with." Seldom mentioned in all the furor over undocumented immigrants in this country is the fact that most of these indigenous and mestizo people would be quite happy not to emigrate if they could earn a decent living at home; many of them are just working until they earn enough to lay the foundations for a decent life in their place of origin, or to support the rest of a family that remains behind.

From outer space, the privileged of this world must look like ants in an anthill that's been stirred with a stick: everyone constantly rushing around in cars and planes for work and pleasure, for meetings, jobs, conferences, vacations, and more. This is bad for the planet, but it's not so good for us either. Most of the people I know regard with bemusement or even chagrin the harried, scattered lives they lead. Last summer I found myself having the same conversation with many different people, about our craving for a life with daily rites; with a sense of time like a well-appointed landscape with its landmarks and harmonies; and with a sense of measure and proportion, as opposed to a formless and unending scramble to go places and get things and do more. I think of my mother's lower-middle-class childhood vacations, which consisted of going to a lake somewhere not far from Queens and sitting still for a few weeks—a lot different from jetting off to heli-ski in the great unknown and all the other models of hectic and exotic travel urged upon us now.

For the privileged, the pleasure of staying home means being reunited with, or finally getting to know, or finally settling down to make the beloved place that home can and should be, and it means getting out of the limbo of nowheres that transnational corporate products and their natural habitats—malls, chains, airports, asphalt wastelands—occupy. It means reclaiming home as a rhythmic, coherent kind of time. Which seems to be what Bacon's Oaxacans want as well, although their version of being uprooted and out of place is much grimmer than ours.

At some point last summer I started to feel as if the future had arrived, the future I've always expected, the one where conventional expectations start to crack and fall apart—kind of like arctic ice nowadays, maybe—and we rush toward an uncertain, unstable world. Of course the old vision of the future was of all hell breaking loose, but what's breaking loose now is a strange mix of blessings and hardships. Petroleum prices have begun doing what climate-change alarms haven't: pushing Americans to alter their habits. For people in the Northeast who heat with oil, the crisis had already arrived a few years back, but for a lot of Americans across the country, it wasn't until filling up the tank cost three times as much as it had less than a decade ago that all the rushing around began to seem questionable, unaffordable, and maybe unnecessary. Petroleum consumption actually went down 4 percent in the first quarter of the year, and miles driven nationally also declined for the first time in decades. These were small things in themselves, but they are a sign of big changes coming. The strange postwar bubble of affluence with its frenzy of building, destroying, shipping, and traveling seems to be deflating at last. The price of petroleum even put a dent in globalization; a piece headlined "Shipping Costs Start to Crimp Globalization" in the *New York Times* mentioned several manufacturers who decided that cheaper labor no longer outweighed long-distance shipping rates. The localized world, the one we need to embrace to survive, seems to be on the horizon.

But a localized world must address the unwilling and exploited emigrés as well as the joy riders and their gratuitously mobile goods. For the Oaxacans, the right to stay home will involve social and economic change in Mexico. Other factors pushing them to migrate come from our side of the border, though—notably the cheap corn emigrating south to bankrupt farm families and communities. The changing petroleum economy could reduce the economic advantage to midwestern corporate farmers growing corn and maybe make shipping it more expensive too. What's really needed, of course, is a change of the policy that makes Mexico a dumping ground for this stuff, whether that means canceling NAFTA or some other insurrection against "free trade." Another thing rarely mentioned in the conversations about immigration is what American agriculture would look like without below-minimum-wage immigrant workers, because we have gotten used to food whose cheapness comes in part from appalling labor conditions. It is because we have broken out of the frame of our own civility that undocumented immigrants are forced out of theirs.

Will the world reorganize for the better? Will Oaxaca's farmers get to stay home and practice their traditional agriculture and culture? Will we stay home and grow more of our own food with dignity, humanity, a little sweat off our own brows, and far fewer container ships and refrigerated trucks zooming across the planet? Will we recover a more stately, settled, secure way of living as the logic of ricocheting like free electrons withers in the shifting climate? Some of these changes must come out of the necessity to reduce carbon emissions, the unaffordability of endlessly moving people and things around. But some of it will have to come by choice. To choose it we will have to desire it—desire to stay home, own less, do less getting and spending, to see a richness that lies not in goods and powers but in the depth of connections. The Oaxacans are ahead of us in this regard. They know what is gained by staying home, and most of them have deeper roots in home to begin with. And they know what to do outside the global economy, how to return to a local realm that is extraordinarily rich in food and agriculture and culture.

The word radical comes from the Latin word for root. Perhaps the most radical thing you can do in our time is to start turning over the soil, loosening it up for the crops to settle in, and then stay home to tend them.

Guiding Questions

1. Solnit opens with a quotation from Gary Snyder: "The most radical thing you can do is stay home," a phrase that Solnit claims remains relevant—if not even more urgent—today. For Solnit, what makes staying home "radical"? Do you agree with her argument?
2. What are the potential advantages to staying home? Are there potential disadvantages? Is there a way to find a balance between staying home and leaving, between conserving and consuming?

Paths for Future Exploration

1. Go to www.myfootprint.org and calculate your carbon footprint. Are the results surprising? Do you feel compelled to make any changes to your lifestyle?
2. Think about where you live. Is "staying home" an option for residents? For instance, are public transportation and sidewalks available so that people have the option not to drive cars? Write an essay in which you examine the place where you live to determine how difficult or easy it is to "stay home"—in every sense of that phrase.
3. Solnit notes, "Another thing rarely mentioned in the conversations about immigration is what American agriculture would look like without below-minimum-wage immigrant workers, because we have gotten used to food whose cheapness comes in part from appalling labor conditions. It is because we have broken out of the frame of our own civility that undocumented immigrants are forced out of theirs." What do you think about Solnit's argument?

Where Are We?

Where *are you?* Really—take a look around. What do you see? What do you hear? What do you smell, what do you feel? What's the first thing you notice, and why? Are you alone or with other people? Are you inside or outside? Are you in a private place, a public place, or a place that is a bit of each? What do you know about the materials and substances around you? What do you know about the history—including the natural history—of the place where you are reading these words? Is it a place designed for reading and studying, or for something else? If you're in a building, do you know who designed it, who built it, when, and why? If you're outside, do you know what trees, flowers, or other plants are around you and whether they are wild, cultivated, or a mix of both? What about any animals nearby—are they native or invasive species, wild or domesticated? If it is a place that you "control," what would someone who does not know you assume about you based on what they could see there?

These questions might seem simple, or even silly, at first. If you are reading this book while in a library on campus, at your desk in a classroom, on your bed in a residence hall, or in a chair in your home, you probably think you have a good sense of where you are. In many ways, you do. But if you are in such a place—a place that is familiar or quickly becoming familiar to you—you have also probably learned to take a number of things for granted, to fail to notice that place consciously.

Of course, we *have* to take some things for granted; if we stopped to notice every small and changing detail of the places we frequent, we would never have time for anything else. We generally reserve careful attention to extraordinary places: those that are new to us (such as a new workplace, deployment, school, or

51

vacation spot), places that we know and will miss (a former home, a favorite hangout far away, a childhood playground or playing field), or places that are under threat of some kind (a changing neighborhood, a beach that is eroding, a patch of woods slated for development). But the ordinary places we move through in the everyday "now" tend to become invisible to us unless we have some reason to look at them with fresh eyes.

Learning not to take *anything* for granted is a crucial part of good writing and of critical thinking. Thinking, researching, and writing about the everyday places we encounter can be surprisingly interesting once we get started, and what we learn about the places we are in now can lead to provocative questions about how these places affect us—and how we shape them, in turn. Knowing where you are goes a long way toward knowing why you're there, where you're going, and even who you might be.

So, let's think this through again: Where are you?

If you are inside "your room" in a residence hall or in some kind of off-campus housing:

- What size is your room?
- What are your walls made of?
- Do you live there alone?
- Who are your neighbors? Do you get along with your roommate(s), floormate(s), or housemate(s) in this space? Can you describe the connections between those relationships and the place itself?
- How does your room affect your education, your social life, your love life, and your sense of a private self?
- Can you think of where or to whom you might go to start finding out more about your room, or about the residence hall, apartment, or house as a whole?
- What ideas might govern the ways residence halls are made, how they're run and organized, and what they look, smell, and sound like? What specific university decisions lie behind your walls, the size of your room, and the number of your roommates?

If you are at your home or your family's home:

- What is going on in the rest of the house or apartment building?
- Do you live with anyone else?
- What is happening right now on your street or in your neighborhood?

- How hot or cold does it tend to get in your house or building?
- Do you feel safe inside your home?
- Is your home structurally sound?
- Is it safe or unsafe to walk in certain areas nearby?
- Who makes the decisions about your home and neighborhood?
- Can you think of specific ways in which some aspects of your neighborhood affect your daily life?
- How far is your home from the other places in your life—your school, job, friends' homes, downtown areas, and so forth?
- Can you guess what people would think of you if they saw your neighborhood before they met you?
- How does what goes on in and around your home reflect larger social or cultural values?

If you are in a library, cafeteria, coffee shop, park, or some other public space:

1. Is it quiet or noisy, and are the noises calming or distracting to you?
2. What kind of light comes to where you are sitting?
3. If you are at a desk or table, is it good for reading and writing?
4. Other than this book, do you have other media—computers, smart phones, and so on—that you are simultaneously viewing, or are you focused only on this text?
5. Does the place get used a lot for studying, or do people use it primarily for other purposes?
6. If there are any students around you, what are they doing? Do certain kinds of students use different spots in the building for different tasks?
7. Are there things of historical or artistic value in the building or space?
8. Where are you in relation to the rest of your college campus?
9. What might you learn about where you are by investigating these questions?

Thinking about place in these more thorough terms may seem difficult and artificial to you at first, but you will get the hang of things quickly. If you are new to school and to the area in which your campus is located, you will find thinking and writing about places near and new to you are great ways to orient yourself—to get a fuller, more informed sense of where you are and of what sorts of things are "at work" in those places.

For example, writing about a particular campus green or quad could lead you to discover the history of some dispute between your school's administration and the surrounding community, or to encounter a particular tradition of the student body connected to that space, or even to a realization of how such open spaces affect education and campus life. If you begin exploring your neighborhood, you might be drawn into a discussion of local politics and zoning decisions, or into an analysis of the cultural heritages found there, or into a discussion of broader issues such as technology, transportation, or local environmental issues. Even writing about something as close at hand as your dorm or bedroom could lead to an exploration of the use of energy-efficient windows to conserve fossil fuels, or to a discussion of the perils of bunk beds combined with alcohol, or to a study of how and why different kinds of students decorate their rooms. Recall some of your answers to the questions we asked earlier: can you imagine any of them leading to a research paper or persuasive essay?

In various ways, the essays presented in this section turn careful attention to ordinary places that the authors make new by looking at them with fresh and deliberate eyes. As the authors describe where they are "now," they discover larger issues and questions, all the while taking care to stay grounded in specific places, to bring them alive to the reader. For example, Julia Corbett's "Robotic Iguanas" essay grows from a simple trip out for a meal with a friend to serve up a detailed description of the restaurant with a side order of philosophical consideration of our culture's relationship to the natural world. Derek Owens ("Where I'm Writing From") and Ron Fletcher ("By Dawn's Early Light") craft their pieces in large part by just deciding to begin walking through and observing particular areas, thus combining the personal experience of and reaction to place with researched facts about local history, culture, and even geology.

Description, then, is one of the key skills you will develop when you write about place; indeed, you will build upon the descriptive skills you began to develop in the last section when you may have been writing largely from memory. As you will see in these essays, good place-based writing depends a great deal upon the writer's ability to convey a sense of the physical reality of the space, and upon his or her ability to know what to leave out. While *one* physical detail may be too small to be effective, a whole list of them would quickly bore the reader, so the careful writer learns how to recognize "choice details," things that will be both particular to that place and evocative of some larger sense of it. As you develop your own writings on place, you'll learn to pay attention to physical details without becoming hostage to them. (Keeping a Place Journal is a great idea—that way you can record any and every minute physical detail that strikes you as you explore a place, and can choose the best or most effective of them later; you might want to discuss what a Place Journal could look like with your instructor and classmates.) When you wrote about the places in your past, you called up memories and used your imagination to enhance the details; now, as you write about the places of your present, you will find ways to generate details grounded in the moment.

As you explore the places around you, you will also learn how to use specialized research sources to help you understand them, from online databases, to dedicated library holdings, to personal interviews with experts, to local newspapers and historical societies. You may learn a bit about art and architecture, infrastructure planning, and even basic sociology as you explore the places around you. Writing about place can also lead you to a more informed knowledge of the natural world, as you may discover that recognizing things like watersheds, tree canopy corridors, native and invasive species, micro climates, and other natural aspects of places is crucial to a fuller understanding of the many forces that create and shape them. Finally, as you learn to spot the human values and choices that lay behind the reality of the places you encounter, you will learn to analyze places like you would a text or a painting, to think and write about the larger ideas that shape places and the ways that places shape our larger ideas.

So, where are you? Enjoy—your explorations are just getting started.

Where I'm Writing From
DEREK OWENS

Derek Owens teaches at St. John's University in Queens, New York, where he is the director of the Institute for Writing Studies and Vice Provost. In his book, Composition and Sustainability: Teaching for a Threatened Generation, *where this essay appears, he asks college writing teachers and their students to discover the links between writing and the environments where we live, work, and study. Owens demonstrates how he has explored where he lives, a suburban neighborhood in Ronkonkoma, Long Island, New York. By combining human history with natural history, Owens attempts to explain what home means for him as a teacher, husband, father, and citizen, and invites his readers to consider how teenagers in particular might respond to such suburban spaces.*

───────────── ✦ ─────────────

Where the hell is Ronkonkomano?

—A character in the film *200 Cigarettes*

I am writing this book at the corner of Lake Promenade and Second Street in the hamlet of Lake Ronkonkoma, in the township of Brookhaven (the largest in New York state), which is located in Suffolk County, a chunk of land that forms the eastern half of Long Island. My house is in the exact center of this island. In 1994 I got a job at St. John's University, which is located in Queens, on the western half of the island, but we moved farther out east because my wife's family is here—her parents, her sisters' families, her aunt and uncle, her cousins—most of them less than five minutes away. Close extended families are always something to celebrate, but such tribal islands are crucial when you live in the middle of a sea of suburban sprawl.[1]

Sixty thousand years ago a mile-high glacier called the Wisconsinan bulldozed its way in slow motion down through Canada and New England and didn't stop until it reached just about where I'm sitting right now. Warmer temperatures caused it to melt and retreat, leaving behind the detritus (mud, sand, gravel, boulders) that geologists now call the Ronkonkoma Terminal Moraine, a line of glacier droppings (including rocks, called "erratics" or "messengers," sheared off of the tops of northern mountains) that extends all the way to Montauk Point, the easternmost tip of New York State. A few thousand years later the very same glacier came back and did it all over again, dumping another string of debris stretching the entire length of the island, this one running from Brooklyn to Orient Point, the northern fork of the island. When the ice began to melt, the land "began to rebound the way a small boat bobs back up when people step out of it" (Isachsen et al. 177). As the ice retreated, mammoth chunks broke loose, got buried, and eventually melted within the ground, forming kettle holes. One of the largest is Lake Ronkonkoma, the freshwater lake that is a fifteen-minute walk from where I sit. Eventually—perhaps as recently as six thousand years ago—Long Island evolved into its present-day shape, making it, geologically speaking, a baby compared with the rest of the state.

The variety of ecosystems caused by the proximity of outwash and moraines led to hardwood forests, salt marshes, and even prairies (a geological anomaly now thought to be the result of periodic burning by American Indians), which, combined, supported an unusual diversity of flora and fauna. Five thousand years ago, the first humans settled in the area—Archaic American Indians of the Orient phase, followed by American Indians of the Woodland phase. These were the first people to clear forests for agricultural purposes. Contact with Europeans occurred five hundred years ago, and, just two centuries later, most of the American Indian population had disappeared or blended with European ethnicities as a result of factors including genocide, slavery, alcoholism, smallpox, and intermarriage. In the seventeenth century, the four American Indian communities around Lake Ronkonkoma were conned into relinquishing water rights (Curtis 5) to settlers who, from the beginning, had a hard time pronouncing, let alone spelling, the name of the area (local historical documents include, for example, references to "Ronconkomy Plains" and "Rocconkkemy Pond").[2] Three separate townships now abut the lake, and the lack of coordination between the localities has contributed to the lake's steady decline since the 1950s.

By 1850 the Long Island Rail Road (LIRR) had already spanned the length of Long Island, making wealthy New Yorkers aware of the lake and turning the area into a "millionaire's playground" around the turn of the nineteenth century. Mansions sprouted around the perimeter of the lake, along with dozens of hotels, lodges, and beach pavilions. Postcards from this period show men lounging in flannel bathing suits and children climbing two-story-tall water slides or scampering like mice in giant water wheels. Summer dances were held on Saturday nights in the halls bordering the lake; in winter, scooters and iceboats raced across the ice. During prohibition, houses of prostitution and speakeasies popped up in the surrounding woods, and one could buy "needle beer" that made one's fingers tingle (Curtis 100). During the 1920s, anti-Catholic sentiment helped create an active Ku Klux Klan presence: one conductor on the Long Island Rail Road actually sold KKK outfits on the Greenport line (Curtis 134).[3]

In the 1940s, MacArthur Airport opened two miles away from   5
the Lake. (Our house is situated along one of the flight paths; you can almost make out the passengers in the windows of the Southwest jets that pass overhead.) An auction sale catalog from 1937 advertised the selling of two hundred lots near the lake, emphasizing the easy commute from this "gem of Long Island" to Penn Station via twenty-four daily trains. The population surged

as summer cottages were converted for year-round living. (My own single-story, two-bedroom home, while not large by middle-class Long Island standards, started out as a bungalow, and has been added onto three or four times in the last four decades.) A local historian writes that "many new developments appeared, and unfortunately some of the promoters emphasized cheapness rather than quality which attracted some buyers who were less desirable," and that "the crowning blow to the town" came when a significant woodland stretch was sold to developers (Curtis 148). Development continued. Lakeside pavilions were sold, and those left abandoned were burned. In the 1960s and 1970s "unrestricted dumping of fill over the banks of the lake destroyed many trees and left unsightly yellow gashes here and there on the east side of the lake": "Large sections of the Great Swamp were filled in and the once beautiful lake was becoming an eye sore." In 1975 the entire lake was closed for three days due to pollution from storm drains carrying runoff into the water (Curtis 161).

Today Lake Ronkonkoma is a working- and middle-class suburb, indistinguishable from a hundred other suburbs on the island, most of them spilling into each other so that one's sense of boundaries comes not from any visual sense of "village limits" but from proximity to highways and strip malls. (In his stand-up days, the comedian Jerry Seinfeld, who grew up half an hour away in Massapequa, joked that the town's name was Indian for "near the mall.")

If you walk out my front door and view the neighborhood, you will see streets that are safe and quiet, except on occasional summer days when neighborhood kids and sometimes their fathers race motorcycles, looking furtively at intersections for signs of cops. Up to 25 percent of the homes in the area are rentals converted into two or more illegal apartments. Despite the fact that when the house next door was rented out the new tenants found the basement littered with vials and syringes, obvious drug activity in the neighborhood is virtually nonexistent, save for an occasional teenager shuffling down the street smoking a joint, or a pipe tossed into the bushes. An abandoned shopping cart across the street is evidence of the "sober house" up the street, a home containing eight apartments (all legal, surprisingly) rented out to men trying to get back on their feet. These men are some of the more visible members of the community, walking (their drivers' licenses have been revoked) six blocks to a minimarket for groceries. Because these men are not permitted to have overnight guests, on a few occasions women have spent the night sleeping in cars outside our house.

Like much of suburbia in Suffolk County, the streets here have no sidewalks, just sandy shoulders. The side streets are often very wide—so wide in fact that five, possibly even six, cars could park side by side across the width of the street and still not touch the lawns on either side.

> It has been established . . . that suburban streets all over America ought to be as wide as two-lane country highways, regardless of whether this promotes driving at excessive speeds where children play, or destroys the spatial relationship between the houses on the street. Back in the 1950s, when these formulas were devised, the width of residential streets was tied closely to the idea of a probable nuclear war with the Russians. And in the aftermath of a war, it was believed, wide streets would make it easier to clean up the mess with heavy equipment. (Kunstler 113–14)[4]

If you walk five blocks north from our house you will come to a service road that runs parallel to the Long Island Expressway (LIE), with its (increasingly slow-moving) current of 24/7 traffic. At night the hiss of cars in the distance spills in through our bedroom skylight.

In 1998 they started widening the highway, extending the HOV lanes. Although HOV stands for "high occupancy vehicle," in this case two people—even if that second person is a baby—are considered "high occupancy." The HOV lanes have been added to decrease congestion by encouraging carpooling. Traffic, even out here, ninety minutes from Manhattan—off peak—is thick: on weekdays as early as 6:30 A.M. the westbound lane of the LIE can crawl at 15 m.p.h. But studies show the HOV lanes to be ineffective. In a car culture like Long Island's, people are reluctant to carpool (the newspapers occasionally report stories of drivers getting caught in HOV lanes with mannequins sitting next to them or cabbage patch dolls in baby seats), and, even when they do, the time it takes to navigate the crowded secondary highways to pick up one's passengers requires people to get up that much earlier.

So you think traffic on Long Island is bad now? Stick around.

In a mere 22 years, it will be unbearable unless something is done.

That's the prediction of a team of consultants hired by the state Department of Transportation.

Their study, released by the department last week, makes it clear that existing and planned HOV lanes on the Long Island

Expressway aren't going to solve anything. . . . The forecasters say that by 2020, the amount of time Long Islanders are delayed in traffic will nearly double. The 1,091 miles of congested lanes during the morning rush will increase by a whopping 75 percent. And it will take longer to get where we're going; the average travel speed during morning and evening rush hours will decrease by 17 percent.

. . . The big problem is that Long Island's highway system is close to overflowing already, according to the experts. Even a small increase in the number of cars on the road can cause big problems. (Adcock)

Yet construction of the new lanes continues. By the time they are finished, the LIE will be twelve lanes wide in places: the outside shoulder, three lanes of traffic, an on-off lane for entering and leaving the HOV lane, and the HOV lane itself—times two. (See Figure 1 for a construction photo.)

10   If you want to walk more than five blocks north from my house you will have to walk under the LIE, which means crossing a busy service road. Continue for another five blocks and you will find yourself looking at Lake Ronkonkoma. Although the lake is described as "the jewel" of the community, there is no boardwalk, sidewalk, or even pathway encircling the lake—just a perimeter road (dangerous to walk on due to lack of shoulders), scattered homes in some areas, a restaurant, low-income apartments, and a trailer park. There are three beaches, but each resides in one of the three localities bordering the lake, so residents are permitted to use only one of them. (See Figure 2.)

If you walk several blocks east or west from my house you will arrive at busy four-lane streets (seven-lane, if you count the wide shoulders and the center turning lanes), which serve as effective pedestrian barriers, boxing in and thereby defining the parameters of our little "neighborhood." Both roads were widened in the last decade. One street has a light that sometimes changes color before you can reach the other side; the other is an artery connecting the expressway to the Long Island Rail Road and, beyond that, Veteran's Highway. I am reluctant to take walks with my son in this direction because the traffic on Ronkonkoma Avenue is constant and fast-moving (I was nearly run over early one morning while walking to the train station). On the other hand, living so close to the Ronkonkoma LIRR station (see Figures 3 and 4) is helpful since I take the train to work. (My daily commute is almost two hours, each way: a fifteen-minute walk

FIGURE 1. May 14, 1998, 3:55 P.M. Looking down at HOV lane construction on the Long Island Expressway from the Ronkonkoma Avenue overpass between exits 59 and 60, about forty-five miles from Manhattan. "The Long Island Expressway was built without rapid transit—and without provision for rapid transit in the future. And as each section of the superhighway opened [beginning in 1955], it was jammed—with traffic jams of immense dimensions. [Robert Moses'] dream became a nightmare—an enduring, year-after-year nightmare—for tens of thousands of other men. Year by year, the huge road bulled its way eastward, through Queens, across Nassau County, deeper and deeper into Suffolk; it would take fifteen years to build it out to Riverhead. And as each section opened, as each piece of Moses' largest road-building achievement fell into place, the congestion grew worse. The Long Island Expressway's designed daily capacity was 80,000 vehicles. By 1963, it was carrying 132,000 vehicles per day, a load that jammed the expressway even at 'off' hours—during the rush hours, the expressway was solid with cars, congealed with them, chaos solidified. The drivers trapped on it nicknamed Moses' longest road 'the world's longest parking lot.'" (Caro, *Power Broker* 949) Photo by Derek Owens.

FIGURE 2. A view of Lake Ronkonkoma (obstructed by low-income housing). Photo by Derek Owens.

to the train station, a one-hour train ride to Jamaica, Queens, a fifteen-minute wait for the Q30 or Q31 bus, and another twenty- to twenty-five-minute ride to campus.)

If you choose to walk south from my house you can go only two blocks before coming to a wooded acre of (for the moment)[5] undeveloped land, which ends at the railroad tracks. A tall fence prevents one from crossing the tracks, which are electrified and will cause third-degree burns and possibly death if one touches the third rail. It is in this wooded plot of land that in the late summer of 1997 I found, hidden amid the black oaks and scrub pines, the remains of a campsite.

They had been living in two ripped tents, the smaller one erected inside the larger one, apparently in an attempt to keep out rain and mosquitoes. Filthy clothes and broken furniture were strewn everywhere. From the smell of the cheese and chopped meat left in a plastic foam cooler, and the remains of a cat coated with maggots and wrapped in a blanket, the site had been abandoned for several weeks. (See Figure 5.) The next day I made an attempt to clean it up but only got so far as to fill a half a dozen garbage bags before I grew too disgusted and gave up. In the

FIGURES 3 AND 4. Abandoned stores and empty lots at the Ronkonkoma train station. In 1995 a new multimillion-dollar train station was built here, this being the busiest LIRR hub east of Queens. But the new station has not led to the revitalization of local businesses. A billboard in the center of an empty lot next to the train station promises future stores as early as 1997, but as of 2001 the lot remains empty. Photos by Derek Owens.

FIGURE 5. Squatters in suburbia. Photo by Derek Owens.

process, I found a shoebox of old photographs and a diary. The two squatters had been teenage girls who had taken to living back here in this tiny patch of woods, subsisting for a time by cashing in on a stepfather's social security checks. I wondered what had caused them to leave so suddenly.

Despite the filth they left behind, part of me admired them. In Ronkonkoma, like most suburbs, teenagers, along with elderly persons, are the ones most victimized by the absence of a public commons, of meeting places, of coffee shops or bookstores or independent movie theaters or parks. As a result, many teenagers skulk around in small bands, knocking over fences, stealing the occasional mailbox, and parking at night in the dark beneath shot-out streetlights to hang out, get stoned, or have sex (twice I've found used condoms on the shoulder outside our house, and, once, a discarded early pregnancy test kit in the bushes).

> As a teenager I visited my old suburban chums back on Long Island from time to time and I did not envy their lot in life. By puberty, they had entered a kind of coma. There was so little for them to do in Northwood, and hardly any worthwhile destination reachable by bike or foot, for now all the surrounding territory was composed of similar one-dimensional housing developments punctuated

at intervals by equally boring shopping plazas. Since they had no public gathering places, teens congregated in furtive little holes—bedrooms and basements—to smoke pot and imitate the rock and roll bands who played on the radio. Otherwise, teen life there was reduced to waiting for that transforming moment of becoming a licensed driver. (Kunstler 14)

One writer has suggested, not completely tongue in cheek, that   15
it is the sameness of the Long Island landscape, perfected early on in that famous suburb of Levittown, that makes Nassau and Suffolk county produce more than their share of kidnappers, serial killers, snipers, teenage killers, spouse murderers, and other dangerous individuals. In "Long Island, Babylon," Ron Rosenbaum implies that the inability to situate oneself psychologically or physically within a specific space distinguishable from other spaces leads to psychosis. Moreover, Rosenbaum sees the percolation of antisocial behavior on Long Island as a harbinger for the rest of the country:

> Long Island, after all, was supposed to be the future *before* the future. We always had a head start on the life cycle of suburban baby-boom culture because we were the first-born burbs of the baby boom; a burbland created almost all at once, very fast and virtually ex nihilo, right after the war, a self-contained social organism. An organism whose sociobiological clock started ticking a little earlier than subsequent burbs, and whose shrill alarms now seem to signal that it has raced through its mature stage and is now rocketing headlong into the social-organism equivalent of senile dementia. (628)

Others have called attention to what some see as a disproportionate number of famous crimes associated with Nassau and Suffolk county (Demoretcky; Jensen; Wacker). Two weeks after the April 1999 high school massacre in Colorado, an article appeared in the *New York Times* speculating about the role of suburban sprawl in fostering the kind of environment where such tragedies occur: "At a time when the renegade sprawl of suburbs themselves is being intensely scrutinized, the troubling vision of a nation re-pioneered in vast tracts of disconnected communities has produced uneasy discussion about the psychological disorientation they might house" (Hamilton, "Suburban Design" F1).

At least the two squatters near my house had made, for a piece of their summer, a hovel of their own away from others' eyes, tucked away by the tracks in a copse of trees sandwiched between the Quality Muffler Shop and a dirt parking lot owned by the LIRR. As disgusted with them as I was for having defiled that place, I am more ashamed of the planners and architects and developers, and their backers, who have bequeathed to other people's children what James Kunstler calls "a landscape of scary places, the geography of nowhere, that has simply ceased to be a credible human habitat" (15). If their community leaders had exhibited no imagination in designing neighborhoods and had polluted the environs with industrial parks and strip malls, one could hardly criticize these girls for desecrating their own hidden home, which was, after all, distinctly *their* mess, and not a copy of a copy of someone else's idea of what a home or neighborhood should look like. Embarrassing as it was, this pathetic campsite had become, for a few weeks, their space, an island constructed in the center of an island marked by unchecked sprawl.

Endnotes

1. Because of the confusing mélange of towns and villages overlapping one another across the island, coupled with the absence of village centers, Long Islanders often identify themselves according to the exit on the Long Island Expressway nearest their home. When people ask me where I live, all I need to say is "near exit 60." For many Long Islanders, our sense of place is often determined by commuting distance—to Manhattan, to work, or to family in the area.

2. In the 1999 film *200 Cigarettes* two teenagers from Ronkonkoma (Christina Ricci and Gaby Hoffman) spend New Year's Eve on the Lower East Side. One of the film's recurring jokes is that no one can understand where exactly the two young women come from or what they say, given the odd name of their town and their impenetrable "Lawn Guyland" accents.

3. This active KKK presence is, sadly, less surprising when one considers that during the 1700s roughly 20 percent of Long Island's population consisted of slaves, mostly Black but also American Indian. One historian (amazingly) equates ownership of slaves with Long Island's contemporary car culture: "Slaveholding was to colonial status on Long Island what car-owning is to contemporary status: prosperous families owned fourteen or more slaves, while poorer residents could afford only one or two" (Bookbinder 39). An insensitive comparison for obvious reasons—car owners around here spend considerable money "detailing" their machines, not torturing, raping, and murdering them—the analogy is also backwards: to live in sub urban sprawl means to be a slave

to one's car, or, rather, to the planners who built these communities designed around automobile transportation.
4. "The influence of the Cold War was profound. In the 1950s, the civil Defense Committee of AASHTO, the American Association of State Highway Transportation Officials, was a dominant force in the determination of street design criteria. Its prescription was straightforward: street design must facilitate evacuation before, and cleanup after, a major 'nuclear event'" (Duany et al. 65). Ironically, fear of the bomb is what drew so many "come-outers" to the suburbs in the first place, away from urban centers that had become atomic bomb targets (Stilgoe 301).
5. Portions of this wooded lot have since been bulldozed to make way for a road widening project; the rest is up for sale.

Works Cited

Adcock, Sylvia. "A Look at Delays to Come." *Newsday* 3 May 1998: A3.

Bookbinder, Bernie. *Long Island: People and Places, Past and Present*. New York: Abrams, 1983.

Caro, Robert A. "The City-Shaper." *The New Yorker* 5 Jan. 1998: 38–50, 52–55.

———. *The Power Broker: Robert Moses and the Fall of New York*. New York: Vintage, 1974.

Curtis, Ann Farnum. *Three Waves: The Story of Lake Ronkonkoma*. Ronkonkoma, New York: Review Publishing. 1993.

Demoretcky, Tom. "Crime in the Suburbs: A Deadly Parade of Violence Brings Pain to Peaceful Neighborhoods." *Newsday* 21 June 1998: H16.

Hamilton, William L. "How Suburban Design Is Failing Teen-Agers." *New York Times* 6 May 1999: F1+.

Isachsen, Y. W., et al., eds. *Geology of New York: A Simplified Account*. Albany: New York State Museum/Geological Survey, State Education Department, State U of New York, 1991.

Jensen, Bill. "A True-Crime Tour." *Long Island Voice* 15–21 October 1998: 16–18.

Kunstler, James Howard. *The Geography of Nowhere: The Rise and Decline of America's Man-Made Landscape*. New York: Simon, 1993.

Rosenbaum, Ron. "Long Island, Babylon." *The Secret Parts of Fortune: Three Decades of Intense Investigations and Edgy Enthusiasms*. New York: Random, 2000: 612–628.

Wacker, Bob. "Why Living Here Can Be Murder." *Long Island Voice* 15–21 October 1998: 154.

Guiding Questions

1. How does it make you feel when Owens keeps addressing "you" in the second person, and tells you what you'd see if you walked north, south, east, or west from his house?
2. Why do you think Owens spends as much time as he does early in the essay on the geological and other natural histories of Long Island and Lake Ronkonkoma?
3. Owens mentions a theory that central Long Island's historic prairies—a natural anomaly—might actually have been caused by the actions of Native American inhabitants. Why do you think he makes sure to include this point? Are there implications here for the rest of his essay?
4. Both Lake Ronkonkoma and the Long Island Expressway figure prominently in Owens's neighborhood and in the essay—how does he describe each of them, and what kinds of contrasts or similarities does he draw?
5. Are you surprised by how long it takes Owens to get to work in Queens (which is also on Long Island, less than forty-five miles away from Ronkonkoma)? Do you think he expects or wants you to be surprised?
6. How would you describe the kinds of research Owens does for this piece? What kinds of sources does he read in order to make sense of his place? How does he integrate these secondary sources with his own observations?

Paths for Further Exploration

1. Write the kind of neighborhood narrative Owens does. Leave your home or residence hall (and get off campus, too, if you can) and walk in all four directions, explaining to your readers what they would encounter if they were to do the same. Take pictures and lots of notes, and do some research on one or two things that particularly capture your interest (an old building, a brook, a busy intersection, an abandoned field, etc.) (See the section "Tools for Getting Places" for tips on how to research local histories). Or, consider the overall "walkability" of the area; consult sites such as www.walkscore.com to get a sense of how the area compares to others you may know in this regard.
2. Find out something about the natural history of your hometown neighborhood or campus neighborhood and write about how those environmental factors may have affected what humans have done with the place, or may even be affecting how you experience it today. (See "Tools for Getting Places" for tips on how to get started on this kind of research.)
3. Write about your own commute—whether it is to classes or to a job you hold now or have held in the past. How long does it take

you? How many different modes of transportation do you have to use, including your own walking? Do you experience the places you commute through in any special way? If you don't think you've got enough to write about, consider writing about someone else's commute. Interview someone to find out as much as you can about how he or she gets to work or school. Try mapping your commute or someone else's in a new way; using tools like Google Maps is one way to get started.

4. Owens discusses the boredom that many teens experience in suburban communities that were not designed with them in mind, and cites various authorities who argue that boredom and sameness can lead to psychosis. If you have been bored in a place you have lived—especially if you have lived in the suburbs—write about why the place was boring, how you tried to make it interesting, and how boredom affected you. Do you understand Owens's depiction of the sameness and nowhereness of suburban teenage life?

By Dawn's Early Light
RON FLETCHER

Ron Fletcher has taught English at Boston College High School, his alma mater, since 1993 and his reporting and op-ed commentary on educational issues regularly appear in The Boston Globe. *This "slice-of-life" article from* The Boston Globe *shows us that familiar places— such as urban neighborhoods—can become essentially different places when we change our perspective on them in even one significant way. Here, Fletcher changes our perspective by taking us through the city at a time most of us never see it. In doing so, he not only makes the everyday urban landscape seem strange, he also encounters a secret second society of neighbors, those up with (or before) the sun.*

———————— ✦ ————————

In a city that does sleep, the pulse of the Charles River slows, its pre-dawn repose a black mirror for solitary headlights that wind down Storrow Drive. Delivery trucks sail through downtown traffic lights that flash yellow above near-empty intersections. The occasional jogger, dog walker, or roller-blader commands an open sidewalk. An empties-laden shopping cart rattles down the alleyways behind Comm. Ave. condos with curtains drawn. And stiletto heels click and clack along the streets of Bay Village, where turning the clocks back means gaining an hour to ply the oldest trade.

"Four a.m. in Boston is another world," says Steve Hobbs, whose work as a floral designer has him up before the sun. "You see everything. Well, everything that those who get to work at 9 a.m. miss."

For those who set their alarms for the small hours, Boston offers ample free parking, a lack of coffee shops, and an expansive calm. Early risers talk often about the ways space and pace shift throughout hours four, five, and six. They turn to recurring sounds and sights rather than clocks or watches for a sense of time.

Last week's return to standard time matters little to them. "When the sun comes up, it wakes a tree full of birds right in front of the shop," says Dave House, co-owner of Flat Black, the coffee shop in Lower Mills. "They chirp away for about 15 minutes. When they stop, the day begins."

5   For Marlon George at the Franklin Park Golf Course, there is the morning ritual of placing 18 blue flags on the dew-dappled or, now, sometimes frosted greens. He drives his cart from hole to hole in the company of other early birds to the course: geese, seagulls, and the occasional hawk. "There's always some kind of activity at the course," says George, "people walking or jogging or looking to get an early nine holes in."

A solid three-iron away from the links, Steve Sullivan pushes a broom along the curb outside the Shattuck Shelter. A resident as well as a member of the shelter's work crew, Sullivan earns minimum wage as he sweeps up damp leaves, cigarette butts, scratch tickets, and a few bottle caps. The hour of 5 a.m. appeals to him.

"I do appreciate a little solitude," says Sullivan, 45, who had worked full time as a truck driver before he lost his license and landed at the shelter last March. "To find a quiet moment when you live with a couple hundred people is pretty nice."

As the black sky lightens to dark blue, Sullivan completes his outdoor chores, walks through the gray cigarette smoke exhaled by a handful of fellow early risers, and prepares the shelter's cafeteria for a 6:40 a.m. breakfast. He moves silently past a row of occupied bunk beds toward the labyrinth of hallways that will lead him to the cafeteria, where trays of scrambled eggs and crates of single-serve OJ and milk cartons await the guests. Sullivan sees little unique in his appreciation of the early-morning hours.

"There are a lot of people staying here who get up very early and go straight off to work or to look for a job," he said, enjoying his own breakfast after having prepared and served more than 100 himself. "When the average rent [in Boston] is over $1,000, what are the chances of someone making minimum wage getting a place? If you're lucky, you find some steady work and make enough to get a room."

Working alongside Sullivan is Peter Lewis, who has spent   10
two years at the shelter. This year, he says, is about continuing to break the habits that hobbled him last year. Progress has opened his eyes to dawn's early light.

"Sunrise didn't mean too much last year," says Lewis, "but I appreciate it now, what it represents something beneficial, something peaceful. Sometimes I catch it while I'm working." He points to the cafeteria's wall of windows. "But most of the time I'm too concerned with what's going on in here to notice it."

Rene Morales has seen his share of sunrises through a window as well. Since 1974, the native of Guatemala has been mixing dough and making breads at Quinzani's Bakery on Harrison Avenue in the South End. Describing himself as a "morning person," Morales, 59, flits around the heavy machinery that cranks out 5,000-plus dinner rolls per hour. He punctuates his 4 a.m. to noon shift with a well-timed break.

"You see that window?" asks Morales, pointing a flour-dusted finger. "When I can, I go there and watch the sun come out. The daylight makes you keep going. It energizes you."

Many who work the predawn shift speak of having two days in one. Restored by a post-work nap, they enjoy an afternoon and early evening all their own. Not Morales.

"I go home, take a shower, have lunch, then go to my second   15
job at South Shore Hospital," says Morales. No boast, no grouse. "At 8 [p.m.], I go home, get some sleep, then come here. That's my life." He smiles, then mentions he has a chance to sleep late on Sundays. "I get up at 9 a.m.," says Morales, "then go out for breakfast with my beautiful wife and my beautiful daughter."

Outside of the bakery, Javier Ayla loads paper bags of still-warm bread onto a delivery truck he will drive from 5 a.m. until 1 p.m. He says that the end of daylight saving time matters little to him. "I'm still working and it's still dark out," says the young father, who rises daily at 2:30. "I just have to make sure that I get up at the right time."

A few blocks away, the alarm clock-like beeping of a delivery truck in reverse gear snaps to attention the small staff of Back Bay

Wholesale Flowers. The loading-dock door is raised like a stage curtain to reveal a choreographed ballet of retrieval, unboxing, plunging into water, refrigeration, and the displaying of flowers picked in Ecuador or Holland less than 24 hours ago. Europe or South America, to New York City, Boston, then, perhaps, your dining room table.

"It's amazing," says Wayne Robinson, who owns a flower shop in Easton. "If it wasn't for these guys here, we'd be selling carnations and mums from oh, I don't know—Woburn." He then points out one of his own creations, a fall floral arrangement in a 4-foot glass vase, filled with eight bags of candy corn.

A whit more subdued is Steve Hobbs, designer for Exotic Flowers of Boston. The 30-year veteran who learned the trade from his father sips a cup of coffee as the staff trots out buckets and boxes of fresh flowers. Color and fragrance fill the room, surfeiting the senses.

20   "This is wonderful, just wonderful," says Hobbs, who eyes a display of gerbera daisies that capture the colors of fall. "People think that autumn in a flower shop is all about gourds, pumpkins, hay, and cornstalks. As you can see, it is not.

"But you have to get here early for the best stuff," adds Hobbs. "Show up at 9 and you're looking at a few boxes of yellow and orange daisies not the glorious colors you see now."

From the flower district to the fish piers, the newsstands to the bakeries, the early -morning hours offer a commerce of daily consumption, a trafficking in the timely and ephemeral. Dawn dramatizes transition. And witnessing dark give way to light each day seems to offer something salutary.

"The light," said baker Rene Morales, "it's like life."

Guiding Questions

1. The autumnal setting of the clock back one hour at the end of Daylight Savings Time seems to have inspired this article. Why do you think Fletcher found that a useful writing prompt? What kinds of things about time, places, and routine do you think it made him consider?

2. Do the people Fletcher encounters at these early hours seem to have certain traits or lifestyles in common? Do the same kinds of places seem to be occupied before dawn as during the regular day? If so, why? If not, why?

3. The natural world seems particularly present in the city at these early hours. Why might that be so?

Paths for Further Exploration

1. Set your alarm for 4 a.m. some morning and write a description in your Place Journal of what your neighborhood or campus looks and feels like at that time of day. Consider writing a 24-hour description of these places, observing the place for at least a few minutes during every hour. (Break this assignment up into several days of observation, though, as doing 24 hours straight probably isn't a healthy or safe idea.) Webcams may help you in this assignment; see "Tools for Getting Places" for the URL address of a directory of public webcams, and check your school's home page and admissions office page to see any webcams that may be on your campus. Tools like Google Earth and Google Maps' Street View may also be helpful, even though they provide static images.

2. Imagine other ways to alter your perspective on a familiar place. How would these change your sense of it? Give yourself an assignment and write up what you observe. For example, what if you could not see or hear in a particular place? What if you could not speak to anyone there? What if you were much shorter or taller? What if you were much older or younger than you are? Be creative.

3. Find out what specific tasks need to be done in your neighborhood or on your campus to make them "ready" for you and interview the people who perform those tasks, such as the workers in a dining hall, cleaning staff, bakers, or delivery drivers. Examine how your sense of the place is different from and similar to theirs. Once you have met some of these people, note how, if at all, your understanding of the places you share is altered.

A Nation Divided
ROSE ARRIETA

Originally from Los Angeles, Rose Arrieta has worked as a writer, editor, producer, and reporter in print, broadcast, online, and community journalism for more than twenty years, including as a news writer at San Francisco's KCBS; a reporter and editor for El Tecolote, *a bilingual, bi-weekly newspaper; and as a producer of KALW's "Crosscurrents," a "public radio news magazine" in the Bay area. In 2002, Arrieta won a grant from the Independent Press Association's George Washington Williams Fellowship for Journalists of Color to report on border issues. In this essay, which first appeared in* Orion *(www.oriononline.org), Arrieta describes the situation of the Tohono O'odham and other peoples who find themselves on the wrong sides of the border laws of the nations and cultures around them.*

───────────── ✦ ─────────────

Ana Antone skillfully maneuvers the four-wheel-drive vehicle, peering over the dash, pausing every so often to negotiate the deep potholes, large rocks, and tree branches scattered on this bumpy dirt road just north of the U.S.-Mexico border. The surrounding desert is dotted with ocotillo shrubs, palo verde trees, and saguaro cacti. Full, heavy mesquite trees hang low. Greasewood bushes, about four feet high and a deep leafy green, hug the earth. Somewhere out there, families of *javelinas* (wild pigs) snort around for seeds and berries; cows poke along the landscape; and white-winged doves, woodpeckers, and hawks swoop through the Sonoran Desert skies.

Antone is headed home. Although she lives in Sells, Arizona, her birthplace and ancestral home is south of the border in the Tohono O'odham community of Ce:dagi Wahia—known in Spanish as Pozo Verde. The village is just twenty miles from the San Miguel Gate, an unofficial border crossing on a route used by the Tohono O'odham for centuries.

"That's the road my people traveled when they went back and forth to visit our relatives, the Pima at Salt River, and Gila River," says Antone softly. "But by the time I started remembering things, that wasn't happening anymore. By then, the boundary was there." Today, the Tohono O'odham Nation straddles the border, with members living on both sides.

Antone, fifty-four, with short dark hair and a pleasant smile, works as a mental health counselor for the Tohono O'odham Health Services Department in Sells. Sitting next to her is forty-five-year-old Lavern Jose, a Health Services health care worker. Jose's job is to bring elders from south of the border to their medical appointments in Sells. A woman of force and vigor, she grinds her own corn masa for the tamales that she cooks over the wood stove at her home in Tecolote, Arizona. She used to help her dad rope cattle and can get a broken vehicle up and running in short order. It is perhaps this strength that steels her against intimidation by U.S. border agents.

5   As tribal members, Jose's patients can receive medical care provided by the Tohono O'odham Nation. But that care, like all

other tribal services, is located at the nation's headquarters in Sells, on the increasingly inaccessible U.S. side of the border. "They have lights in the front, spotlights—that's how they pull us over," Antone says, referring to the vans of border agents. "Lot of time they will just follow us for a long distance and never turn on the spotlights. Some will even drive alongside your vehicle. In November it happened almost every week. I was stopped once; other times I was followed all the way to my house in Sells."

With a reporter in the car and no patients as passengers, there is a good chance we won't get stopped on our way back into the U.S. But Jose and her patients aren't always so lucky. "I tell them things will be okay," Jose says, recalling the fear in the eyes of patients who are well into their eighties or nineties. "We've had different agencies point guns at us. Whatever they learned in training—they shouldn't be using it on the elderlies. The agents have no respect."

***

Antone and Jose are maneuvering in a militarized zone. Since 1994, when Congress passed the immigration-control measure Operation Gatekeeper, a record number of border agents have been descending on the Tohono O'odham Nation. Border officials acknowledge that the tribe's seventy-five-mile section of the border is now patrolled by seventeen hundred agents, the largest number ever—not including a battalion of customs agents.

Operation Gatekeeper, designed to crack down on illegal immigration in the San Diego area, diverted migrants to the less crowded Sonoran Desert and Tohono O'odham land. Within a year or two, hundreds of tribe members "started calling the vice chairman's office because they were being stopped and asked for documents," says tribal general counsel Margo Cowan. "Some of them were roughed up—dragged out of their cars, spoken to with profanity, told they had to get documents or they would be arrested and deported. Some were arrested. Some were deported."

Among other activities, tribal officials report an increase in   10
vehicle surveillance, gunpoint questioning, and the use of helicopters, which roar overhead to spot migrants. Like migrants, Tohono O'odham tribe members are subject to arrest and detention in any one of a handful of jails along the border. Some detainees are held up to twelve hours before they are released in the border city of Nogales, Arizona. Others are transferred to detention facilities in Florence or Eloy for stays of up to six weeks, according to border patrol spokesman Frank Amarillas.

Cowan says the nation has filed at least one hundred written complaints with U.S. border authorities in the past nine years, on allegations ranging from wrongful detentions to property damage. While Mario Villareal, spokesman for the U.S. Bureau of Customs and Border Protection, says he is not familiar with the complaints, Clyde Benzenhoefer, a border patrol official who worked in the Tohono O'odham region until 2000, acknowledges having received written complaints, although "nowhere close to a hundred."

In 1997, agents arrested a seven-year-old Tohono O'odham boy traveling to a heart specialist at the Sells clinic, says Cowan. The boy and his grandparents were jailed and deported for lack of documentation, their vehicle seized. In February 2003, a woman was turned away for prenatal care for similar reasons; she later miscarried, Jose adds. Many of Jose's patients are elderly, and require regular visits to the health clinic. "A lot of our people have diabetes," she says. "My heart is there for them."

The Tohono O'odham tribe, with a Connecticut-sized reservation on the U.S. side, has twenty-eight thousand members, fourteen hundred of whom live south of the international border that has bisected their homeland for one hundred fifty years. Since the 1930s, that divide has been marked by barbed-wire cattle fences; so far, tribe members have been spared the imposing metal walls that seal the border in areas like San Diego. But the country's recent immigration-control policies have drastically changed every facet of Tohono O'odham life.

Because of the border and its enforcement, ancestors' graves are unvisited; relatives go years without seeing family; and fiestas, wakes, and ceremonial offerings go unattended. Elders, hampered from crossing for a number of reasons, fail to share traditional stories, and to pass on knowledge about the past, about plants and animals, and about caring for their desert home—knowledge that is vital to the tribe. "We were brought into this world for a purpose," says Joseph Joaquin, Tohono O'odham cultural resources specialist, "to be the caretakers of this land."

15 Even the gathering of native plants, a mainstay of traditional culture, is no longer without hassle. Tohono O'odham women just north of the border still go out early in the morning to collect saguaro to make jams and ceremonial wines. "But now the border patrol often pulls up and starts asking for identification," says Jose.

"From time immemorial this has been our land," says tribal vice chair Henry Ramon. "It doesn't make sense that we should be questioned about who we are—we know who we are."

The Tohono O'odham is the only border tribe whose Mexican members are officially recognized by the U.S. government. But members of the Yaqui, Cocopah, Quechan, Kumeyaay, and Kickapoo nations have also traversed the two-thousand-mile border that runs from California to Texas in order to maintain ties with tribe members in Mexico.

Before 1994, members of all these nations could cross the border both ways with little trouble. Operation Gatekeeper, which followed on the heels of Texas's Hold the Line initiative at the El Paso crossing, ended the informal recognition of tribal peoples' right to travel within their traditional homelands. The 1999 federal Operation Safeguard, targeting the Nogales border south of Tucson, intensified the clampdown. September 11 further heightened the tensions, sending the number of border agents to an all-time high, from 7,300 in 1998 to 10,200. "Everyone," as one Yaqui cultural leader puts it, "becomes a suspected terrorist now."

Last January, the Department of Homeland Security folded an array of functions from several border-related agencies into two bureaus: the Bureau of Customs and Border Protection handles inspections, while the Bureau of Immigration and Customs Enforcement handles enforcement. Warren McBroom, associate general counsel of the enforcement bureau, says that some fifteen hundred undocumented non-O'odham migrants could be occupying the U.S. side of the nation's land on any given day. The O'odham generally accept that estimate. Their own police force cooperates with the border patrol and has been shot at by drug runners, according to Cowan. But this ramped-up border security, meant to curtail illegal immigration, drug trafficking, and terrorism, is causing trouble for the Tohono O'odham.

Ana Antone got a sense of the new Homeland Security 20 Department's policies late one night in November of 2002, as she was returning home from a ceremony in Pozo Verde honoring the ancestors. Antone's group had just pulled through the San Miguel Gate. "A border patrol van drove right in front of us," she says. "My friend had to slam on her brakes." Agents in four separate vehicles approached their vehicle on foot and pointed guns at them. "This is our home," she says in a quiet, firm tone. "Who gave them the right to treat us the way they do?"

In 1999, following complaints about harassment at the border, the U.S. government agreed to issue visas to facilitate passage to and from the fourteen O'odham communities in Sonora, Mexico. The program has had limited success. Visas were issued during a ten-week period from November, 2000 to January, 2001. Many tribe members didn't apply during that period, and since then have reported difficulties obtaining the document, according to Cowan. To apply, members from south of the border were required to display Mexican passports, but about four hundred O'odham had never obtained passports. Some refused to apply for them because "to do so was to deny their own nation," Cowan explains. On the U.S. side, many didn't apply for the visas because they feared deportation; several hundred tribe members born south of the border now live in Arizona, where they are as vulnerable to arrest as undocumented immigrants.

The Tohono O'odham Nation also estimates that seven thousand members, a quarter of its population, were born on U.S. soil but cannot prove it. The reason: they have no birth certificate. "We were born in our own homes by a special medicine woman who does births," says Ramon. "Now we are paying the penalty." Some, like Antone, have served in the U.S. military, which is open to noncitizens, but now find they cannot even apply for a passport.

Tribe members also complain about the indignity and inconvenience the visas represent. The required documents are only accepted at official U.S. ports of entry, but the nearest ones are outside the nation's land, reached by miles of poorly maintained roads, says Silvia Parra, executive director of the nation's Health and Human Services Department. Most people are accustomed to using a number of traditional crossings, many of them cattle guards like the San Miguel Gate, which are no longer legal. And once they make the trek to an official port of entry and show proper documentation, tribe members must still obtain and carry a special immigration permit, usually good for only one day.

Warren McBroom contends that the agencies have a good relationship with the tribe. "If you cross by a port of entry using your documents," he says, "you won't have any problems."

25   Yet even documented members from Mexico have reported trouble. According to Joaquin, border patrol agents don't always honor the U.S. visas, saying that "it's not a passport." That charge is denied by U.S. officials. Neither the U.S. border patrol nor the tribe has counted how many tribe members have been turned away from crossing the nation's border points, or determined the reasons.

To tribe members, the situation is increasingly unacceptable. "These gatekeepers are telling them they can't come on their own land," says Cowan. "That is very offensive. They are not Mexican. They are Tohono O'odham."

For their part, border guards have little patience for nuanced explanations about tribal identity, missing documents, or historical passageways, says Cowan. Many agents have no experience with the desert, indigenous culture, or the border area, she says. "The agents are typically sent in for six-week tours of duty from all over the United States," Cowan explains. "You [often] have rookies, and people itching for a fight." Not surprisingly, O'odham elders respond with dismay. "These people are very private. They believe that they were created from the sand of this sacred desert," says Cowan. "For them, harsh words and harsh actions and people who don't belong disrupt the harmony."

Before the border was established, Tohono O'odham villagers in places like Quitovaca, Bacoachi, Caborca, Pitiquito, or Pozo Verde freely moved south and north to visit their relatives, to barter, to share stories. According to tribal cultural affairs manager and archaeologist Peter Steere, some modern border-crossing roads follow prehistoric trade routes along the river valleys. They connected the Tohono O'odham, who lived in the western desert, with the Akimel O'odham (Pima), who lived along the Santa Cruz and nearby rivers. The tribes spoke a mutually understandable dialect. The Tohono might trade baskets, beans, foodstuffs, or labor for "pottery, basketry, meat, deer hides, or mesquite or ironwood carvings," Steere says.

The network of ancient trade routes covered a large swath of territory. "One of the great traditions was going to bring salt from the Sea of Cortez," says Raquel Rubio-Goldsmith, adjunct professor of Mexican-American studies at the University of Arizona. "It was a rite of passage [for] young men. And it indicates the range of land they moved in."

That range of land was bisected following the 1853 Gadsden 30 Purchase, which imposed a string of six-foot-tall metal pillars across Tohono O'odham territory, and opened the way for the U.S. to build a southern transcontinental railroad. The Gadsden Purchase added thirty thousand square miles south of the Gila River to the vast stretch of the Southwest that Mexico had ceded six years earlier, through the Guadalupe Hidalgo Treaty that ended the Mexican War.

"No one showed the Tohono O'odham the respect to invite them to the table," says Cowan. "It was bought and sold out from under them."

By the 1930s, according to Steere, the U.S. had built cattle fences and border inspection stations to prevent the entry of hoof-and-mouth disease from Mexican cattle. Following World War II, the U.S. began establishing border checkpoints. And around that time, the pilgrimage to the Sea of Cortez was halted when U.S. border agents refused to let the salt into the country, says Joaquin.

But for the most part, people still traversed the border freely, even when Lavern Jose was a young girl going to visit relatives in Mexico. "My grandparents never said 'We're in Sonora,'" she recalls, "just that they were going back to the ranch."

Today, because of the threat of detention, deportation, harassment, or just inconvenience, Tohono O'odham travel less freely. Many are blocked or discouraged from making the trek to honor what is perhaps the O'odham's most revered mountain— seventy-seven-hundred-foot Baboquivari Peak. It rises high above the lands overlooking the Tohono O'odham Nation on the U.S. side. Each March, Felix Antone, Ana's brother, leads a pilgrimage there to make offerings before the start of the Unity Run from Pozo Verde to Salt River, a ritual he initiated five years ago to connect O'odham youth with their elders.

35   Antone, sixty-seven, is considered a healer. Wearing a white cowboy hat, dark blue plaid shirt, Levis, and boots, his skin the color of polished mahogany, Antone speaks thoughtfully about Baboquivari Peak. "There is a cave there where the creator we call I'itol lives. That's where we take the young children and where we talk to them about our old way of life," he says. "We go out there and camp all night, and sing and tell stories. Every morning, we go to the cave, and make offerings to the creator." Such offerings preserve a ritual the tribe has practiced "forever."

Now a shadow hangs over ceremonies that require cross-border travel. Antone says that when he was a young boy, "that border line didn't mean anything to me. Or maybe for those of us who live on both sides of the border it really didn't exist. But now, as the years go by, things are getting harder."

For Antone and the Tohono O'odham Nation, the solution may rest with a bill reintroduced by Arizona Congressman Raul Grijalva in February. It would amend the Immigration and Nationality Act of 1952 to grant U.S. citizenship to all enrolled tribal members who carry a tribal card. That card—not a U.S. or Mexican passport—would then authorize all crossings, reinforcing the tribe's identity as a nation. Since 9/11, the bill, H.R. 731, has been held up in the House Immigrations and Claims subcommittee. But the tribe has 112 co-sponsors from forty states including California, Arizona, New Mexico, and Texas. Border patrol spokesman Russell Ahr points out that the U.S. grants residency status, and permanent rights of passage, to all officially recognized North American Indians born in Canada. "If there is already a norm for Canada," he asks, "why is there no discussion of applying that to Mexico and that country's Indians?"

The indigenous nations along the U.S.-Mexico border are asking that same question. Leaving the quest for a citizenship bill to the O'odham, other border tribes are pursuing their own methods for maintaining cross-border links.

Yaqui ceremonial leader Jose Matus helps coordinate cultural exchanges as co-founder of the Tucson-based Alianza Indigena Sin Fronteras (Indigenous Alliance Without Borders), which defends the right-of-way of indigenous peoples on their lands. About ten thousand Yaquis live in southern Arizona, but about forty thousand live in Mexico, where they practice a traditional subsistence lifestyle. They have no running water, electricity, or paved roads, and little experience with U.S. bureaucracy. An agreement hammered out by the Alianza, the Pasqua Yaqui tribal government, and the Yoemem Tekia Foundation waives strict visa requirements for Yaqui cultural events.

In December 2002, Matus followed the protocol of the agreement, informing border agents that he would be crossing with a contingent of his tribe's dancers and singers from Rio Yaqui, Sonora—about four hundred miles south of the border. Matus and his group got through. Still, "three or four of them were heavily questioned about what they were doing and why," says Matus. "We realize that passports could be confiscated at any given moment on the whim of a border agent, especially from a person who can't answer the questions or understand them. They get very intimidated."

Cultural relations were severely strained in 1994, when a group of Yaqui deer dancers was coming across the Nogales port of entry. They were on their way to perform a traditional ceremony involving a sacred deer head, which can only be touched by the dancer using it. A border agent broke open the deer head to make sure there were no drugs inside. "We believe it is an omen when something happens like that," says Matus. "The dancer did not participate in the ceremony, and it is something that they prepare for all year."

In 1998, the tribe met with border officials for a series of cultural sensitivity workshops that improved relations, says Matus. "But we are braced for the ramifications of the border patrol now being part of Homeland Security as they build forces at the border and clamp down even more."

That clampdown has already affected the federally recognized Kumeyaay tribe, whose lands stretch from San Diego and Imperial counties in California to sixty miles south of the Mexican border. Four years ago, the Kumeyaay Border Task Force established a "pass/repass" plan with the U.S. Immigration and Naturalization Service (INS). It was supposed to allow the Baja Kumeyaay to apply for visas that would facilitate cross-border cultural exchanges. A year after the 9/11 attacks, the INS, without consulting the tribe, terminated the agreement, citing security reasons. So far only about three hundred Baja Kumeyaay visas have been processed, with about a thousand more to go.

Despite such obstacles, all the border nations are determined to maintain free travel within their own territories. "To us, everything is a whole; it is one piece," says Dale Phillips, the vice chairman of the Cocopah Nation, located just outside of Yuma, Arizona, about twelve miles from the border. "That line has nothing to do with us; it has to do with two foreign countries who came in and divided [the nation] in half. If it wasn't for that line, maybe we would have a lot of the elders be free to come here to tell the [traditional] stories."

45 As Ana Antone, Lavern Jose, and I approach the San Miguel Gate, vendors in t-shirts, Levis, and long-sleeved flannel shirts are selling pop, juices, and snacks from blue and white and red ice chests. Border patrol agents wearing reflective sunglasses and military garb stare out of parked vans. Nearby, migrants wait to make their way north when darkness falls. We cross the wooden cattle guard slowly, bumping and rocking toward the dusty dirt road that will take us south.

It is late afternoon when we arrive at Pozo Verde. Set amid a cluster of small wooden buildings, Ana Antone's home is simple, clean, and comfortable. It has dirt floors and no running water. An altar in one corner holds white candles, marigolds, a buffalo skull, gourds, sage, rosaries, a cross, and an exquisite statue of the Virgen de Guadalupe. The statue has been in her family for years.

"I was born and raised here," says Antone, gazing out at the desert land. "My parents, grandparents, and other relatives are buried here. I still consider it home."

That sense of home, disrupted by a political boundary, lies at the heart of the identity of the Tohono O'odham, and all the border tribes who are intent on maintaining their traditions. "We are a broken vase," says Louie Guassac, tribal coordinator for the Kumeyaay. "There are pieces of our lifestyle and ways on both sides of the border. Preserving our culture is our priority."

Guiding Questions

1. Do you think this essay is journalism, advocacy, or both? Does Arrieta present the situation of the Tohono O'odham tribe and other "border nations" in a balanced way? If not, why?
2. Why do you think Arrieta begins and ends the essay with her journey toward and across the border with Ana Antone and Lavern Jose, while putting the larger historical and political discussions in between?
3. Why do you think the American border policy toward Canadian-born Indians differs from the one toward Mexican-born Indians and American-born Indians coming from Mexico?
4. One of the ways we define a place is by understanding it to be separate from another distinct place. But what happens to people whose sense of themselves is deeply connected to a place when outsiders redraw the lines that define it? And in an increasingly small and threatened world, how do we strike the right balance between being able to be secure within borders but free enough to cross them?

Paths for Further Exploration

1. Write about how a border you know affects your sense of place and identity. The border might be a national border, state border, city line or even something as unofficial as the "lines" between neighborhoods.
2. Investigate the history of an official, significant border. Who drew it or declared it? Based on what values? Using what technology or techniques? What cultural, natural, social, or economic realities helped determine that border? How were they, in turn, shaped by it?
3. Research the immigration issue and argue in favor of some "best practices" you think should be used to regulate the comings and goings of border tribes and nations such as the Tohono O'odham.
4. Write an analysis of the different sets of values that seem to determine where various kinds of people depicted in the essay decide to enforce borders.

King's Chapel and Burying Ground

ROBIN DUNN

Robin Dunn is from Southington, Connecticut, and graduated from Boston College in 2006. She earned an MSA at the University of Connecticut, and she currently works as a certified public accountant in

*Boston. Her other interests include traveling, reading, writing, and,
of course, the Red Sox. In this essay, written in response to a college writing assignment that sent students out to various interesting
or historic places in Boston, Dunn places her sense of intimidation
about the city next to her growing sense of awe concerning one of
its most historically significant spaces. A reluctant observer at first,
Dunn comes to recognize the unexpected pleasures of exploration,
and discovers connections between her studies and the place she is
visiting.*

✦

I somehow motivate myself to rise out of bed early (a college student's "early") on a Saturday morning, onto a bus (or three), and
into the heart of the city of Boston to observe King's Chapel and
Burying Ground. My adventure begins, well, rather slow. Here
I sit, wedged into a bus seat among a throng of college students who are heading into the city, most likely directed toward
Newbury Street or the Fenway Theater, and I'm traveling downtown as part of a homework assignment. Soon I become "deeply"
involved with an *Us* magazine, still wishing that I were in bed and
praying that I will find my way to the chapel without getting lost.
In fact, I'm more interested in the spasmodic moth attacking the
subway floodlight than the church I am soon to discover.

Sigh of relief. I made it—through the busses and the T, and
with a little help from a handy pocket map my parents provided
when they dropped me off at school just a few short weeks ago.
Onto Tremont Street. It is obvious I am located within a tourist
trap of Boston. I begin to feel like the nonconformist without a city
map in one hand, a camera in the other, and a fanny pack around
my waist. However, I proceed onward and begin to finally grasp
the effects the city is having on me. I have not even reached the
chapel yet when I begin to realize that waking up was well worth
the effort. I pause for a moment. I will admit that the smell of
subway beneath me doesn't exactly enhance the atmosphere, yet
the early fall temperature, the beaming sunshine, and the sounds
of the city life are almost too much to take in. Here I stand, on my
own, and loving every minute of it.

The corner of Tremont Street and School Street. King's
Chapel and Burying Ground sneaks up on my right. Doors open
and a soothing breeze flows peacefully throughout the massive
and handsome structure as if an angel were whispering secrets
of its past behind every open window. An animated woman in
her late fifties sits behind the front desk eager to meet and greet

all those preparing to take the self-guided tour of the church. I can hardly help but to strike a conversation with this woman. Her smile alone is persuasive enough to get me to introduce myself.

Gail, as she introduces herself, tells me of myriad tales that date back to the 1600s in relation to the church and the burial grounds that lie to its side. She tells me about the Puritans, explains the essentials of Unitarian ideals and, what interests me most, conveys the stories of individuals who once stood where I am currently standing.

I learn from Gail and from the brochure she slips into my hand that King's Chapel was the first Anglican Church in New England (now a Unitarian church) and was founded in 1686 by the Royal Governor of the Province of New England. Gail tells me this church represented all that the Puritans stood for—their beliefs as well as their hopes to escape the religious oppression they faced in England. I am officially bound to Gail's words when she speaks of the thousands of Boston settlers, including many anchoring members of Boston's seventeenth and eighteenth century society, whose final resting place is within this cemetery. Among these honorable men and women we can find John Winthrop, the first Governor of Massachusetts Bay Colony; Hezekiah Usher, the first book seller in Boston; Reverend John Cotton and Reverend John Davenport; William Dawes, who rode with Paul Revere to Lexington on April 18, 1775; Elizabeth Pain, who many believed was the prototype for the Hester Prynne character in Hawthorne's *The Scarlet Letter*; and Mayflower descendents such as Mary Chilton, the first woman to set foot off ship in 1620.

I am having some difficulty hinting to Gail to finish her story-telling so I can proceed onward, yet eventually I manage to break away from her company and begin my "self-guided tour" of King's Chapel. Immediately I am taken in by the hand-carved facades on every column, the ivory color that flows throughout the chapel, and the echoes of the other visitors who are whispering and pointing at the artifacts and monuments that line the church walls. I am especially fascinated by the cozy booth-like pews lined with plush red velvet seat coverings and accented with ancient yet well preserved leather-bound books of worship and song. The pews remain segregated from one another yet fit up to eight people per booth. I read on to discover the pews were purchased by families of the town who would pay a fee to occupy a particular pew each week. Funny how a church would separate one family from another when its beliefs promoted unifying the community as a whole.

I proceed onward. As I approach the pulpit, I notice its wine-glass shape Gail had mentioned. I spot the hand-carved balusters

5

(noted by my most helpful tour book) that lead to the high pulpit and to a suspended canopy that hovers over an area meant to amplify the preacher's voice. I am amazed at the design, yes, but at this point I figure my trip is at its end and I have seen all I need to see to write a decent descriptive analysis. Yet, as I turn around to trace my steps, I am overwhelmed by an ornate organ that rests within the choir loft. This tremendous structure is ornamented by a magnificent crown, detailed miters, and intricately designed carvings. I gaze up at it and wonder what brilliant composers and musicians once tickled its keys and imagine how wonderful the music must sound throughout the chapel's unyielding walls.

As I'm looking up, I notice the chandelier that hangs from the chapel's ceiling. It dominates the entire hall with multiple tiers of light fixtures upon light fixtures, illuminating the whole of the chapel. However, it is the embroidered leaf pattern surrounding the chandelier's fixture that catches my eye. I wonder what incredible care and continual hours of labor must have gone into the task of creating and maintaining such an elaborate piece of art.

I make a move toward the walls of the chapel and clumsily trip on a raised tile from the church floor. This stumble forces me to look to the ground and take notice of the aged, worn stone that is marbleized with a greenish tone. Again, I begin to wonder if those many names Gail ran by me once stood where I find myself positioned at this moment. I feel a chill throughout my body and I notice the hair on my arms defy the forces of gravity.

10 Again I believe I have absorbed enough for one day's journey and do my best to make a quick exit for the burying ground. I cannot seem to avoid bumping into chatty Gail once again. She refuses to let me leave until I take a look at the Bede Book that rests to the left of the Vestry. I do as she asks and take the time to glance at this small book. Anyone is invited to enter requests for prayers to be included at the upcoming weekend service. I believe the book is meant more for prayers of remembrance for those who have passed, but I proceed to write a short prayer for my boyfriend who attends Fordham University. Later I'll wonder if they mentioned my prayer in the following day's service: "Here we pray for the deceased souls of Mary Smith and Joe Brown, and for Robin's boyfriend Will who is most likely having a grand old time in N.Y. at F.U." It's the thought that counts, right?

I finally slip out of the chapel (not without a quick smile from my good friend Gail), and gradually I pass through the wrought-iron gates that mark the entrance to the burial grounds. I step upon an ash-colored stone path that winds its way around the graveyard, ending where it initiates, reminding me of that famous yellow brick road. I begin my journey along the bricks and take notice of the composure and order of the colorless, skeletal tombstones that give the graveyard its eerie spirit. Each tombstone looks as if it could crumble to a million pieces with one gentle gust of wind or accidental human touch. Like dominoes, I imagine one knocking over its neighbor if disturbed by any sudden movement such as the vibration of the subway that I now feel beneath my feet. I cannot help but to wonder if such a movement is at all disturbing to those who are now laid to rest among these grounds. Here lies John Winthrop, first governor of Mass Bay, with the T riding by at forty miles per hour every ten minutes to pay its respects.

I take a moment, turn my head from left to right, and capture the site in its entirety. I am standing on one of New England's most hallowed ground, yet all I hear and see beyond the gates is commercial activity at its height. I notice construction to the left of the gravesite, alongside a brick building at the graves' edge. Green ivy crawls up the sides of the wall in a fruitless effort to hide its unattractive bricks. I walk a bit farther and come across a metallic blue object. I find it to be nothing more than a crumpled Doritos bag, neatly placed among the greenery and adjacent to a sign that reads "Please Protect our Heritage." I force myself to believe the wind carried the bag to this resting place.

I soon approach the tombstone of Elizabeth Pain. Is this not the model for a character I had read about in one of Hawthorne's most renowned novels? I read this book, I remind myself. I have read this author's work and now I stand where his inspiration lies. I find this the most monumental moment of my travel, as if I am walking the Hollywood Walk of Fame and fitting my hands within those of the most talented entertainers of our time. I fantasize what greater tales and secrets this ground has held for over 300 years. And that's just it. The church and grounds have hundreds of years on the local Starbucks. Its history will be forever preserved by all those who walk the path of faded engravings, attend the ongoing services, take the self-guided chapel tour, and treat themselves to a quick chat with Gail.

I finally make my way back to the T-station, and realize that *Us* magazine is not nearly as appealing as it had been only hours earlier. While on the T I find that everything I set my eyes on reminds me of the incredible site I have just left. The dreary and sinister stone walls that line the subway tunnels resemble the deteriorating gravestones that line the fading grass of the burial

grounds. The dim lighting of the Boylston Street T-stop is compa-
rable to that of the light that rested on the serene alter. And finally,
I stop to notice the repulsive smudge mark on the glass window
to my right that immediately reminds me to where I am sitting
once again.

15   Newton Campus. I àm back within my dorm room, gathering thoughts and attempting to make something of all I have witnessed today. I reflect on my day and smile at how my morning
began and how my afternoon ended. I have gained a greater interest for the beautiful and amazing aspects of city life, of its history
and the endless tales that stretch back hundreds of years. I wonder what another hundred years will do to King's Chapel and its
burial grounds, and hope that its mystery and atmosphere will be
forever preserved despite all that activity the surrounding stores
and restaurants provide and despite the tourists who share this
sacred space with those who still use it as a site of worship. I dwell
on how different times are for those who once walked those aisles
and the paths of the cemetery from those who now tour in years
exceeding the millennium. How remarkable a difference, yet the
paths walked are one and the same.

Guiding Questions

1. Why does Dunn seem so apprehensive about going into Boston on her
   own, and when do those feelings begin to diminish? Can you relate to
   how she feels in some way?
2. What techniques does Dunn use to anchor you in the scene? What
   attention does she pay to sensory detail? What use does she make of
   simile and metaphor?
3. Why do you think Dunn includes the little "friendship" she strikes up
   with Gail, the woman at the information desk?
4. How important is Dunn's sense of history and literature to her appreciation of King's Chapel and Burying Ground?

Paths for Further Exploration

1. Dunn seems to sense the serendipity of many of her discoveries during
   the trip. Write about a serendipitous moment you have experienced,
   especially if it was on a visit to a tourist site or on vacation.
2. One of the things that Dunn notices is the close juxtaposition of this
   historic site to all the bustle of modern urban life. Write about a place
   you know where a similar juxtaposition occurs.
3. Compare Dunn's essay to Ron Fletcher's "By Dawn's Early Light,"
   which is also an exploration of Boston. What do these two essays share

in their approach? How do they differ? Write an analysis of how both Dunn and Fletcher undertake the task of exploring a specific aspect of the city that is new to them.

The Silence of the Lambswool Cardigans
REBECCA SOLNIT

Rebecca Solnit is an art critic, activist, museum curator, and the author of Motion Studies: Time, Space and Eadweard Muybridge, Wanderlust: A History of Walking, *and* Hollow City: The Siege of San Francisco and the Crisis of American Urbanism. *In this essay, which originally appeared in* Orion *(www.oriononline.org), Solnit investigates the alienation between the products we buy and the places and people who made them, often at greater costs than they will recoup.*

———————— ✦ ————————

There was a time not so long ago when everything was recognizable not just as a cup or a coat, but as a cup made by so-and-so out of clay from this bank on the local river or woven by the guy in that house out of wool from the sheep visible on the hills. Then, objects were not purely material, mere commodities, but signs of processes, human and natural, pieces of a story, and the story as well as the stuff sustained life. It's as though every object spoke—some of them must have sung out—in a language everyone could hear, a language that surrounded every object in an aura of its history.

"All commodities are only definite masses of congealed labor-time," said Marx, but who now could dissolve them into their constituent histories of labor and materials, into the stories that made them about the processes of the world, made them part of life even if they were iron or brick, made them come to life? For decades tales of city kids who didn't know that milk came from cows have circulated, and the inability of American teenagers to find Iraq on a map made the rounds more recently, but who among us can picture precisely where their sweater or their sugar comes from?

I've been thinking about that because a new shopping mall has opened up at the eastern foot of the Bay Bridge, in what was once, according to the newspaper, the biggest shellmound in northern California (though the town I grew up in claimed the same distinction for the Miwok mound it bulldozed without excavation for a shopping center in the 1950s). From the 1870s to the 1920s, this place was Shellmound Park, an amusement park, racetrack, dance hall, and shooting range, but Prohibition put the pleasure grounds out of business and the mound was bulldozed for industry. The remains of seven hundred Ohlone people that an archaeologist snatched from the construction site in 1924 are still at the University of California at Berkeley. Meanwhile, the industrialized site hosted paint and pesticide factories that eventually made it into a wasteland so toxic that those venturing into it wore moonsuits. It was reclaimed for shopping, and the cleanup disturbed the Ohlone remains that hadn't already been bulldozed.

The street that goes out there is still called Shellmound, but the mall itself hosts all the usual chains that make it impossible to know if you're in Phoenix or Philadelphia: Victoria's Secret, Williams-Sonoma, Express, all three versions of the Gap corporation, including Old Navy and Banana Republic, all laid out on a fake Main Street. Anti-Gap protestors haven't arrived yet, though they are frequent presences in downtown San Francisco, decrying both the Gap's reliance on sweatshop labor and the clearcutting of old-growth redwood forests in Mendocino owned by the Gap's CEO (see Gapsucks.org). But the day the mall opened, activists from the International Indian Treaty Council handed out flyers protesting the desecration of a burial ground. As a substitute for protecting the actual site, the city of Emeryville has offered a website with information about it, as if a place could be relocated to cyberspace. The mall is a distinctly modern site, a space that could be anywhere into which commodities come as if out of nowhere.

In *The Making of the English Working Class*, Engels recounts 5 the crimes behind the production of everyday things—ceramics, ironware, glass, but particularly cotton cloth. He wrote in a time when objects were first becoming silent, and he asked the same thing that the activists from Gapsucks.org do, that we learn the new industrial languages of objects, that we hear the story of children worked into deformity and blindness to make lace, the story of the knifegrinders with a life expectancy of thirty-five years, or nowadays the tales of sweatshop, prison, and child labor. These industrial stories have always been environmental stories too, about factory effluents, cotton chemicals, the timber industry, the petrochemical industry.

Somewhere in the Industrial Age, objects shut up because their creation had become so remote and intricate a process that it was no longer readily knowable. Or they were silenced, because the pleasures of abundance that all the cheap goods offered were only available if those goods were mute about the scarcity and loss that lay behind their creation. Modern advertising—notably for Nike—constitutes an aggressive attempt to displace the meaning of the commodity from its makers, as though you enter into relationship with very tall athletes rather than, say, very thin Vietnamese teenagers when you buy their shoes. It is a stretch to think about Mexican prison labor while contemplating Victoria's Secret lavender lace boycut panties. The Western Shoshone rancher and landrights activist Carrie Dann, whose own family graveyard has been flooded by a goldmine pumping out groundwater to get at the gold below, once remarked to me that everyone who buys gold jewelry should have the associated spent ore delivered to their house. At Nevada's mining rates, that would mean a hundred tons of toxic tailings for every one-ounce ring or chain you buy.

The objects are pretty; their stories are hideous, so you get to choose between an alienated and ultimately meaningless world and one that makes terrible demands on you. Most consumers prefer meaningless over complicated, and therefore prefer that objects remain silent. To tell their tales is to be the bearer of bad news—imagine activists as Moses coming down from Sinai but cutting straight to Leviticus, the forty thousand prohibitions: against shrimp (see www.montererybayaquarium.org), against strawberries (methyl bromide, stoop labor), against gold (see www.greatbasinminewatch.org), and on and on. It's what makes radicals and environmentalists seem so grumpy to the would-be consumer.

Maybe the real question is what substances, objects, and products tell stories that don't make people cringe or turn away. For the past half century the process of artmaking has been part of its subject, and this making becomes a symbolic act that attempts to substitute for the silence of all the other objects. But nobody lives by art alone. There's food from the wild, from your own garden, from friends, ancient objects salvaged and flea-marketed, heirlooms and hand-me-downs, local crafts, and a few things still made with the union label, but it's not easy for anyone to stay pure of Payless and Walmart. Good stories too—pricey organic and free-range and shade-grown food that is only available in the hipper stores of the fancier regions—can be a luxury.

Some of the enthusiasm for farmer's markets, which are springing up like mushrooms after rain, is of meeting objects that aren't mute, because you see the people who grew the produce and know the places they come from are not far away. This alternative economy feeds people who want to be nourished by stories and connections, and it's growing. Some farmer's markets are like boutiques with little bunches of peas or raspberries displayed and priced like jewels, but I go to an intensely multiethnic mobscene called Heart of the City Farmer's Market. The food, even some of the organic stuff, is pretty cheap and everyone is present, including the homeless who hang out in that downtown plaza all week anyway, and the locals who use the market to make up for the way supermarkets boycott poor neighborhoods. Seeing the thorn scars on the hands of the rose growers there was as big a step in knowing what constitutes my world as realizing that, in this town where it never snows, our tapwater is all Sierra snowmelt.

10　　What bothers me about the mall is its silence, a silence we mostly live in nowadays; what cheers me are the ways people are learning to read the silent histories of objects and choosing the objects that still sing.

Guiding Questions

1. Do you think it is possible to return to the pre-industrial world Solnit describes, one where every object told a particular story of where it was made and by whom? How would your daily habits change if you knew who made the products you buy and where these items were produced?

2. Solnit describes the mall at what used to be Shellmound Park as "a place that could be anywhere into which commodities come as if out of nowhere." Why do you think people design shopping areas to be uniform? In what ways do we make places the same ways we make products? Are there benefits to designing these areas to be similar, to making consumers feel that they are at once anywhere and nowhere?

Paths for Further Exploration

1. Listen to the voice of an object you have purchased and trace the processes by which it came to you. If you can, find out the specific areas where the raw materials of the object came from, and what kind of

person or people likely worked to create it. If you want to go further, try comparing something you bought at a big chain store with a similar object bought at a local craftsperson's business. Go online and investigate the chain store at which you bought the product, looking for the countries in which the company manufactures. What do the tags on the product reveal about its history?

2. Analyze some advertising by Nike, Apple, Starbucks, McDonald's, or another major retailer to see whether the ads try to create a sense of connection between you and some specific place and/or people, then think about what connections the advertising may be designed to hide or to distract you from.

3. Imagine you have been hired by a group of environmentalists and/or anti-globalization activists to assist with a public relations campaign. The campaign is to publicize the connections between what we buy and the way places and people are treated. Your job is to help get this message across while avoiding the "grumpy" trap that Solnit describes. Write a proposal for the campaign, explaining (with examples) how you'll attempt to educate and motivate without alienating.

Robotic Iguanas
Julia Corbett

Julia Corbett is a professor of communications at the University of Utah, specializing in environmental communication and mass media issues. Her essays have appeared in Orion *(www.oriononline .org), where this piece first appeared, and various scholarly journals in the science and communication fields. Her book,* Communicating Nature: How We Create and Understand Environmental Messages, *was released in 2006. "Robotic Iguanas" describes a place that has become familiar to many of us in urban and suburban areas: a commercial experience structured around a "natural" theme.*

---- ✦ ----

On a ledge in a cliff face, a small brown iguana raises his head and says to the chartreuse iguana perched above him, "So, you wanna piece of me or what?" Soon the iguanas, joined by some toucans and macaws, burst into song: "Right here in the jungle mon, that's the life for me." Lights strobe, the toucans flap their wings, and the iguanas bob their robotic heads. On cue, waiters and waitresses join in the singing, waving strips of brightly colored fabric. A toucan shouts, "Hasta la vista baby!" as our waiter leans over and asks, "Who had the shrimp?"

Coming here was my idea. I had returned to Salt Lake City from a summer of outdoor experiences while millions of my fellow humans tuned into "Survivor" and hundreds stood in line at the new Mayan theme restaurant in the suburbs. A combination of stifling late August temperatures, unhealthy levels of smoggy ozone, and thick smoke from dozens of wildfires raging in the West left me feeling lethargic and listless. I called a colleague. "Chris," I said, "as people who teach environmental communication, we really ought to check out this restaurant with the Mayan jungle theme." To my surprise, she didn't hesitate.

Our table is on the third level of the restaurant next to a railing with a good view down to the "stage," a cliff face about two stories high adorned with tropical plants made of plastic. A gentle waterfall pours from the cliff into a large aqua pool. The rocks are molded concrete and the pool reeks of chlorine. Under clear resin, our tabletop bears a colorful design of the Mayan alphabet and calendar. Down one level to the right is an area with carpeted steps and a large video screen playing cartoons—a sideshow for children not sufficiently captivated by robotic iguanas. High above in the middle of the cliff wall is an office window, light seeping from behind closed blinds.

The house lights—already dim—grow dimmer. On the lower cliff face, steam starts pouring from holes in the rock and two red eyes begin to glow, eventually illuminating a large fiery face in the stone. A deep voice booms, "I am Copac, behold the power. . ." The message is foreboding and a bit evil, something about heat from the center of the Earth. To break the tension, one of the toucans announces that it is about to get a lot hotter. The waiters and waitresses agree, chiming in with a chorus of, "Feeling hot, hot, hot!"

Chris and I laugh; we are seated under an air conditioning   5
vent. By way of contrast, I tell Chris about a Guatemalan jungle I visited, and how even at 3 a.m. lying perfectly still, sweat would trickle from my face into my ears and hair. As the "hot, hot, hot!" number winds down a macaw asks for a cold towel. "I feel Mayan and I'm not even tryin'," it squawks, instructing diners to order another drink.

The owner of the Mayan—a quirky Mormon guy with his own little Intermountain empire of car dealerships, an NBA team, mega movie-theater complexes, and the new theme restaurant—said in a newspaper interview that he took great pains to give his patrons an authentic experience. He sent his architects to Mexico and Central America to ensure that the restaurant could recreate the experience of visiting an ancient Mayan community. They returned with proposals for plastic banyan trees, thatched huts covering computerized cash registers, and chlorinated waterfalls. According to a recent lawsuit, what Salt Lake's Mayan restaurant allegedly recreated was not an ancient Mayan community but a nearly identical Mayan theme restaurant in Denver.

The lights dim again. A disembodied female voice speaks soothingly about standing on sacred ground, hidden in the jungle. Two young men in loin cloths and tall, feathered headdresses emerge on an upper cliff ledge and bang on tall drums, the slap of their hands occasionally out of step with the drumbeat of the amplified soundtrack. An image of a young woman appears on the rock wall, a water goddess of sorts with bright red lipstick. Her name is Tecal. "The spirit of the jaguar calls and I awaken," she says, urging us to return to a lost paradise, to the Earth, to celebrate, rejuvenate, and rebirth. As her speech crescendoes, lightning flashes, thunder booms, and the once-placid waterfall gushes noisily into the pool, spraying the plastic ferns but not the diners beyond. People stop their conversations and turn toward the water.

Chris and I compare notes on our food (her taco salad with iceberg lettuce is unexceptional and my shrimp are tough) and discuss the "flood." She recalls how, in 1983, abundant mountain snowfall and an abrupt spring melt sent City Creek roaring through downtown, past department stores and pawn shops, a muddy torrent of debris and fish slapping against a channel of sandbags. Like many such floods, it was caused by a combination of weather events and failed human attempts to control and divert runoff. Both that flood and the Mayan one, I point out, demonstrate a similar human desire for (and belief in) control of natural elements that by their very nature are largely uncontrollable and highly unpredictable.

The warriors return, wearing only Speedos and asymmetrical face paint. The crowd has been anticipating this, the most talked-about part of the show. From the highest point on the cliff, the young men alternate fancy dives into the pool, swim around the side of the cliff, and disappear to reappear at the top for another dive.

10   Shortly after the restaurant opened for business, the *Salt Lake Tribune* did a profile on a diver, who like all the divers was a member of a high school swim team in the valley. The diver they

interviewed had immigrated from Guatemala when he was eight, and it was suggested that perhaps he had some Mayan blood in him. The story also mentioned that some restaurant patrons have asked whether the cliff divers are fake like the cliff they jump from and the lagoon they land in.

When I was a naturalist in Olympic National Park, I was frequently asked whether the deer wandering through the parking lot snarfing up Cheetos and sandwich crusts were real. Tourists also asked me what time it would rain in the coastal rainforest, as if there were a button we pressed, or as though, like Old Faithful, we could predict the rain. (Their interest was not so much in the natural patterns of a rainforest but in not getting wet.) Although the gulf between the real and artificial is vast, we have accomplished the illusion of no gulf at all, like silk flowers you must touch to determine whether chlorophyll lies within. We remake and remodel the natural world and its elements into more predictable and controllable versions, our own little themepark paradise where flowers never fade on the vine and bubbling brooks never run dry.

There is more than humor or sadness in this degree of disconnect; there is danger. We grow increasingly ignorant of the natural original and risk not valuing it—or valuing its replacement more. When Salt Lake's foothills are abloom in early spring with allium, balsamroot, vetch, and sego lilies, most residents are aware only of imported tulips and daffodils. Numerous western cities have gone so far as to codify the imports, making green grass and thirsty flowers not just a cultural imperative but a legal one.

"You wannanother margarita?" asks our waiter.
"Is that what the Mayans drank?" I ask in reply.
15   The skinny young man with spiky platinum hair stares blankly.
"No thank you," I say.

He leaves a small, black notebook on the table and says he'll take it when we are ready.

While paying up, I wonder if my fellow diners believe they are experiencing nature or just some wholesome family entertainment that comes with a mediocre meal. Can someone who knows only censored and stylized depictions of the natural world— Disneyland, PBS, The Nature Company—ever love and understand the wonderfully complex original? Can we care deeply about the jungle or the foothills or an untamed mountain creek if we've never truly known them? The love and compassion I have for the

West is rooted in decades of discovery, from brushing against a thousand sagebrush to know its potent perfume and reading the summer sky for signs of late afternoon storms. Such experiences remind me that my control is minuscule, my volition matters little, and the capacity for wonder and entertainment is infinite. Chris and I contemplate what the Mayan has to teach us. Jungles are colorful, comfortable, and sublime. Ancient gods and goddesses—some benevolent, some not—control the weather. Nature is predictable and friendly. Animals (with human voices) are merely there to amuse us. And you can buy pieces of the jungle in the gift shop to take home. In the end, the Mayan is not so much about nature as it is about a culture that prefers plastic picket fences over wood ones, robotic animals over wild ones, reality TV over real life.

The lights on stage grow bright and the birds start jabber- 20 ing again. One introduces herself as Margarita Macaw; another, Pierre, wears a beret and says he is from Paris. Iguanas Marvin and Harry ask the macaws if they've seen their sunglasses. A bird informs us that "it's always perfect weather" in the jungle. We leave a tip on the table; the entire show is beginning again.

Guiding Questions

1. What is the effect of Corbett's first paragraph? How does she set the scene, and what absurd and incongruous sights does she quickly draw our attention to?
2. How does Corbett use her experiences in real jungles to explain her response to the restaurant?
3. What is Corbett's overall tone in this essay? Does she find *anything* to like about the place? Is she at all sympathetic to what drives the design of the location, to the desire to control nature—or at least to give the illusion of control?
4. Are there any benefits to these themed restaurants? Do they, for instance, invite some curiosity about places that might otherwise remain unknown?

Paths for Further Exploration

1. Corbett's analysis of this peculiar restaurant may remind us of casinos or theme parks we have been to, of television shows and advertisements we watch, of books and magazines we read, and of vacations we have taken—all of which seek to put us in a close relationship with

nature while letting us keep a sense of control. How much control over the natural world do *you* like to have in the places you go? Do you prefer at least the illusion of control, or do you prefer to experience the natural world more directly? Present an argument for or against a highly controlled encounter with nature.

2. What do you think it would be like to work at one of these nature-themed restaurants or theme parks? What would it be like to be Corbett's waiter or one of the divers? Do you think she would experience such places differently if she worked at one of them? What about commercial places structured around other themes, such as history, music, culture, and so on? How does a theme constitute a place?

3. Write about a *non-commercial* place you know that seems to make the natural world artificial. Think about places like campus greens, city parks, and even building atriums.

The Effects of Fast Food Restaurants on the Caribbean People

Alayne Brown

Alayne Brown is of Jamaican origin and is currently a junior at Wesleyan College in Macon, Georgia. She is enrolled in an environmental engineering program. Her ultimate goal is to establish a consultancy firm that focuses on environmental issues in the Caribbean. Brown feels strongly about the social, political, and economic woes of her fellow Caribbean people, and she believes that a viable way of overcoming these difficulties is through the enhancement and maintenance of the beautiful natural environment. In the following essay, she examines the impact of fast food on the eating habits of the Caribbean people.

◆

The Caribbean, my home, is well known for its lively people, beautiful scenery, and exotic food. Jerk chicken, curry goat, and peppered seafood are traditional delicacies that inspire tourists to flock to our shores. However, the past two decades have seen a shift in the eating habits of ordinary Jamaicans. Gone is the produce from local poultry and crop farmers that has fed the region for centuries; it has been replaced by foreign fast food imports from the industrialized world, namely the United States. The Caribbean Community, or CARICOM, is a government body that consists of all the Caribbean heads of state. In 2007, CARICOM issued a report in which it stated that these new foods, while delicious, contain high levels of fat and sugar. In this same report, CARICOM also noted that since the beginning of the mass food importation, the population of the Caribbean has experienced a huge increase in obesity and obesity-related diseases such as diabetes, hypertension, stoke, and cardiovascular disease.

As a Jamaican, I have witnessed these fast food restaurants overtaking the Caribbean and replacing our precious traditional foods. From reading the CARICOM report and conducting further research , it is clear to me that fast foods are directly responsible for the high levels of obesity in the population. Critics to my argument may point to urbanization and lack of exercise for the mass shift, but I remain convinced that a high level of fast food intake is the root cause of obesity in the Caribbean, and that steps need to be taken, by both the government and consumers, to reverse this trend and get the region back to a healthier way of eating, and ultimately, living.

A Bit of Caribbean History

The beginning of the fast food shift in the Caribbean started in the 1980s. A chain of small islands with very few natural resources, the Caribbean region has always been poor. Realizing that it would be better to represent the Caribbean on the world stage as one unit instead of multiple states, the heads of government came together and created CARICOM in 1973. Trade and big business were identified as the best avenues to improve the Caribbean economies and to take full advantage of globalization, and so the Caribbean Single Market and Economy (CSME) was born in 1989 (CARICOM, 2007). CSME's primary purpose is to promote the free trade of people, money, and products among the Caribbean countries. However, emphasis was not only placed on items made in the Caribbean, but also on products imported into the region by Caribbean countries to be sold to their neighbors.

Tamu Sadler (2009), a researcher for the Sala Interactiva de Salud Internacional – Interactive International Health Room, argues that a key to allowing CSME to work is the removal of various trade barriers that separated the countries. These new trade agreements, he explains, also helped facilitate the introduction of transnational food co-operations, such as Kentucky Fried Chicken (KFC) and Burger King, as they sought to target new locations to expand. While these companies have introduced many job opportunities to the Caribbean, they have also paved the way for the adoption of westernized eating habits. Since the first introduction of these restaurants, the number of fast food franchises has grown exponentially. For example, the 4,243 square miles that is Jamaica now houses 32 different branches of KFC alone (KFC, n.d.). The fast food restaurants in my town are always packed, especially in the evenings and on the weekends. My family used to only venture out to eat on special occasions or if we were in a rush. Now, we eat out more often than we stay in to cook. Jamaica is also the world leader in per capita consumption of Ocean Spray Cranberry Juice, a liquid that contains high levels of sugar (Sadler, 2009). Clearly this shift in consumption will have some consequences.

For instance, one consequence is the shift in farming practices. Up until the late 1990s, the motto of the Jamaican food culture was "eat what you grow and grow what you eat." Farming was a family activity, and everyone had responsibilities. My grandmother, Dorothy Griffiths, owns her own farm where she raises cows, chickens, goats, and pigs. Fruit trees and ground provisions such as mango, cherry, yam, and sweet potato grow in abundance. Since before my birth, she has religiously kept a vegetable and herb garden that was left for her children to tend. Every Saturday, she has told me, was market day, where all the farmers would convene to sell their produce (Griffiths). Her generation engaged in a form of bartering: If one neighbor produces a certain food, he or she would swap their excess for something they needed. The community was viewed as a self-sustaining entity. That is no longer the case.

Granted, it would seem that the culture of the Caribbean is changing in ways that would support a fast food culture; after all, the Caribbean society has become a virtual copy of the United States. Emphasis is no longer placed on individuals growing their own food, as there is neither the time nor the interest to farm (Griffiths). The majority of the young adults have desk jobs and work from nine to five. They eat when they have time and what they can afford, which is more often than not fast food. In the Caribbean, as in other places around the world that have become westernized, people have discovered that it is cheaper to eat from a fast food establishment than it is to buy food at the market and go home to cook. Such are the inequalities of our trading laws that they completely undermine our local farmers, as similar laws do in other parts of the world. Because of the vast numbers of the imported goods and the lack of competition from the local market, the government makes much more money collecting the taxes that result from companies bringing in goods than they make from taxes that are applied to farming goods. The farmers are demoralized as they cannot sell enough produce to earn a decent living. As my grandmother often reminds us, "Farmers are a dying breed." This is a worrying development as farmed foods are generally lower in fat content and sugars and are therefore less likely to cause obesity than the foods from fast food restaurants.

The Facts

Obesity affects both developed and underdeveloped countries alike. According to The World Health Organization (WHO) (2011), "overweight" and "obese" are defined as "abnormal or excessive fat accumulation that may impair health." The Body Mass Index (BMI) is a scale of weight-for-height that is used to measure the two. A BMI greater than or equal to twenty-five is considered overweight and a BMI of thirty or greater is considered obese (WHO, 2011). Obesity levels have doubled worldwide since 1980, with 1.5 billion adults overweight in 2008 and 500 million identified as obese (WHO, 2011). Approximately 43 million children under the age of five were found to be overweight in 2010 (WHO, 2011). Together, the conditions of being obese and overweight rank as the fifth highest risk of global death (WHO, 2011). Bert Wilkinson (2007), a contributor to The CBS International Business Network, stated that in the Caribbean region, the number of deaths caused by obesity is said to be ten times higher than those caused by HIV-AIDS. This is a shocking estimate, as HIV-AIDS is as affiliated with the Caribbean as it is with Africa. Clearly obesity is indeed a problem in the Caribbean.

In 2009, the National Bureau of Economic Research (NBER), a leading American research organization, conducted research to determine if fast food restaurants contribute to obesity. In its follow-up report, NBER determined that in the United States, since the early 1970s, the number of children aged six to nineteen classified as "overweight" has more than tripled from 5% to 17%, and the adult obesity rate also jumped from half to two-thirds of the population (2011). During that same time period, the number of fast food restaurants more than doubled (NBER, 2011). The research examined over three million school children and one million pregnant women. The results were conclusive: proximity to a fast food restaurant greatly increases the risk of obesity (NBER, 2011). "For children, having a fast food restaurant within 0.10 miles of school increases the probability of obesity by 1.7 percentage points, or 5.2 percent. Interestingly, there is no significant effect of having a restaurant 0.25 or 0.50 miles from the school" (NBER, 2011). In the case of pregnant women, living 0.1 miles from a fast food restaurant increases the possibility of gaining about 20 kilos or 44 pounds (NBER, 2011). These results clearly show that the closer an individual is to a fast food establishment, the greater the chances of becoming obese. Consider the tiny islands of the Caribbean and the multitude of fast food restaurants that inhabit them. Is there little wonder that up to 70% of women in Barbados are obese and 15% of all Caribbean children are approximated as being fat or obese (Wilkinson, 2007)?

A Calorie Counter (2007), an online calorie comparison database for fast food restaurants, provided a list of fast foods and their corresponding calorie count:

One slice of large cheese pizza from Pizza Hut	390
One cheesy breadstick	200
One serving of onion rings from Burger King	500
One single cheese Whopper from Burger King	760
One double cheese Whopper from Burger King	990
One triple cheese Whopper from Burger King	1230
One order of regular fries from McDonald's	570
One Big Mac from McDonald's	540
1 Chicken Selects Premium from McDonald's	630

These companies are all prominent franchises in the Caribbean. Using the traditional 2,000 calories a day diet, one fast food meal a day will rack up anywhere between 600 and 1,200 calories in just one sitting. Most people eat three meals a day; it would be absolutely disastrous if all or most of those meals consisted of fast food.

The Science Behind the Scenes

Some critics challenge these results by claiming that the people who live in such close proximity to fast food restaurants just have more opportunity to eat from them and that it would not matter if it were a fast food restaurant or a fresh vegetable market; given enough of anything to eat, one is bound to get fat. However, this is not the case. Eating fast foods is the same as eating high-fat foods. Foods high in fat have a very high calorie density (WHO, 2011). According to Matthew Gaus (n.d.), a writer for eHow Health, one gram of fat has approximately nine calories and one gram of carbohydrates or protein has only four. This means that if a person were to eat the same amounts of both a meal at Burger King and a bowl of cereal, the higher calorie density of the fast food would cause more calories to be consumed in the same quantity of food. The extra calories that the body fails to use right away are stored as body fat for both carbohydrates and fatty foods (Gaus, n.d.). However, as Gaus (n.d.) reports, studies have shown that it is easier for the body to burn calories from carbohydrates than calories from fat. The calories from fat are more likely to directly become body fat, causing the person to become overweight and eventually obese. This is a clear link between fast foods and obesity. It is obvious that any amount of fast food eaten will not bode well for the body, and the more fast food one eats the more prone one is to becoming obese.

Being overweight or obese is not only about the appearance of extra weight on the body. Hossain, Kawar & Nahas (2007), researchers for the *New England Journal of Medicine*, found that conditions such as cardiovascular disease, type 2 diabetes, stoke, and hypertension are also strongly linked to obesity. Since the introduction of fast food restaurants into the Caribbean, deaths caused by cardiovascular disease, diabetes, obesity and cancer have risen to 51% (CARICAM, 2007). The American Heart Association (2011) described cardiovascular disease as heart and blood vessels disease. It can be attributed to different bodily functions, but the main cause is a process whereby plague builds up on the walls of the arteries, causing them to narrow and making it harder for blood to pass to and from the heart. This condition often results in heart attacks, caused when blood is blocked from flowing in a part of the heart, and ischemic strokes, caused when blood is prevented from reaching the brain (The American Heart Association, 2011). Exact figures of cardiovascular disease in the Caribbean were not readily available in any report because of the lack of proper investigations into the subject; however, research has shown that the disease is much more prevalent among those who suffer from obesity (Hossain et al., 2007).

According to a 2006 report published by the Caribbean Commission on Health and Development (CCHD), type 2 diabetes is a chronic disease that manifests because of high levels of sugar in the blood. It can cause cardiovascular disease, strokes, and blindness. Again, the number of people in the Caribbean suffering from the condition is unknown, mainly because of lack of education on the diseases and lack of government initiative in the area. However, it is known that approximately 90% of type 2 diabetes cases are attributed to excess weight and about 197 million people worldwide have impaired glucose tolerance, which is most common because of obesity (Hossain et al., 2007).

Hypertension is the official name for high blood pressure. It is the pressure at which the heart pumps blood against the walls of the arteries (Hossain et at., 2007). Hypertension can cause serious damage to the arteries, heart, kidneys and brain, and over one billion people had it in 2000 (Hossain et at., 2007). Presently, approximately 25% of the populations of St. Lucia, Barbados, and Jamaica suffer from hypertension (CCHD, 2006). Although a direct link has still not been found among hypertension, obesity, and fast food, it is an established fact that a person is up to five times more likely to contract hypertension if he or she is obese (Hossain et at., 2007). These different conditions are all fatal, and while fast food may not be a direct cause, there is a very strong correlation. An increase in one means an increase in the other.

Counter Argument

Donna Bryson (2010), a writer for *The Huffington Post*, has argued that while fast food has a role in causing obesity, most of the blame for obesity and its related diseases should be placed on urbanization and lack of exercise. She argues that more and more people are moving from rural into urban areas in search of better educational and employment opportunities. There is no more time to stay at home and cook three healthy meals a day; people have to be up by the sound of the alarm and hurry to get wherever they need to be. There is no time to waste in this new world or one will be left behind (Bryson, 2010). In the dash to get to work or school, people eat what they can when they can. The lunch break is not much better. In most places, employees get an hour for lunch and they cannot afford to be picky. The cheapest and most easily available food is fast food, and that is no fault of the establishment or the customer—it's just the way the world is

(Bryson, 2010). This argument relates to a point I discussed earlier: the current culture of the Caribbean is indeed being molded to fit into the fast food culture of the westernized world. It would seem that urbanization and fast foods are two links in the same globalization chain.

Bryson (2010) also notes that people have stopped walking. For centuries in the developing world, such as Africa and the Caribbean, people have not had cars to transport them to work or school. There were no elevators to ride on the way to the top floor of a building. People had to rely on their own two feet and would exercise without knowing it. Bryson (2010) points out that some youngsters in Africa had to walk for miles to get to school every morning and back home every evening, five days a week. They would come home and play with the children next door, burning even more energy. Furthermore, they were eating home-cooked meals every day. Therefore, they had no excess body fat and were quite healthy. Nowadays, Bryson (2010) argues, everyone rides a vehicle to school or work, purchases a meal from a fast food restaurant on the way home, and watches the television until they go to bed. She argues that this pattern is a far cry from the lifestyle just a decade earlier, and remains adamant that the shift in the general lifestyle of people is what is to blame for the increase in the general unhealthiness of the population.

I acknowledge that Bryson's points are compelling, and I agree that modern technology has changed the way we work and play; after all, I have seen this shift in the Caribbean, and I listen to my older family members, like my grandmother, recall the days when there were no PlayStations or elevators and people were forced to walk that extra mile to visit their neighbors. However, I still maintain my argument that the primary cause of obesity is the increase in consumption of fast foods. The evidence is clear. Fast food contains much more calories from fat than from carbohydrates and proteins. Whether it is the way it is produced or the additives added to preserve and flavor the food, they reek of unhealthiness, and those who consume these foods, especially in excess, should be prepared to face major health consequences when their bodies can no longer digest the massive amounts of fat. This excess fat can manifest itself as obesity, but obesity can lead to an increase in cardiovascular disease, strokes, diabetes, and hypertension. That obesity-related deaths in the Caribbean have increased since the introduction of fast food into the culture cannot be a coincidence.

Recommendations for the Future

The dependency on fast food cannot continue, as the World Health Organization believes that the situation is only projected to get worse for both the region and the wider world. My research, along with the reports from CARICOM and WHO, is not only about highlighting the problem but also about providing some recommendations as to how to rectify the situation. First, I agree with the calls from various independent health organizations in the Caribbean that there should be a massive education campaign throughout the Caribbean, funded by the governments and the fast food companies, to teach people about the dangers that arise from bad food choices. Such a campaign would also offer recommendations for eating healthily, including appropriate portion sizes and regular exercising. Second, as the problem is not only affecting adults in the Caribbean but our children as well, the government needs to step in and ban certain high-calorie fast foods from all schools. Some children only get to eat when they attend school, and because most schools are public the government has a responsibility to make sure that the food they are paying to be served to the children is as healthy as possible. If the Caribbean government took this initiative, it would follow in the footsteps of consumer advocacy groups in the United States; in recent years, for example, the Bill Clinton Foundation convinced major beverage companies to withdraw all non-diet soft drinks from public school vending machines, and there have been efforts to discourage schools from purchasing beef and other meat products with the additive "pink slime" in an effort to make the food provided by schools healthier.

Lastly—and this step is the most important for the long road to recovery and sustainability—there needs to be more support from Caribbean governments for local farmers. Farm programs need to be introduced to help protect our local farmers from huge fast food chains so that their prices can be more competitive in the eyes of the public. Eric Schlosser and other food activists are currently taking similar steps in the United States so that more farm goods can be found in the average home and school. Farmers need to be educated in the latest farming techniques so that they can become more efficient in their farming practices, which would also help to reduce their prices. Also, the government should start introducing heavy taxes for the companies who are importing and producing these high fatty and sugary foods. From my point of view, if these fast food establishments are helping to make us sick, they should help us to foot the bill so that we can become healthy again. The Caribbean has wonderful food traditions that are both delicious and healthy. It would be a shame if, in the bid to become globalized, the region abandoned these traditions in favor of the fast food dominance that has gripped a lot of the developed world. If this were to happen, the Caribbean would surely lose its flavor.

References

A Calorie Counter. (2007). [Table illustration the calorie, fat and serving size per fast food choice]. Fast Food Restaurants & Nutrition Facts Compared. Retrieved from http://www.acaloriecounter.com/fast-food.php

American Heart Association. (2011). What Is Cardiovascular Disease? Retrieved from http://www.heart.org/HEARTORG/Caregiver/Resources/WhatisCardiovascularDisease/What-is-Cardiovascular-Disease_UCM_301852_Article.jsp

Bryson, D. (2010, October 24). Global Obesity: Africa's Middle Class Hit with Diabetes, Weight Gain. *The Huffington Post.* Retrieved from http://www.huffingtonpost.com/2010/10/25/global-obesity-africas-mi_n_773277.html#

Caribbean Commission on Health and Development. (2006). Report of the Caribbean Commission on Heath and Development. Retrieved from http://www.who.int/macrohealth/action/PAHO_Report.pdf

Caribbean Community. (2007). Caribbean Unity to Fight Chronic Diseases Epidemic: Obesity a Major Target. Retrieved March 16, 2011, from http://www.caricom.org/jsp/pressreleases/pres194_07.jsp

Hossain, P., Meguid, N, & Kawar, B. (2007). Obesity and Diabetes in the Developing World A Growing Challenge. *The New England Journal of Medicine,* (356), 213–215. doi: 10.1056/NEJMp068177

Kentucky Fried Chicken. (2011). M Gaus. (n.d.). What Happens If You Eat Too Much Fatty Foods? [Web log comment]. Retrieved from http://www.ehow.com/about_5100796_happens-eat-much-fatty-foods.html

The National Bureau of Economic Research. (2009). Do Fast Food Restaurants Contribute to Obesity? Retrieved from http://www.nber.org/aginghealth/2009no1/w14721.html

Sadler, T. (2009). Tackling the Obesity Epidemic the Impact of Food Trade and Commerce. *International Health Board Interactive*. Retrieved March 16, 2011, from http://72.249.12.201/wordpress-mu/jamaica/?page_id=4

Wilkinson, B. (2007). Caribbean to Tackle Obesity, Diabetes, Hypertension. *The CBS Interactive Business Network*. Retrieved March 13, 2011, from http://www.bnet.com/?tag=header;header-pri

World Health Organization. (2011).

Guiding Questions

1. Brown argues that fast food restaurants are primarily responsible for escalating obesity rates in the Caribbean. Do you agree? Who is responsible for the obesity epidemic, here in America and abroad?
2. Compare the approach in this essay to that taken by Chiori Santiago's essay "The Flavor of Hope," in the next section of this reader. Is one essay more descriptive than the other? More argumentative? What similar or different techniques do the authors use to discuss issues of food, community, and place?
3. What kinds of authorities does Brown draw upon to make her argument? Does she blend these other voices with hers throughout the essay?

Paths for Further Exploration

1. If you can, spend an hour or so driving or walking around your current town. How far/close is the nearest fast food restaurant? As you look around, count how many fast food restaurants you see. How does this number compare to the number of fast food restaurants located around your hometown? Likewise, how far/close is the nearest grocery store? Is there a farmer's market nearby?
2. Try to trace as many ingredients of one of your meals at home or at school as far back as you can. Who prepared or delivered the food? Who cooked or assembled it? Who grew or raised its raw ingredients? What places did the food come from and move through on its way to you? Now try to perform that same investigation with a meal you purchase at a fast food restaurant.

Refugees Find Hostility and Hope on Soccer Field

WARREN ST. JOHN

Warren St. John has written for the New York Observer, The New Yorker, Wired, *and* Slate, *in addition to his work as a reporter for* The New York Times. *The following article on the refugee community in Clarkston, Georgia, appeared in* The New York Times *shortly before his book* Outcasts United: An American Town, a Refugee Team, and One Woman's Quest to Make a Difference *was published. The book has been published in seven countries and is being taught in first-year college curriculums throughout the country. St. John is from Birmingham, Alabama, and currently resides in New York City.*

————————— ✦ —————————

CLARKSTON, Ga., Jan. 20 — Early last summer the mayor of this small town east of Atlanta issued a decree: no more soccer in the town park.

"There will be nothing but baseball down there as long as I am mayor," Lee Swaney, a retired owner of a heating and air-conditioning business, told the local paper. "Those fields weren't made for soccer."

In Clarkston, soccer means something different than in most places. As many as half the residents are refugees from war-torn countries around the world. Placed by resettlement agencies in a once mostly white town, they receive 90 days of assistance from the government and then are left to fend for themselves. Soccer is their game.

But to many longtime residents, soccer is a sign of unwanted change, as unfamiliar and threatening as the hijabs worn by the Muslim women in town. It's not football. It's not baseball. The fields weren't made for it. Mayor Swaney even has a name for the sort of folks who play the game: the soccer people.

Caught in the middle is a boys soccer program called the Fugees—short for refugees, though most opponents guess the name refers to the hip-hop band.

The Fugees are indeed all refugees, from the most troubled corners—Afghanistan, Bosnia, Burundi, Congo, Gambia,

Iraq, Kosovo, Liberia, Somalia and Sudan. Some have endured unimaginable hardship to get here: squalor in refugee camps, separation from siblings and parents. One saw his father killed in their home.

The Fugees, 9 to 17 years old, play on three teams divided by age. Their story is about children with miserable pasts trying to make good with strangers in a very different and sometimes hostile place. But as a season with the youngest of the three teams revealed, it is also a story about the challenges facing resettled refugees in this country. More than 900,000 have been admitted to the United States since 1993, and their presence seems to bring out the best in some people and the worst in others.

The Fugees' coach exemplifies the best. A woman volunteering in a league where all the other coaches are men, some of them paid former professionals from Europe, she spends as much time helping her players' families make new lives here as coaching soccer.

At the other extreme are some town residents, opposing players and even the parents of those players, at their worst hurling racial epithets and making it clear they resent the mostly African team. In a region where passions run high on the subject of illegal immigration, many are unaware or unconcerned that, as refugees, the Fugees are here legally.

"There are no gray areas with the Fugees," said the coach, Luma Mufleh. "They trigger people's reactions on class, on race. They speak with accents and don't seem American. A lot of people get shaken up by that."

Lots of Running, Many Rules

The mayor's soccer ban has everything to do with why, on a scorching August afternoon, Ms. Mufleh—or Coach Luma, as she is known in the refugee community—is holding tryouts for her under-13 team on a rutted, sand-scarred field behind an elementary school.

The boys at the tryouts wear none of the shiny apparel or expensive cleats common in American youth soccer. One plays in ankle-high hiking boots, some in baggy jeans, another in his socks. On the barren lot, every footfall and pivot produces a puff of chalky dust that hangs in the air like fog.

Across town, the lush field in Milam Park sits empty.

Ms. Mufleh blows her whistle.

"Listen up," she tells the panting and dusty boys. "I don't care how well you play. I care how hard you work. Every Monday and

Wednesday, I'm going to have you from 5 to 8." The first half will be for homework and tutoring. Ms. Mufleh has arranged volunteers for that. The second half will be for soccer, and for running. Lots of running.

"If you miss a practice, you miss the next game," she tells the boys. "If you miss two games, you're off the team."

The final roster will be posted on the bulletin board at the public library by 10 Friday morning, she says. Don't bother to call.

And one more thing. She holds up a stack of paper, contracts she expects her players to sign. "If you can't live with this," she says, "I don't want you on this team."

Hands—black, brown, white—reach for the paper. As the boys read, eyes widen:

I will have good behavior on and off the field.
I will not smoke.
I will not do drugs.
I will not drink alcohol.
I will not get anyone pregnant.
I will not use bad language.
My hair will be shorter than Coach's.
I will be on time.
I will listen to Coach.
I will try hard.
I will ask for help.
I want to be part of the Fugees!

A Town Transformed

Until the refugees began arriving, the mayor likes to say, Clarkston "was just a sleepy little town by the railroad tracks."

Since then, this town of 7,100 has become one of the most diverse communities in America.

Clarkston High School now has students from more than 50 countries. The local mosque draws more than 800 to Friday prayers. There is a Hindu temple, and there are congregations of Vietnamese, Sudanese and Liberian Christians.

At the shopping center, American stores have been displaced by Vietnamese, Ethiopian and Eritrean restaurants and a halal butcher. The only hamburger joint in town, City Burger, is run by an Iraqi.

The transformation began in the late 1980s, when resettlement agencies, private groups that contract with the federal government, decided Clarkston was perfect for refugees to begin new lives. The town had an abundance of inexpensive apartments, vacated by middle-class whites who left for more affluent suburbs. It had public transportation; the town was the easternmost stop on the Atlanta rail system. And it was within commuting distance of downtown Atlanta's booming economy, offering new arrivals at least the prospect of employment.

At first the refugees—most from Southeast Asia—arrived so slowly that residents barely noticed. But as word got out about Clarkston's suitability, more agencies began placing refugees here. From 1996 to 2001, more than 19,000 refugees from around the world resettled in Georgia, many in Clarkston and surrounding DeKalb County, to the dismay of many longtime residents.

Many of those residents simply left. Others stayed but remained resentful, keeping score of the ways they thought the refugees were altering their lives. There were events that reinforced fears that Clarkston was becoming unsafe: a mentally ill Sudanese boy beheaded his 5-year-old cousin in their Clarkston apartment; a fire in a crowded apartment in town claimed the lives of four Liberian refugee children.

At a town meeting in 2003 meant to foster understanding between the refugees and residents, the first question, submitted on an index card, was, "What can we do to keep the refugees from coming to Clarkston?"

A Coach with a Passion

Luma Mufleh, 31, says she was born to coach. She grew up in Amman, Jordan, in a Westernized family, and attended the American Community School, for American and European expatriates and a few well-to-do Jordanians. There, Muslim girls were free to play sports as boys did, and women were permitted to coach.

Her mentor was an American volleyball coach who demanded extreme loyalty and commitment. Ms. Mufleh picked up on a paradox. Though she claimed to dislike her coach, she wanted to play well for her.

"For the majority of the time she coached me, I hated her," Ms. Mufleh said. "But she had our respect. Until then, I'd always played for me. I'd never played for a coach."

Ms. Mufleh attended college in the United States, in part because she felt women here had more opportunities. She went to

Smith College, and after graduation moved to Atlanta. She soon found her first coaching job, as head of a 12-and-under girls soccer team through the local Y.M.C.A.

On the field, Ms. Mufleh emulated her volleyball coach, an approach that did not always sit well with American parents. When she ordered her players to practice barefoot, to get a better feel for the soccer ball, a player's mother objected on the grounds that her daughter could injure her toes.

"This is how I run my practice," Ms. Mufleh told her. "If she's not going to do it, she's not going to play."

Ms. Mufleh's first team lost every game. But over time her methods paid off. Her players returned. They got better. In her third season, her team was undefeated.

When Ms. Mufleh learned about the growing refugee community in Clarkston, she floated the idea of starting a soccer program. The Y.M.C.A. offered to back her with uniforms and equipment. So in the summer of 2004, Ms. Mufleh made fliers announcing tryouts in Arabic, English, French and Vietnamese and distributed them around apartment complexes where the refugees lived.

For a coach hoping to build a soccer program in Clarkston, the biggest challenge was not finding talented players. There were plenty of those, boys who had learned the game in refugee camps in Africa and in parking lots around town. The difficulty was finding players who would show up.

Many of the players come from single-parent families, with mothers or fathers who work hours that do not sync with sports schedules. Few refugee families own cars. Players would have to be self-sufficient.

On a June afternoon, 23 boys showed up for the tryouts.

From the beginning, the players were wary. A local church offered a free basketball program for refugee children largely as a cover for missionary work.

Others simply doubted that a woman could coach soccer.

"She's a girl — she doesn't know what she's talking about," Ms. Mufleh overheard a Sudanese boy say at an early practice.

She ordered him to stand in the goal. As the team watched, she blasted a shot directly at the boy, who dove out of the way.

"Anybody else?" she asked.

In Brutal Pasts, a Bond

Jeremiah Ziaty, one of those early players, is a typical member of the Fugees.

In 1997, in the midst of Liberia's 14 years of civil war, rebels led by Charles Taylor showed up one night at the Ziatys' house in Monrovia. Jeremiah's father was a low-level worker in a government payroll office. The rebels thought he had money. When they learned he did not, they killed him in the family's living room.

Beatrice Ziaty, Jeremiah's mother, grabbed her sons and fled out the back door. The Ziatys trekked through the bush for a week until they reached a refugee camp in the Ivory Coast. There, they lived in a mud hut and scavenged for food. After five years in the camp, Ms. Ziaty learned her family had been accepted for resettlement in Clarkston, a town she had never heard of.

The United States Committee for Refugees and Immigrants in Washington estimates that there are now more than 12 million refugees worldwide and more than 20 million people displaced within their own nations' borders. In 2005, only 80,800 were accepted by other nations for resettlement, according to the United Nations.

The Ziatys' resettlement followed a familiar script. The family was lent $3,016 for one-way airline tickets to the United States, which they repaid in three years. After a two-day journey from Abidjan, they were greeted in Atlanta by a case worker from the International Rescue Committee, a resettlement organization. She took them to an apartment in Clarkston where the cupboard had been stocked with canned goods.

The case worker helped Ms. Ziaty find a job, as a maid at the Ritz-Carlton Hotel in the affluent Buckhead section of Atlanta, one that required an hour commute by bus. While walking home from the bus stop after her first day, Ms. Ziaty was mugged and her purse stolen.

Terrified of her new surroundings, Ms. Ziaty told her son Jeremiah never to leave the house. Like any 8-year-old, Jeremiah bristled. He especially wanted to play soccer. Through friends in the neighborhood, he heard about tryouts for the Fugees.

"When he tell me, 'Mom, I go play soccer,' I tell him he's too small, don't go out of the house," Ms. Ziaty recalled. "Then he would start crying."

Ms. Ziaty relaxed her rule when she met Ms. Mufleh, who promised to take care of her son.

That was three years ago. At age 11, Jeremiah is a leader of the 13-and-under Fugees, shifting among sweeper, center midfielder and center forward.

Other members of the Fugees also have harrowing stories. Qendrim Bushi's Muslim family fled Kosovo when Serbian soldiers torched his father's grocery store and threatened to kill them. Eldin Subasic's uncle was shot in Bosnia. And so on. The Fugees, Ms. Mufleh believed, shared something intense. They knew trauma. They knew the fear and loneliness of the newcomer. This was their bond.

"In order to get a group to work together, to be effective together, you have to find what is common," she said. "The refugee experience is pretty powerful."

• • •

Ms. Mufleh made a point never to ask her players about their pasts. On the soccer field, she felt, refugees should leave that behind.

Occasionally, though, a boy would reveal a horrific memory. One reported that he had been a child soldier. When she expressed frustration that a Liberian player tuned out during practice, another Liberian told her she didn't understand: the boy had been forced by soldiers to shoot his best friend.

"It was learning to not react," Ms. Mufleh said. "I just wanted to listen. How do you respond when a kid says, 'I saw my dad shot in front of me'? I didn't know."

As a Jordanian in the Deep South, Ms. Mufleh identified in some ways with the refugees. A legal resident awaiting a green card, she often felt an outsider herself, and knew what it was like to be far from home.

She also found she was needed. Her fluent Arabic and conversational French came in handy for players' mothers who needed to translate a never-ending flow of government paperwork. Teachers learned to call her when her players' parents could not be located. Families began to invite her to dinner, platters of rice and bowls of leafy African stews. The Ziatys cut back on the peppers when Coach Luma came over; they learned she couldn't handle them.

Upon hearing of the low wages the refugee women were earning, Ms. Mufleh thought she could do better. She started a house and office cleaning company called Fresh Start, to employ refugee women. The starting salary is $10 an hour, nearly double the minimum wage and more than the women were earning as maids in downtown hotels. She guarantees a 50-cent raise every year, and now employs six refugee women.

Ms. Mufleh said that when she started the soccer program, she was hopelessly naïve about how it would change her life.

"I thought I would coach twice a week and on weekends— like coaching other kids," she said. "It's 40 or 60 hours a week—coaching, finding jobs, taking people to the hospital. You start off on your own, and you suddenly have a family of 120."

Off to a Rough Start

On a Friday morning in August, the boys come one by one to look for their names on the roster at the public library. Many go away disappointed, but six do not.
The new players are:

> Mohammed Mohammed, 12, a bright-eyed Iraqi Kurd whose family fled Saddam Hussein for Turkey five years ago and who speaks only a few words of English.
>
> Idwar and Robin Dikori, two rocket-fast Sudanese brothers, 12 and 10, who lost their mother, sister and two younger brothers in a car crash after arriving in Clarkston.
>
> Shahir Anwar, 13, an Afghan whose parents fled the Taliban and whose father suffered a debilitating stroke soon after arriving in this country.
>
> Santino Jerke, a shy 11-year-old Sudanese who has just arrived after three years as a refugee in Cairo.
>
> Mafoday Jawneh, a heavyset boy of 12 whose family fell out of favor after a coup in Gambia, and who has a sensitive side; his older brother ribs him for tearing up during "The Oprah Winfrey Show."

Ms. Mufleh is uncertain of her team's prospects. She will have to teach the new players the basics of organized soccer. There are no throw-ins or corner kicks in the street game they have been playing.

In her occasional moments of self-doubt, Ms. Mufleh asks herself: Can I really get these boys to play together? Can I really get them to win?

• • •

The Fugees' first practice this season is on a sultry August afternoon, with thunderclouds looming in the distance. After 90 minutes of studying, the team runs for half an hour and groans through situps, push-ups and leg lifts.

But the Fugees have no soccer goals. The Y.M.C.A., which sponsors the team, did not place the order, despite a $2,000 grant for the purpose. Ms. Mufleh quietly seethes that a team of wealthy children would probably not have to wait for soccer goals. She likens practice to "playing basketball without a hoop."

The team's first games portend a long season. The Fugees tie their first game, 4-4. In their next game, they surrender a lead and lose, 3-1. The team isn't passing well. Players aren't holding their positions.

On a sweltering afternoon in early September, the Fugees prepare to take the field against the Triumph, a team from nearby Tucker. Even before the game, there is a glaring difference between the Fugees and their competition. The Triumph have brought perhaps 40 parents, siblings and friends, who spread out with folding chairs and picnic blankets and are loaded down with enough energy bars and brightly colored sports drinks for an N.B.A. team.

Though this is technically a home game, no one is on the Fugees' side. During the course of the season, only one Fugees parent will make a game.

The Fugees lead, 2-0, at halftime. In the second half, they put on a show: firing headers, bicycle kicks and a gorgeous arcing shot from 30 yards out. Even the parents of the Triumph gasp and clap in appreciation. At the final whistle, the Fugees have won, 5-1.

"Not bad," Ms. Mufleh tells her team. "But next week will be a much better game, O.K.?"

A Call for Change

Ms. Mufleh has a list of complaints about the Fugees' practice field: little grass, no goals. Neighborhood children regularly wander through the scrimmages, disrupting play.

But after a gang shooting in an apartment complex behind the field in late September, she concludes that the field is not safe. She cancels practice for two days. Fed up, she storms into Mayor Swaney's office, demanding use of the empty field in Milam Park.

When Lee Swaney first ran for City Council in Clarkston more than 15 years ago, he did so as an unabashed representative of "Old Clarkston"—Clarkston before the refugees. It was certainly the more politically viable stance. Because few of the refugees have been in the country long enough to become citizens and vote, political power resides with longtime residents. The 2005 election that gave Mr. Swaney a second four-year term as mayor of this town of 7,100 was determined by just 390 voters.

As mayor, Mr. Swaney has frequently found himself caught between these voters and the thousands of newcomers. But he has also taken potentially unpopular steps on behalf of the refugees. In 2006 he forced the resignation of the town's longtime police chief, in part because of complaints from refugees that

Clarkston police officers were harassing them. Mr. Swaney gave the new chief a mandate to purge the Police Department of rogue officers.

Within three months, the chief, a black man of Trinidadian descent named Tony J. Scipio, fired or accepted the resignations of one-third of the force.

Soccer is another matter. Mr. Swaney does not relish his reputation as the mayor who banned soccer. But he must please constituents who complain that refugees are overrunning the town's parks and community center—people like Emanuel Ransom, a black man who moved to Clarkston in the late 1960s.

"A lot of our Clarkston residents are being left out totally," Mr. Ransom says. "Nobody wants to help," he says of the refugees. "It's just, 'Give me, give me, give me.' "

Mr. Swaney encourages Ms. Mufleh to make her case at the next City Council meeting. So in early October she addresses a packed room at City Hall, explaining the team's origins and purpose and promising to pick up trash in the park after practice.

Mr. Swaney takes the floor. He admits concerns about "grown soccer people" who might tear up the field. But these are kids, he says, and "kids are our future."

He announces his support of a six-month trial for the Fugees' use of the field in Milam Park.

The proposal passes unanimously. At least for six months, the Fugees can play on grass.

Getting Back in the Game

Early on the morning of Oct. 14, Jeremiah Ziaty is nowhere to be seen. The Fugees have a 9 a.m. game an hour from Clarkston, against the Bluesprings Liberty Fire, one of the top teams. Ms. Mufleh had told her players to meet at the library by 7.

Ms. Mufleh usually leaves players behind if they aren't on time. But she knows Jeremiah's mother is now working nights at a packaging factory; she gets home at 3 a.m. and won't be up to wake Jeremiah. So the coach orders the bus driver to the Ziatys' apartment. Jeremiah is sound asleep. Awakened, he grabs his uniform and fumbles toward the bus.

From the outset of the game, the Fugees, and especially Jeremiah, seem groggy. They fall behind, 1-0. But in the second half, they tie the score, fall behind, and tie it again, 2-2. Jeremiah is now playing fearsome defense. With minutes to go, the Fugees score. They win, 3-2.

"We played as a team," says Qendrim Bushi, the boy from Kosovo. "We didn't yell at each other. Last game, when they scored, all of us were yelling at each other. And Coach made us do a lot of stuff at practice. That's why we win. Only because of Coach."

As the Fugees leave the field, a man on the Bluesprings sideline yells to them, "I'd have paid money to watch that game!"

• • •

The Fugees have a knack for inspiring such strong reactions, both positive and negative. After one game Ms. Mufleh thought for a moment she was being chased by a rival parent.

"We've heard about your team," the man said when he caught up with her. "We want to know what we can do to help."

The rival team donated cleats, balls and jerseys.

Then there was the game in rural Clarkesville last season at which rival players and even some parents shouted a racial epithet at some of the African players on the Fugees.

After being ejected from a game against the Fugees in November, a rival player made an obscene gesture to nearly every player on the Fugees before heading to his bench. And opponents sometimes mocked the Fugees when they spoke to each other in Swahili, or when Ms. Mufleh shouted instructions in Arabic.

There were even incidents involving referees. Two linesmen were reprimanded by a head referee during a pregame lineup in October for snickering when the name Mohammed Mohammed was called.

Ms. Mufleh tells her players to try their best to ignore these slights. When the other side loses its cool, she tells them, it is a sign of weakness.

Ms. Mufleh is just as fatalistic about bad calls. In her entire coaching career, she tells her players, she has never seen a call reversed because of arguing.

The Fugees are perhaps better equipped to accept this advice than most. Their lives, after all, have been defined by bad calls. On the field, they seem to have a higher threshold for anger than the American players, who often respond to borderline calls as if they are catastrophic injustices. Bad calls, Ms. Mufleh teaches her players, are part of the game. You have to accept them, and move on.

On Oct. 21, Ms. Mufleh is forced to put this theory to the test. The Fugees are on their way to Athens, an hour's drive, for their biggest game, against the undefeated United Gold Valiants. A win will put them in contention for the top spot in their division. Ms. Mufleh sets out in her yellow Volkswagen Beetle, the back seat crammed with balls and cleats. Her team follows in a white Y.M.C.A. bus.

Just outside Monroe, Ms. Mufleh looks to her left and sees a Georgia State Patrol car parallel to her. She looks at her speedometer. She isn't speeding.

The brake light, she thinks.

Ms. Mufleh noticed it early in the week, but between practices, work and evenings shuttling among her players' apartments, she neglected to get it fixed. The trooper turns on his flashing lights. Ms. Mufleh eases to the side and looks at her watch. If this doesn't take too long, the team will make the field in time to warm up.

It isn't so simple. Because of a clerical error, a ticket Ms. Mufleh paid a year before appears unpaid. Her license is suspended. The trooper orders her from her car. In full view of her team, he arrests her.

In the bus, the Fugees become unglued. Santino Jerke, in the country only a few months, begins to weep, violating the unwritten team rule that Fugees don't cry. Several of the Fugees have had family members snatched by uniformed men, just like this. They have been in the United States too little time to understand court dates or bail.

Ms. Mufleh tells the team's manager and bus driver, Tracy Ediger, to take the team to Athens. They know what to do. They can play without her.

Coachless, though, the Fugees are lost. Athens scores within minutes. And scores again. And again. The final score is 5-0.

After the game, Ms. Ediger drives the team back to Monroe. She puts together the $800 bail for Ms. Mufleh and signs some papers. In a few moments, the coach appears. Later, Ms. Mufleh says she thought at that moment about all the times she had told the Fugees to shake off bad calls, to get back in the game, to take responsibility. She walks straight to the bus and her players.

"This was my fault, and I had no excuse for not being there," she tells them. "I should have been there and I wasn't, and the way it happened probably messed you guys up."

Ms. Mufleh asks about the score.

"It was a really hard team, Coach," says Idwar Dikori, the Sudanese speedster.

"Were they better than you?"

"No!" the Fugees shout in unison.

"Come on, guys—were they?"

"No, Coach," Robin Dikori says. "If you were there, we were going to beat them."

Back in Clarkston that night, Ms. Mufleh takes some sweet rolls to the family of Grace Balegamire, a Congolese player. Grace's 9-year-old brother has heard about the arrest, but doesn't believe it.

"If you were in jail," the boy says, "you wouldn't be here."

Ms. Mufleh explains that she gave the people at the jail some money and promised to come back later, so they let her out.

"How much money?" he asks.

"Enough for 500 ice creams."

"If you pay 500 ice creams you can come out of jail?" he asks.

Ms. Mufleh grasps the boy's confusion. The boys' father is a political prisoner, in jail in Kinshasa, under circumstances that have drawn condemnation from Amnesty International and the Red Cross. The government there has issued no word on when, or if, he will be released.

At the Ziatys' home, the arrest has a similarly jarring effect. Jeremiah locks himself in his room and cries himself to sleep.

Battling to the End

It's late October, and with just two weeks left in the season, a minor miracle occurs in the arrival of two 10-foot-long cardboard boxes: portable soccer goals for the Fugees. The administrator at the Y.M.C.A. finally put in the order. Ms. Mufleh and Ms. Ediger assemble the goals in Milam Park.

The goals and the new field offer Ms. Mufleh new opportunities to coach. On grass, players can slide-tackle during scrimmages, a danger on the old, gravelly field. A lined field makes it easier to practice throw-ins and corner kicks. And goals: well, they provide a chance for the Fugees to practice shooting.

A disturbing trend has emerged in recent games. The Fugees move the ball down the field at will, but their shots are wild. They tie two games despite dominating play.

Perhaps the Fugees are missing shots for the reason other teams miss shots: because scoring in soccer, under the best conditions, is deceptively difficult. But Ms. Mufleh also wonders if the absence of goals for most of a season doesn't have something to do with it.

Even so, the Fugees end the regular season on a misty Saturday with a 2-1 victory, to finish third in their division with a record of 5-2-3, behind undefeated Athens and the Dacula Danger, a team the Fugees tied. The season finale will be a tournament called the Tornado Cup. To a player, the Fugees think they can win.

"What makes us work as a team is we all want to win bad—we want to be the best team around," Qendrim says. "It's like they're all from my own country," he adds of his teammates. "They're my brothers."

• • •

The Tornado Cup comes down to a game between the Fugees and the Concorde Fire, perhaps Atlanta's most elite—and expensive—soccer academy. The Fugees need to win to advance to the finals.

Standing on the sideline in a sweatshirt with "Soccer Mom" on the back, Nancy Daffner, team mother for the Fire, describes her son's teammates as "overachievers." One is a cellist who has played with the Atlanta Symphony. Her son wakes up an hour early every day to do a morning radio broadcast at his school.

The Fire are mostly from the well-to-do Atlanta suburb of Alpharetta. They have played together under the same coach for five years. They practice twice a week under lights, and have sessions for speed and agility training.

Over the years, the parents have grown close. During practice, Ms. Daffner says, she and the other mothers often meet for margaritas while the fathers watch their sons play. The team has pool parties and players spend weekends at one another's lake houses. In the summer, most of the players attend soccer camp at Clemson University. Ms. Daffner estimates that the cost of playing for the Fire exceeds $5,000 a year per player, which includes fees, travel to tournaments and, of course, gear. Each player has an Adidas soccer bag embroidered with his jersey number.

There is one other expenditure. The parents of the Fire collectively finance the play of Jorge Pinzon, a Colombian immigrant and the son of a single working mother. He isn't from Alpharetta, but from East Gwinnett County, a largely Latino area outside Atlanta. Fire parents go to great lengths to get Jorge to games, arranging to meet him at gas stations around his home, landmarks they can find in his out-of-the-way neighborhood. Jorge is the best player on the team.

Ms. Mufleh gathers the Fugees before warm-ups.

"Play to the whistle," she tells them. "If the ref makes a bad call, you keep playing. O.K.? You focus on the game and how you're going to win it. Because if you don't, we're going to lose your last game of the season, and you're going home early."

Just before the opening whistle, some of the Fugees see a strange sight on the sideline. A teacher from the school of Josiah Saydee, a Liberian forward, has come to see him play. Some older refugee children from the complexes in Clarkston have managed rides to the game, an hour from home. Several volunteers from resettlement agencies show up. For the first time all year, the Fugees have fans.

The Fugees come out shooting—and missing—frequently. They lead, 1-0, at the half. In the second half, it's as if a force field protects the Fire's goal. After a half-dozen misses, the Fugees score again midway through the second half, to lead by 2-1.

Then, with just minutes to go, Jorge Pinzon of the Fire gets free about 25 yards from the Fugees' goal. He squares his shoulders and leans into a shot that arcs beautifully over the players' heads. Eldin Subasic, the Fugees' Bosnian goalie, leaps. The ball brushes his hands and deflects just under the bar, tying the game.

The final whistle blows moments later. The Fugees' season is over.

"You had them," Ms. Mufleh tells her team after the game. "You had them at 2 to 1, and you wouldn't finish it."

The Fugees are crushed.

"We lost, I mean, we tied our game," says Mafoday Jawneh, the sensitive newcomer to the team. "It was so. . . ." His voice trails off. "I don't know what it was."

An Unpleasant Holiday Gift

The holidays are a festive time in Clarkston. Santa Claus arrives by helicopter at City Hall. The mayor is there to greet him, as are some of the Fugees.

They have other concerns besides Christmas. The Fugees have held two carwashes in town, to raise $1,000 to go to a tournament in Savannah in late January. They have come up $130 short, and Ms. Mufleh tells them that unless they raise the money, they are not going. When one player suggests asking their parents, Ms. Mufleh says that any player who asks a parent for tournament money will be kicked off the team.

She tells them, "You need to ask yourselves what you need to do for your team."

• • •

"You need to ask yourself what you need to do for your team," Jeremiah Ziaty says.

He is at home in his kitchen, talking with Prince Tarlue, a teammate from Liberia, making a case for a team project. Some of the boys are to meet at Eldin Subasic's apartment. They can knock on doors in town and offer to rake leaves to raise the money to get to Savannah. No need telling Coach, unless they raise enough cash. Prince says he is in. Grace is in, too. Some older boys in the refugee community offer to help out as well. Late on a Sunday morning, they set out.

That afternoon, Ms. Mufleh's cellphone rings. It's Eldin, who asks if she will pick up Grace and take him home. They have been raking leaves all day, he says, and Grace does not want to walk home in the dark. Oh, Eldin adds, he wants to give her the money.

"What money?" she asks.

"You said we needed $130," he tells her. "So we got $130."

• • •

Ms. Mufleh and Ms. Ediger, the team manager, spend the holiday vacation visiting the players' families. On Dec. 26, Ms. Mufleh receives a fax on Town of Clarkston letterhead.

Effectively immediately, the fax informs her, the Fugees soccer team is no longer welcome to play at Milam Park. The city is handing the field to a youth sports coordinator who plans to run a youth baseball and football program.

Questioned by this reporter, Mayor Swaney says he has forgotten that in October the City Council gave the Fugees six months. A few days later, he tells Ms. Mufleh the team can stay through March.

In early January, Ms. Mufleh logs on to Google Earth, and scans satellite images of Clarkston. There are green patches on the campuses of Georgia Perimeter College, and at the Atlanta Area School for the Deaf, around the corner from City Hall. She hopes to find the Fugees a permanent home.

Correction: February 1, 2007

A front-page article on Jan. 21 about a soccer program for refugee boys in Clarkston, Ga., rendered incorrectly a quotation from *The Atlanta Journal-Constitution* in which Mayor Lee Swaney of Clarkston commented on the use of a town park. He said, "There will be nothing but baseball down there as long as I am mayor." He did not say "baseball and football."

Editors' Note: March 4, 2007

A front-page article on Jan. 21 reported on a soccer program for refugee boys in Clarkston, Ga., and how it has come to symbolize the passions that run high in the area over the issue of immigration. The article included a statement that Clarkston's mayor, Lee Swaney, had forced the resignation of the town's longtime police chief, in part because of complaints from refugees that police officers were harassing them.

The former police chief, Charles Nelson—who was not identified by name in the article—called *The Times* on Feb. 5 to say that he had resigned voluntarily. Mayor Swaney says that Mr. Nelson left on his own accord.

The Times tried several times to contact Mr. Nelson for comment before publication. The article should have said that he could not be reached, and it should have attributed the information about the circumstances of his resignation to those who provided it.

This editors' note was delayed for research.

Guiding Questions

1. St. John explains that in many ways, Clarkston was an ideal location for refugee resettlement: "The town had an abundance of inexpensive apartments, vacated by middle-class whites who left for more affluent suburbs. It had public transportation; the town was the easternmost stop on the Atlanta rail system. And it was within commuting distance of downtown Atlanta's booming economy, offering new arrivals at least the prospect of employment." However, what have been some of the challenges Clarkston has presented to the refugee community?

2. St. John describes the Clarkston mayor's insistence that fields around town be used only for baseball. He also describes the refugees' complaints that the local police were harassing them. Are there racial tensions within your hometown? Are there (perhaps subtle) ways in which your hometown alternately increases or decreases these tensions?

3. Do you know of any refugee communities near you? Do you have any interaction with these communities? How is it that these particular refugees ended up in your area?

4. What does St. John gain (or lose?) by structuring this portrait of a town struggling with an influx of diverse refugee cultures around the relatively small question—and literally small space—of an athletic field? How does the field work for St. John as metaphor, case study, and organizing principle for the story?

Paths for Further Exploration

1. Do some research on countries in which people are currently being persecuted (e.g., Rwanda, Burundi, Sudan, Indonesia, Pakistan, Burma). Choose one country, and write a research paper that describes the process from refugee camp to resettlement. What did you learn from your research? What kinds of problems did you find within this process?

2. Consider reaching out to local refugee resettlement agencies in your area to investigate, and help address, the chief problems facing refugees in your area. Work with the agencies' administrators to come up with the most appropriate way for you to interview those involved in many sides of the issues and conduct your research as you also participate in the agency's efforts.

3. What does it mean for a community to be selected by outside agencies to fulfill a particular role, whether as a refugee resettlement area, the site of an industrial park, the site of a new national wilderness area, or some other major use? In Clarkston's case, or others you might consider, are there reasons beyond the obviously troubling ones (such as racism) that a community might resist such changes?

Where Are We Going?

Where are you going to be in five years? Ten years? Fifty years? Though you may not often ask yourself this question so directly, it is one many of us keep in the back of our minds, a question that subtly shapes the decisions we make and our outlook on life. We might envision various answers:

- "I want to move back to my rural hometown in Illinois."
- "I want to be an actor living in a big city like New York."
- "I want be in medical school on the West Coast."
- "I want to be doing business and making it big in China."
- "I have no idea."

When we talk about the future, we often speak both literally ("move back to my rural hometown in Illinois") and metaphorically ("making it big in China") about what we'll be doing then. Indeed, the two modes often blur together, partly because the metaphors we use to talk about time are very spatial:

- "She's really going places."
- "I'm going nowhere fast."
- "There goes the neighborhood."
- "I'm just trying to get ahead."
- "The future is out there."
- "Life is passing me by."

If it's true that *who* we are is intimately tied to *where* we are, then it makes sense that *who we become* is connected to *where we are going*.

Thinking about the future, or our own futures, can be just as disorienting as trying to navigate a new place because the future represents change. Many of us feel uprooted for the simple reason that we move so often. In 2009–2010, according to the U.S. Census Bureau, 37 million Americans moved—13 percent of the population—and one-third of people in their twenties moved. Transportation technologies allow us to get around more cheaply, and communication technologies like smartphones, email, instant messaging, video chats, and thousands of location-based apps and websites make geographic distance seem almost irrelevant. Such new technologies change so rapidly that we find ourselves in a constant state of relearning and retooling, always trying to keep up with the newest version or the latest device.

Even if we keep up with technological change and stay in the same physical place, we can still become dislocated in our own neighborhoods. The various locations that we inhabit change all the time. Sometimes the changes are planned (which is not to say always welcomed by all), such as neighborhood redevelopment or gentrification. Other times, the changes come about slowly, as in the decline of Main Street areas in some rural towns or the effects on native flora and fauna from changes in climate. Many times, however, change is rapid, unexpected, and even catastrophic, as in the case of natural disasters, fires, toxic spills, or acts of terrorism. In other words, the future is uncertain because even if the ground underneath us feels solid, it too is constantly changing. As the Greek philosopher Heraclites said, "You cannot step into the same river twice."

We can wake one morning and realize that the place we thought we knew has changed dramatically. Suburbs expand into the country or decline and fracture, urban neighborhoods change both slowly and overnight, a Walmart opens, or a shopping center closes, and communities struggle to deal with the various kinds of waste that rapid expansion or decline produce. Whether we move or stay put, the world keeps spinning.

So how do we get our bearings in the midst of rapid and ongoing change? How do we make sense of where we as individuals and communities are going and where the places we inhabit are heading? What we really need is a critical perspective that will allow us to see and weigh the costs of our choices and actions. The essays in this chapter assume that writing and reading about places as they change can help us assess the potential gains and losses of their changes. In this sense, this section picks up where the previous two left off: Before we can figure out where to go next, we have to figure out where we have been and where we are now. As you read, you'll begin to notice some recurring themes throughout the essays, themes that tend to bring us back to the basics:

Food: Producing food is one of the most place-based activities in the world, and yet we seem to know less and less about where our food comes from and how it is grown. (Though recent years have seen a possible reawakening of local food movements, slow food movements, and pursuing more conscious connections to what we consume in some parts of American culture.) If we are what we eat, what do we need to know about how the food we consume and how it affects us and the places around us? How can we feed the world with seven billion inhabitants? Where do we want our food to come from in the future?

Work: Most of us will spend much of our lives on the job, often in particular workplace settings. On one hand, our jobs often affect where we live; on the other hand, where we live often determines what kind of job opportunities we have. What do we need to know about the kinds of jobs that await us and how they will affect our quality of life? What kinds of workplaces are safe and attractive, equitable and profitable? And, when modern communications technology lets you be "in touch" 24/7/365, what's happening to the boundaries between workplaces and homes, between public and private spaces, and between commercial activities and those not specifically intended to get ahead, produce, or turn a profit?

Transportation: How we get around is closely tied to the energy we consume, the jobs we have, and our sense of community. How does what we drive or how far we commute— and how—affect our future homes, neighborhoods, towns, cities, and the larger world environment?

Technology: Many products that we buy make it possible to live almost anywhere we want, while still being able to communicate with others and get work done. However, making and disposing of these products nearly always creates pollution and conflict somewhere else, affecting the health of someone else's place. Do the new technologies we use help us figure out where we are going or just disorient us more? Do they connect us or isolate us? To paraphrase an old question: If you go to the woods, but don't check-in on foursquare, are you really there?

The essays in this chapter each represent a different way of making sense of changes and trying to imagine what is coming. Eric Schlosser in "On the Range" portrays the impact that large cultural and economic forces are having on rural agricultural and ranching communities. In "Social Movements in the Age of Social Media: Participatory Politics in Egypt," S. Craig Watkins writes about the evolving role of Twitter, Facebook, and other media in global politics. Jerry Herron's "Borderland/Borderama/ Detroit" explores the past, present, and future of a struggling city. None of these authors claims to accurately predict the future— clearly an impossible task. Instead, they make arguments about what they think is coming and try to imagine alternatives. Because the future by definition does not exist yet, writing about what is coming always involves a measure of speculation. Sometimes mind-bending visionaries help us imagine the future in completely novel ways (the best science fiction often does this); more often, convincing visions of the future are grounded in close attention to what is going on right now, as well as the insights of history.

Arguing about the future is important because we would not be where we are now if someone had not made a persuasive case for it. For every subdivision or electronic gadget or software application, there are thousands of pages of words put to paper: memos, policy statements, legislative bills, science-fiction novels, op-eds, PowerPoint presentations, academic essays, business plans, websites. When thinking about what makes the future happen, it is easy to think most of it is out of our control and inevitable, unless we are the ones personally designing buildings and subdivisions, creating new computer technologies, or running large corporations. We may feel powerless in the face of rapid and sweeping changes. However, much of the future appears first in the words we use to imagine alternative possibilities and to persuade others to make these visions realities.

When we write about the future, it is important to view our texts as more than just leisure activities or, worse, as academic exercises designed to earn a good grade. Rather, the texts we create are statements that *do* something in the world; you are designing things that are meant to affect people. As you read the essays in this chapter, you will encounter texts designed to affect *you*. Your job is to pay attention to how they are designed, and then create your own texts, pieces of writing that not only help you make sense of the future but also attempt to persuade others to think differently about what is coming.

Ultimately, the work of imagining alternative futures is important because it forces us to think about what kind of future we are passing on to the next generation, to our children and grandchildren. As the Kenyan proverb says, "We didn't inherit the Earth from our parents; we borrowed it from our children." The ethic of sustainability involves trying to meet our current needs without crippling the ability of future generations to meet their needs—needs we cannot accurately predict. This ethic of sustainability requires us to re-imagine how we live: how we make and consume things, how we design our buildings and neighborhoods, and how we communicate, travel, work, and play.

Although designing a sustainable future may seem like an overwhelming project, it is a project infused with hope, hope based on the belief that human energy and inventiveness might still enable us to find a healthy way to inhabit the world. In the same spirit, the essays in this section express the hope that the more we read and write critically about the future, the better the chance we will know where we are when we get there—and that it will be a place worth knowing.

Elm City
Kevin Savage

Kevin Savage is a student at Boston College, where he majors in International Studies. Born and raised in the small town of Jacksonville, Illinois, in this essay, he reflects on his decision to leave home for college and the impact of that decision on his relationship to his hometown. Kevin is an avid reader and plays the guitar.

———————— ✦ ————————

The colorful lights of the old theater sign are burned out now, and its age shines through its many cracks and broken bulbs. Before the box office was boarded up, the majestic Times Theater was booming, with nightly shows on two giant screens and two-dollar matinees drawing crowds from all over Morgan County. But today the old theater has gone the way of many other things in town, and is closed for business. The grandeur of the old marquee has faded now, and the once stately display hangs in a state of defeated disrepair. Its paint is chipped and birds nest litter its every crevasse. Not even a "Thanks for your business" sign hangs where show times and ratings were once displayed. Across the town square, the twin towers of the county courthouse loom impressively over the storefronts below. Above the arched entrance, an inscription reads "Jacksonville, Illinois. Erected A.D. 1868."

The courthouse, too, is long removed from its glory days. The roof under which men like Steven A. Douglas and Abraham Lincoln once served as attorneys now leaks melting snow to marble floors below each winter. But in its age, the building seems to have taken on a new identity. It's embraced its eroding façade and aging clock tower and has become an entirely new sort of beautiful. Like the theater, like the town, the building's history still shines through in its almost defeated state. But while it's easy to stand back and admire the impressive bell tower, you can't help but feel that you've come too late, that Lincoln and the movie projector and the radiance of the place have all skipped town.

• • •

The two narrow lanes of College Avenue are lined with ancient elms, their outstretched limbs creating a natural tunnel through which we'd drive every morning in our family station wagon. We'd pile into our '86 Volvo, my brothers and sister and I, and my father would drive us to school before continuing on to work. We'd drive through the stately elms standing guard in front of old Victorian houses lining the street. The trees, so great in size and number, are littered throughout the small town, earning it the nickname "Elm City." At the eastern end of the street, lying at the edge of the rows of elms, sits our school. Over one hundred years old, the old parochial school is separated into two buildings—grade school and high school—which sit at opposite ends of a blacktop parking lot, across the street from our Catholic church. As we graduated from addition to calculus, the nuns and priests who taught us, and generations before us, were gradually replaced by lay teachers.

Upon dropping us off, my father would turn around and drive back down College Ave. a few blocks to his shop. His business, an independent pharmacy that he'd opened with my mother, has now been operating for over twenty-five years, and a recent retirement across town has left it with the title of Longest Running Pharmacy in Jacksonville. Blue-collar customers from all over town stop in to have their prescriptions filled and to shoot the breeze. Many customers know my parents from church, where we'd fill a pew each Sunday. In the pharmacy, they'd ask about us kids.

They'd ask, and my parents would have plenty to tell; we were the kids who were always busy. Between us, we captained teams, won spelling bees, and earned merit badges. We were MVPs, valedictorians, and class presidents. We went door-to-door selling popcorn and candy bars for fundraisers, mowed lawns for neighbors, and worked as delivery staff for the pharmacy. We drove through town in our distinctive station wagon, rode in homecoming parades, and made headlines in the local newspaper. We were the do-everything kids typical of American suburbia. But in the small town of Jacksonville, we were especially visible.

• • •

Once a booming center of industry, today Jacksonville is a shadow of its great history. Many of the three-storied brick storefronts downtown that once housed mom-and-pop bookstores, laundromats, hardware stores, and boutiques now lie mostly vacant, replaced by the massive cement buildings of discount stores. Restaurants and diners closed, forced out of business by fast-food chains and a dwindling population. Factories like EMI, AC Humco, and Pactiv have shut their doors or replaced many of their employees with machines. The state mental hospital, once the most dominating presence in town, and the largest employer, was shut down and most of its buildings demolished. The town library, ornately built and funded by a donation from Andrew Carnegie, no longer sees many faces pressed in its books. Many residential neighborhoods are going the way of the business districts. Dotted amongst well-kept homes lie a growing number of unkempt ones. Aging houses sit perched upon disheveled lawns, weeds and crabgrass inching up the fading wooden siding. Old cars with deflated tires lie defeated in front yards. The town square now harbors more weeds in its cracked sidewalks than patrons in its stores, as most of the business was drawn to the cheap prices of superstores at the edge of town. Despite an ongoing downtown restoration project, an attempt to return to the town square its previous distinction as a center for both commerce and community, the town's population continues to bleed. The Jacksonville of today has fallen victim to the double-edged sword of modernization.

A constant throughout the changing identity of the town, though, has been the rolling farmland pressed all the way against the city limits. The fields seem so limitless that the town seems out of place, stuck arbitrarily in the middle of the spread of nature, a needle in a haystack. Vast fields of corn and soybeans surround the town and spread for miles, with small towns littered here and there throughout the entire southern half of the state. The flat plains of the American Midwest allow for miles and miles to be seen at once. Tractors and combines drive down highways and through city streets without a second look, as if they were sedans, and crop yields and planting seasons are the talk of the town from barbershops to the grocery store. Rough country boys look forward to starring on high school football teams each fall after long summers of baling hay and detasseling corn; trading one field for another. The farmers' market is still busy each Saturday morning, selling sweet corn and peaches in the summer, and pumpkins and apples in the fall. The state of the town's meager economy still lies in the hands of the fields beyond it.

• • •

In a region falling behind the times, we grew up to become the family that seemed to outgrow our small town. We became those students not often seen in our school. We went beyond the local community colleges and state schools within driving distance. We cashed in our successes and went east, growing apart from friends who stayed close. While many old classmates graduated or quit school and moved back home to start lives down the street from childhood houses, we moved plane rides away. Holidays suddenly became the only times we returned to the small community. We went abroad, with each of us studying and then volunteering overseas. At first it was met with amusement, these hometown kids trying to make a name for themselves. But soon, each college acceptance and Peace Corps placement and job in some new city was brushed off as another of the Savage kids forgetting where they came from. As the youngest, I witnessed these sentiments being generated much more toward my siblings; my decisions were unsurprising in light of theirs. Still, my decision to explore the world far outside of our town was confusing to some. Often, people would have a hard time understanding the allure we found in faraway places, the adventures to be had. "Isn't it dangerous over there?" we were asked. "Wouldn't you rather stay home?" And even though we've chosen to leave home, we all share a common sense of pride in our hometown, and retell stories of small-town misadventures to anyone that will listen.

• • •

At the heart of Jacksonville, at the corner of the intersection of its two main streets—with stoplights and all—sits the pride of the town: the Ferris wheel. Though quite understated for a Ferris wheel, with seats enough for maybe twenty riders, the Ferris wheel is easily the town's most distinctive feature. The Ferris wheel, dubbed Big Eli, was built downtown at the Eli Bridge Company and moved to the park long before I was born. Legend has it that the Ferris wheel was invented in Jacksonville, and most locals still hold that to be true. The truth, in fact, is less glamorous, as Eli Bridge saw the first Ferris wheel at the Columbian Exposition in Chicago like everyone else. Despite the inaccuracy of the small-town lore, the Eli Bridge Company *has* been making Ferris wheels in Jacksonville for 110 years.

• • •

As others came home to take over family farms or businesses, more and more customers began to ask my parents which of their children was to inherit the pharmacy. Surely, they thought, the oldest pharmacy in town would be passed on to the next generation. We kids must be fighting over ourselves, each vying for the right to carry on the family business that had served our parents so well. But when none of us enrolled in pharmacy school, and each of us decided upon a different path, always outside of Jacksonville, the patrons couldn't believe it. There were *four* of us after all; surely at least *one* of us wasn't so stupid as to pass up a guaranteed spot as owner of a successful business in a quiet town. What could be better than picking up where we left off and returning home to live out our lives in the shadow of Big Eli?

Despite the obvious mindsets of many customers, peers, and others in town, I've found it difficult to pinpoint exactly why I'd never really considered staying home and starting a life amongst the towering elms and sparsely trafficked roads. It was, after all, a delightful place to spend my childhood and adolescence; it allowed my siblings and me opportunities we wouldn't have been offered in more urban settings. A big back yard and a close-knit school community; safe neighborhoods and sidewalks on which to ride bikes or draw with chalk; fresh air, and that indefinable but always recognizable feeling of belonging unique to small towns across the country. Even today, nothing thrills me quite like the chance to go home. To drive down College Avenue in the same old station wagon as years before, to see old friends and visit old hangouts, still puts me at ease and instills a contentedness that can only be truly felt at home. But something harder to define exists in the town; a sense of complacency, of isolationism, is almost omnipresent. And the ubiquity of this feeling, I think, was enough to start me searching for new horizons. Home, for me, was a fantastic place to grow up, but a place in which I don't imagine myself growing old.

• • •

Once a year, in early October, Jacksonville hosts Cruise Night, where people come from across the county to drive their old cars from the '50s and '60s down Morton Avenue, right in front of Big Eli, while the rest of the town lines the road in lawn chairs and admires them. The antique cars drive past the ancient elms and the vacant storefronts, where entrepreneurs and small business owners had tried and largely failed to bring life to the small economy. Though the cool October air is thick with automotive exhaust you might expect in a city, the night maintains the town's distinctly small-town feel. But the main attraction is Big Eli. Cruise Night is the one night a year that the wheel runs. For one night, every October, the wheel shakes off its rust and turns on its axle, reminding everyone that it still moves, however slowly. For one night each year, as the cars passing before it grow ever older, the wheel turns delicately forward, and then slows back into its familiar, inert resting place.

Guiding Questions

1. Compare Savage's essay on Jacksonville, Illinois, to Jerry Herron's essay on Detroit, Michigan. What are some of the similarities and differences between the two cities?

2. How would you describe Savage's relationship to his hometown? Point to places in the text that seem to capture this relationship. Compare Savage's relationship with Tim Lindgren's and Kathryn Carey's relationships with their hometowns.

3. Savage describes the gradual growth of a sense of distance between his generation of his family and their hometown: "In a region falling behind the times, we grew up to become the family that outgrew our small town. We became those students rarely seen in our school. We made it beyond the local community colleges and state schools within driving distance. We cashed in our successes and went east, growing apart from friends who stayed close. While old classmates graduated or quit school and moved back home to start lives down the street from childhood houses, we moved plane rides away." Describe your current geographic proximity and emotional relationship with your hometown, and then imagine your future connection with it.

4. Why might it be important for community members to see one or more of the Savages return to run the family business? What's at stake for a community when some of its most prominent or promising members seem to want to be elsewhere? How could communities hold onto more residents who grow up in their confines? Should they try?

Paths for Further Exploration

1. Savage writes, "The Jacksonville of today has fallen victim to the double-edged sword of modernization." If you grew up in one city or town, think about how it has changed over the course of your lifetime—if, in fact, it *has* changed. What are some of those changes? What needs to change? Write an editorial to your local newspaper in which you describe the ways in which the place has changed for better or worse over the years, and call for action accordingly.

2. Rebecca Solnit in "The Most Radical Thing You Can Do" discusses the luxury of a future of staying put. Do you imagine your future leading you to stay in your hometown or to move away from it? Why? Can you research what changes are facing your home place now that will affect what it's like in the future?

My Fake Job
RODNEY ROTHMAN

Rodney Rothman is a screenwriter, television producer, and author. He graduated from Middlebury College in Vermont and, at age twenty-four, became the youngest head writer for The Late Show with David Letterman. *At twenty-six, he gained notoriety with a* New Yorker *essay in which he described his experience posing as a worker in a New York start-up company. Written as the "dot-com" craze of the late 1990s—when all anyone seemed to need to start a business was a company name and a URL that ended in ".com"— was starting to become the dot-com crash of the early 2000s, "My Fake Job" is a reflection on the changing nature of work in an economy altered by the explosive growth of the Internet.*

✦

I don't smoke, but I still take a cigarette break every day at four o'clock. I stand there and let the cigarette burn down. I pretend to inhale, lightly, so I don't trigger a coughing fit. The office smokers never notice; they're too busy complaining about their newly worthless stock options, or how the latest reorg left them with a job title they don't even understand, like "resource manager." I never speak up, because there is a crucial difference between my colleagues and me: I was never hired to work at this company.

I don't have stock options here. I don't have a job title here. *I don't have a job here.* A few weeks ago, I just walked into the office.

It was the first Internet office I'd ever seen. It takes up five floors of an old warehouse in downtown Manhattan's Silicon Alley. No one stopped me when I came in. The sense of transience was overpowering. Hundreds of employees worked at identical workstations. They sat in thousand-dollar ergonomic office chairs, but their nameplates were made with paper and Magic Marker. The message was clear: the chairs could be resold; the employees were expendable.

Twenty-five-year-olds in T-shirts and cutoff fatigues pinballed from computer monitor to coffee machine, staring at their feet. Scattered desks were unoccupied because of April's NASDAQ implosion. It struck me that somebody could easily just start showing up for work at this office. Sitting at an empty desk, minding his own business, he would never be noticed.

DAY 1, 10:30 A.M.

5   I recently left a sixty-hour-a-week job so I could have more free time and do freelance writing. It hasn't been going well. I have no free time, because I'm always trying to write. I get no writing done, because I'm always wasting time. What counts as wasting time? How about dozing off midday while reading *InStyle*? How about spending six hours deciding how best to spend six hours?

The building's lobby is a gray expanse of faux marble, sucking up daylight. There's no security guard. A small group of people wait for the elevator and sip iced coffee. Standing among them, I feel like a CIA operative, albeit one who scares easily and is wearing Teva sandals.

I spent the early part of the morning concocting a false identity. I decided that I had just been transferred from the company's satellite office in Chicago (I'd read about it on the Web site). Then I selected a fake job title. The more I thought about it, the more I liked the sound of "junior project manager." It seemed vague, perfect for flying under the radar.

The elevator empties into an airy loft, filled with desks. In front of me, a young receptionist is talking on the telephone. I try to look distracted, as if I were junior-managing a project deep inside my mind. I see her staring at me, but her face registers no concern. She turns back to her phone conversation, and I walk in undisturbed.

I have no idea where to go. I follow everyone down a hallway and into a bustling kitchenette. The kitchenette is spacious and revolves around a large common table that nobody sits at. There is a communal refrigerator stocked with a dozen brands of soft drink, but I take a sodium-free seltzer. I have never, ever liked seltzer. Everyone loads up on caffeine and moves on. People clutch mugs that say "Omnitech" or "Digitalgroup.com" instead of those "You Want It When?" Dogbert ones.

I drift freely around the office. It's like a campaign headquarters without buttons. The workstations are low to the ground and clustered in fours. Everyone is on the phone. I see a man in his forties with bare feet up on his desk. I see nose studs. Nobody looks at me twice. After a few laps around the office, I decide I've worked hard enough for today. As I walk out, I turn to the receptionist and say, "See you tomorrow."

Day 2, 10:50 a.m.

There is a different receptionist today, and I walk by her too quickly to notice anything interesting. Everything feels different today, in a bad way. Back in the kitchenette, I take another repulsive sodium-free seltzer. It's now part of my office routine. Then I see a sign-up sheet posted on a bulletin board:

FEELING STRESSED? JOIN US FOR LUNCHTIME YOGA!

It's too much to resist. I sign "Mike Kramer." As I finish, I realize someone is behind me, looking over my shoulder. "You don't have to sign up, you know," she says. "Only, like, four of us go."

I turn around. She's pretty, of course, even in harsh fluorescent lighting. The collar of her blouse is charmingly askew.

I briefly imagine us doing downward dog pose on adjacent mats. Her name is Katie. (Actual names have been changed.) "Are you new here?" she asks.

"I've been here a week," I say. "I transferred from the Chicago satellite office."

I realize that employees my age probably don't use bland corporate-speak like "satellite office." "I'm a junior project manager," I add.

"Really?" she says. "I'm a project manager. What projects do you work on?"

It occurs to me now that I could have been more prepared. Perhaps I could have *learned what this company does.*

"I'm still finishing up Chicago projects." I begin shifting from foot to foot. Katie asks me where I live, and I tell her, "Downtown, with friends."

"No," she laughs, "where do you live *here?*"

20 "I, uh, don't have a desk yet," says the brilliant junior project manager, having worked for a week in an office with fifty empty desks.

DAY 2, 10:53 A.M.

I introduce myself to the receptionist. My thinking is that if I get her on my side, I'll be able to come and go as I please. Her name is Donna. "Nice to meet you, Donna," I say. "I'm Rodney Rothman." I immediately realize my mistake and panic. I've been here for three minutes and I've managed to establish two separate false identities, one of which is technically my real identity.

"Rodney, have you met Lisa yet?" she asks, motioning to a sturdy woman in a cardigan chatting ten feet away from us.

"Yes," I lie.

"Good. So you got an ID card?"

25 "Yes," I lie.

"Good. You'll need that after six." Donna's phone is ringing, and she's not picking it up.

"Do you have an extension yet?"

"They haven't given me one."

"And that's R-o-d-n-e-y?"

30 "Actually . . . it's Randy."

"Randy Rothman?"

"Ronfman. R-o-n-f."

Donna writes my name down on a pad of paper. Donna's phone is ringing. She's not picking it up. *Pick it up. Pick it up.*

Donna extends her hand toward my sweaty palm. "Welcome to the office, Randy."

DAY 3:

"Randy" is taking a much-needed personal day from fake work. I'm at an afternoon Yankee game with my friend Jay. Like many of my friends, Jay can't believe I'm really doing this; he regards me with a mixture of awe and concern. Jay was recently let go by an Internet startup. In between pitches and beers, he explains things like production tools and C++. Jay tells me that some of his former colleagues are continuing to go to work, even though they're not getting paid anymore.

Last night I checked out Web sites for some of the hundreds   35
of Web consulting companies like mine. I learned about maximizing my knowledge system. I boned up on branding, decision support, and integrated E-solution deployment. Now, as I watch Tino
Martinez take batting practice, I relate to his work ethic. We are
strivers. We are brothers. We are improving our skill sets.

DAY 4, 7 P.M.

I ride up in the elevator with a tiny West Indian security guard in
a heavy wool uniform. I'd like to see him try to wrestle me to the
ground. I remember too late that the office is locked after six, but
it doesn't matter. The guard swipes his own card and *holds the
door open for me.*

I've always liked offices during the fringe hours, early morning and in the evening. It's liberating to spend peaceful time in a
place that's normally frantic. To me, the sound of a night cleaning
crew is like a rolling country stream.

The office is quiet and freshly mopped. I walk around and
shop for my desk. It's hard to tell which desks are unoccupied.
Some people refrain entirely from decorating their workspace.
That way, they can pack up and leave quickly when the axe comes
down. Other desks are decorated lavishly, although I can think of
harsher words to describe a green plastic M&M playing a trumpet.

I hop from desk to desk. I sit in each chair, maximizing, de-
ploying, wanting it to feel right. I finally select a desk at the end
of a large room with thirty workstations. It's well situated, facing
the entire room, with nobody in back of me. It has an operational
computer, perfect for taking notes. I put my feet up and close my
eyes, thinking of rolling country streams.

DAY 5, 10 A.M.

There's no seltzer in the kitchenette this morning. I have to take   40
a Fresca, a beverage I loathe. It's a bad omen, considering what I
have to do: sit down at my new workstation in front of an office
full of employees.

I'm purposeful as I steam through the place, steering around
bodies and desks. Nobody looks up. I reach my chair and sit down.
I wait. I let out a loud sigh. I scan the room. Everyone is typing
or on the phone. Two women in their early twenties huddle at a
desk, eating breakfast and talking: "But what if I worked six hours
on one, three on the other . . . I don't know, that's just what *they*
told me to do."

Whoever *they* are, I don't see them. Nobody acknowledges me. The office has swallowed me up without a burp.

DAY 5, NOON

The phone rings. My imagination gets the better of me. I picture a squadron of security guards mobilizing upstairs. ATF agents clamber through air ducts, closing off my available exits. I wonder whether Teva sandals would cushion a twelve-story fall. I answer the phone. "This is Randy?"

"Randy. It's Donna."

45   I consider grabbing a spare rubber band for self-defense.

"Just confirming your extension."

"This is it."

"Great. Let me know if you need anything."

"Okay."

50   I know what I need. I need to take a break. I need to go outside and pretend to smoke a cigarette.

DAY 5, 6 P.M.

Today I followed a strict schedule of affectation. Every three minutes: stare dreamily into the distance. Every five minutes: flamboyantly rub eyes or chin, or tap finger thoughtfully on upper lip. Every ten minutes: make eye contact with someone across the room and nod in empathy. Every fifteen minutes: fill cheeks with air, then exhale while making a quiet *puh-puh-puh-puh* noise.

I take a beverage break every half-hour. Consequently, a bathroom break every hour. Establishing my own hourly bathroom routine within the pre-established routines of my coworkers is crucial to assimilation.

My small-talk break in the kitchenette was supposed to be every two hours, but sometimes I skipped it because of nerves. A smalltalk break is a massive endeavor of strategizing. Every word is premeditated. A perfectly executed small-talk break goes like this:

> ME: How crazy is this coffee machine?
> WOMAN IN KITCHENETTE: Ha-ha, I know.
> ME: It tastes like General Foods International Coffees.
> WOMAN: Does it? Ha-ha.
> ME: Ha-ha.

I've been at my desk for eight hours, and it already feels like home.

DAY 6, 8:45 A.M.

I came in early to beat the rush. The only other person here is a   55
guy my age in a Mr. Bubble T-shirt. He sits under a large dry-erase
board with an acronym-laden flowchart labeled "The Closed Loop
Process." I'm noticing things I didn't yesterday, like the abandoned fire extinguisher on the floor next to my desk, and the office
in the converted warehouse across the street, which looks nearly
identical to this one. I find myself faintly bored, waiting for all the
people to come in so I can act like I'm ignoring them.

DAY 6, 2 P.M.

When you work in a room with twenty other people, talking on the
phone can be tricky. Every word you say can be heard and digested.
It doesn't take much mental calculus for your neighbor to decipher
the other end of the conversation. You learn to maximize your deployment of pronouns: "I got it . . . She said that? . . . Send me it
before you do that with them there." Or you can be like the Mr. Bubble T-shirt guy and try to whisper inaudibly. His whisper was pretty
audible this morning: "It's like, 'We're a news aggregator! We're a
portal! We're a B2B thingy! Let's buy UPI!' *Total lack of focus!*"
  My phone calls fall into three categories. Most of them are
straight-up personal. I don't feel bad about this, because I believe
that my colleagues would be more suspicious of me if I didn't
spend half the day calling friends and family. Other phone calls relate to my real professional life: agents, other writers, etc. Because
I work mostly in television, it's easy to make these calls sound
Internet-related. I just use the word *network* as much as possible.
My favorite phone calls are the ones that relate to my fake job. I set
these up in advance by asking a few friends to call me. These calls
make no sense at all, on either end, but they make me look busy.
  "This is Randy."
  "Randy, it's, uh, Kurt at LogiDigiTekResources dot com, dot,
uh, org."
  "Hey, Kurt. The links are all crapped out. I think we need to   60
check the URL again."
  "Rodney, do I talk technical on this end, too?"
  "Ha-ha-ha, Kurt. Good idea. I'll check that through with client
services."
  "Does it even matter what I say? Blah blah blah, la la la."
  "Perfect. Cc. That to me. G'bye."
  It all adds to the noise: the voices, the ringing, the hum of the   65
air-conditioning, the clicking of heels on wood.

DAY 7, 7 P.M.

The Girl with Long Brown Hair has bar graphs on her computer. Bar graphs! I can see her through the glass partition next to my workstation. When I go to the bathroom, she looks up and says "Hi." *Dear Penthouse:* Every so often, she leans back in frustration, and her tailored white dress shirt tightens against her chest.

I generally avoid interoffice romances, but it's different when you're a guy working at an office without an actual job. As I think about the Girl with Long Brown Hair, though, a discomfort settles in. I increasingly feel that I've taken refuge in a self-constructed crappy high-concept movie. I picture us having a secret tryst. Then my conscience gets the better of me, and I tell her about my scam. She storms out, of course. I follow her down to Tampa, to the regional meeting. I stand on the conference room table with flowers and tap shoes, singing "My Cherie Amour." Then she forgives me, we embrace, an updated version of "My Cherie Amour" by the Goo Goo Dolls kicks in, the credits roll, and we thank the Toronto Chamber of Commerce.

Enough. I pack up my laptop and go home.

DAY 8, 10 A.M.

I ride up on the elevator with a fortyish-looking guy. He goes to five, I go to twelve.

70 "Morning," he says.

"Morning," I say.

Getting into the spirit of it, I add, "Hot one out there."

This is going great. He responds, "You work on twelve?"

"Yeah."

75 "What are you guys doing up there?"

"Uh . . . I have no idea."

He nods in understanding. He's been there. We hit floor five, and he steps off.

"Have a good one," he shouts over his shoulder.

DAY 8, 11:30 A.M.

The Man in the Blue Oxford Shirt is glaring. Every time he walks across the office, he fires a double-take at me. I have a premonition that he will be the dark agent of my downfall here. The Man in the Blue Oxford Shirt is doughy, with thinning, shiny hair. You get the feeling that his body type went from baby fat to middle-aged paunch all at once. He looks so ill at ease, I wonder whether he's a fake employee, too.

The Red-Haired Lady worries me even more. She's one of   80
the older staff members. The more silent and inoffensive I am,
the more I seem to threaten her. She probably thinks I'm an Ivy
League consultant, here to observe her and weed her out. I see her
reflection in the window whenever she creeps behind me. We've
developed a little tango, she and I. She cranes her neck to look at
my computer screen, and I lower my shoulder to block her view
of my notes. Her oversized eyeglasses make me feel like I'm being
cased by Sally Jessy Raphael.

Day 8, 4 P.M.

While taking a cigarette break today, I meet a colleague named
Lawrence, one of what seems like five hundred guys in my office
who wear black nerd-chic eyeglasses. Lawrence says that his of-
fice responsibilities have recently been expanded beyond what he
was hired for.
  "What were you hired for?" I ask.
  "Overseeing office support programs."
  "What kind of programs?"
  Lawrence takes a big drag off his cigarette. "Mostly Wellness."   85

Day 9, 11:30 A.M.

Today I'm decorating my desk with whimsical junk I bought in a
Sixth Avenue Chinese variety store. I arrange it precisely on the
desk surface. On the right are two filthy pieces of rubber fruit: a
smiling orange and a frowning pineapple. On the left is a pirated
Winnie-the-Pooh figurine, for a touch of approachability. Last,
I add a plastic Virgin Mary clock, to make sure I'm not too ap-
proachable. Nothing puts people off like the promise of spontane-
ous sermonizing. I figure the clock alone has added three days to
my stay here. At the end of the day, I put a labeled personal item in
the communal fridge. Hint: it was brewed in Latrobe, PA.

Day 10, 7 P.M.

The Girl with Long Brown Hair is working late, so I am, too. A few
minutes ago her boss was down here, standing over her, pacing. I
struggled to hear what he was saying, but could make out only a
few phrases and an undertone of irritation:
  "Are you doing all this in Photoshop? I want to do it in Quark.
. . . There's no dialogue happening . . . Someone should go down
to Staples and get this really sticky double-sided tape. . . . We have
to put this out."

Before he exited, he must have sensed that he was acting like an Old Economy jerk boss, because he turned and said, "You know, you don't have to do this tonight."

90   "Good." She laughed. "I have dinner plans."

"Groovy. Bye, sweetie!"

She packs up her handbag and walks up the steps. I watch her go, and stay another hour, glad I'm not a guy who says "groovy" or "bye, sweetie."

DAY 11, NOON

When I get back from lunch, there is a meeting of at least thirty staff members in the big conference room. Why am I not part of the company's knowledge-management system?

I work the resentment out through my work: an afternoon spent devising ways to deceive the increasingly menacing Red-Haired Lady. First I open up a Microsoft Excel spreadsheet document on my computer. I've never used a spreadsheet before, but I have no problem filling it in with random numbers. Whenever I see the Red-Haired Lady's reflection in the window, I click from my word-processor file to the spreadsheet file, drumming my fingers distractedly on the mouse. My only concern is that she'll think I'm auditing her expense reports and go on the warpath.

95   I also draw a meaningless flowchart, labeled "Starwood Project," on a legal pad, and leave it out on my desk to give me management credibility. I invent some acronyms, box them, and connect them with arrows. Then I write "August 2001" in big letters underneath, and underline it three times. This lets her know that I am very much on schedule, whatever it is that I am doing.

DAY 11, 5:30 P.M.

This afternoon, a group of middle-aged men show up in our work area and go from desk to desk talking to employees. Everyone looks terrified. I don't notice that they're approaching my desk until it's too late. "How are ya?" says one with swept-back hair. "Don't mind us, we're just taking a tour." I focus as hard as possible on my spreadsheet. My fingers dance a John Bonham solo on the mouse.

A member of the tour group speaks up: "Can I ask you a question?"

"Go right ahead."

"Is it true that there's massages on this floor?"

"That is true." And it is. Scattered throughout the office are 100
fliers advertising "Back Massage by Melissa!" It's all part of chain-
smoking Lawrence's Wellness empire. I've been building up the
nerve to get one for days.

"Oh," the man says, already snickering. "Which floor has body
piercing?"

The whole tour group explodes with laughter. I join in cau-
tiously, then enthusiastically when I see that the tour group has
begun riding the wave of hilarity to the next room.

"Take care, now," the man with the swept-back hair says, still
laughing.

Day 12, 10 a.m.

It's my twelfth day here, and the anonymity, once a pleasure,
has become maddening. I feel a bubbling, reckless desire to
make my existence known. Maybe that's why I've started sign-
ing my name to every sign-up sheet I see. Today I signed up for
a charity walk. Yesterday I signed one labeled "May the E-Force
Be with You."

Day 12, 2 p.m.

This week, Lawrence and Team Wellness posted the first two pages 105
of *Moby-Dick* by the elevator, under the heading "Elevate Your
Life with Literature!" I'm not sure if they have a nine-year plan for
posting the rest. I am troubled by the implication that our elevator
waiting time needed to be more useful. God forbid employees stop
maximizing for a few seconds.

Did anyone bother to read the first two pages of *Moby-Dick* before posting it? Ishmael takes to the open sea on a whale-hunting
expedition because he is fed up with the drudgery of office life, "of
week days pent up in lath and plaster—tied to counters, nailed to
benches, clinched to desks." Try thinking about that on the subway
home from work.

What was Ishmael so afraid of, anyway? Are scurvy, whale
attack, and pirate rape so much better than working in an office? At least our office is air-conditioned. At least our compli-
mentary Thursday morning doughnuts haven't been befouled by
bilge rats. Ishmael, poor sucker, was born a hundred years too
early. He could have opened "the great flood gates of the won-
derworld" right here in this wonderful wave tank of an Internet
office.

DAY **12**, 3:30 P.M.

". . . and so the universal thump is passed round, and all hands should rub each other's shoulder-blades, and be content."— Herman Melville, Chapter 1, *Moby-Dick*.

Melissa's hands are rubbing my shoulder blades. "You have a lot of tension in your neck and shoulders," she says. "You should get more massages." I couldn't agree with her more. I've been avoiding the massage room, perhaps because of a fear that Melissa would somehow sense my ruse through the deceitful flow of my lymphatic fluid. As she navigates her knuckles around my back, I meditate blissfully. Free massages. Free beverages. Companionship, flirtation, E-mail access. No disruptive phone calls, no meetings, no boss, no questions, no decisions to make. A perfect job, perfectly undisturbed by having a job.

110 "Sorry, Randy, back to work," Melissa says, finishing up with that weird karate-chop thing. "Lots of tired backs out there. Drink water."

DAY **12**, 4:45 P.M.

I started the conversation, so I have only myself to blame. Laura, a friendly woman in her thirties with a broken wrist, has been working next to me all week long, and I haven't said a word to her.

"What happened to your arm?" I ask.

Laura skips the part where she got injured and just tells me her medical horror story. Andy, her "arm guy," wants to take bone from another part of her body, and she's mistrustful and scared.

"And who are you?" she adds.

115 "I'm Randy Ronfman."

"What do you do here?"

Lately, when I get this question, I lean heavily on the word *stuff*. I find it has a narcotizing effect.

"I'm here from the Chicago satellite office. I'm doing a bunch of stuff. Project managing stuff. Branding stuff."

"Branding stuff. *Really.*" Laura leans her good arm on the desk eagerly. "I'm in marketing and recruiting here. Do you mind if I pick your brain?"

120 A week ago this question might have terrified me, but now it excites me. I'm starting to believe that I actually do this for a living, that I am capable of having my brain picked about branding. Laura's question is a cataract of jargon: "Launching a B2B . . . E-commerce . . . inventive user experiences . . . success factors . . .

so if you know any branding people in Chicago that could help us out with that, I'd really appreciate it."

"You don't want to work with the people there," I tell her conspiratorially. "They're not so great."

Laura's brow furrows in genuine disappointment. "Well . . . maybe you could come up with some people? Do you have a few minutes?"

"Not right now," I answer. "I have a meeting at five." This is not a lie. I do have a meeting, for a real job. Typically, I've nearly missed it. "I should be back later. When do you leave?"

"Six." 125

I make a mental note to come back at six-thirty. "Think about people you know who are very well connected," Laura calls after me as I run out. "Who could send me off into *their* network of people."

Day 13, 5 p.m.

It's been twenty-four hours since my conversation with Laura, and I haven't seen her since. This doesn't surprise me. The office has a seizure-inducing strobe effect. People appear and disappear, switch desks, switch jobs. Today Rick, the head of the office, is walking around, asking where Lawrence is. He is informed that Lawrence has recently been "reshuffled" into a new department. Lawrence is now sitting fifteen feet from Rick's office, on the floor below us, a floor that has fewer than twenty people. *The head of the office.* And you wonder how I've been able to stay here for two weeks?

Day 13, 8 p.m.

If it's possible to be a workaholic at a job you don't actually have, that's what I've become. The thought of going back to my apartment is loathsome, and I don't even have a family I'm trying to avoid. In this office I feel productive, even when I'm doing nothing. In my apartment, even when I'm working, I'm idle, lazy, and always a hairsbreadth away from masturbation. In her book *The Overworked American*, Juliet Schor writes about workers at an Akron tire plant who won a six-hour day. Many of them used their increased leisure time to take on second jobs. I'm beginning to think that a second, or even a third, fake job sounds like a fine idea. How tremendous it would be, traveling from fake job to fake job, taking only Fresca, leaving only flowcharts.

Day 14, 2 p.m.

To make myself feel better, I've started holding my own meetings. All day long today, friends come in, in groups of varying sizes. Sometimes I hold the meeting at my desk, in full view of the office. I like this because it gives the impression that I'm bringing in my own department. It's usually small talk and the occasional "Well, it's great to finally meet you!"

130 Mostly, though, we meet in the barren, glassed-in conference rooms. We close the door and gossip. For authenticity, I pace around the room and gesticulate madly. It's a Kabuki theater rendition of how I think meetings should look. At one point a woman interrupts our meeting. It turns out that we weren't in an empty conference room. We were in her office. I swear you can't tell the difference.

Day 15, 10 a.m.

Today I walk in and there's a staff-wide meeting in the conference room. Everyone is in there. My immediate concern is that they are meeting about me, preparing some form of ghastly homicidal vengeance, like locking me in the Xerox machine until I asphyxiate on toner powder.

There will always be drywall between me and them. That's the limitation of my perfect job. I can never join the inner circle. I can never become indispensable, because, no matter how hard I try, I don't really exist here.

Day 15, 4 p.m.

There's no such thing as Casual Friday in a company that's casual all week long, but don't tell that to the Man in the Blue Oxford Shirt. He's wearing a short-sleeved blue polo shirt today. Recently I found out that he's a junior project manager, like me. His name is Dennis. It's hard to maintain an adversarial relationship with a guy named Dennis, particularly one who stopped caring about me a week ago. At this point, I'm rental furniture. I haven't seen the Red-Haired Lady for days. Maybe some Ivy League consultant sent her home to New Rochelle with the rest of the forty-year-olds.

Day 16, 2:30 p.m.

The office smokers are abuzz today. Word is spreading that the rest of the fifth floor is going to be let go. Apparently the New

York office is now officially the worst in the company. We're even lagging behind Denver, because "they're small market, but at least they control it." Each person present seems to have a compelling reason that they're the next in line for dismissal. Everyone is ticked off that most of the senior staff is conveniently on vacation and the mass firings are being handled by middle managers. Some new young guy with a patchy beard looks at me accusingly and says, "They're going after the high-salaried ones first." I don't get that. So I'm "high salaried"? Just because I happen to be the only smoker here who bothers to wear a belt?

Day 17, 7:45 p.m.

When I arrive this morning. I sense that this will be my last day 135 at fake work. What clinches it is the new phone list. Many names are no longer on it. My name is: Randy Ronfman, with my phone extension directly beside it. I feel an intense wave of emotion, guiltless and giddy. But before too long I start thinking about the Peter Principle and decide I have been promoted past my point of competency. I know how to be a fake employee, but this is too legitimate. The only thing left for me to do is actual work, with actual coworkers who will rely on me. I've done that before. It's not as much fun.

Someday, if I'm ever a death row inmate, or a guy who sneaks into prison and pretends to be a death row inmate, I know what my last meal will be. It will be sodium-free seltzer. I like how it cleans you out. I sip one as I go from desk to desk, telling my coworkers that I'm "going back to the satellite office." Many of them have never met me before, or seen me, for that matter, but they react cordially. They assume it's their mistake, not mine.

"Lucky bastard!" one guy says.

"Your own choice, or are you 'resigning'?" another says, making quotation marks with his fingers.

"Nice working with you," the Girl with Long Brown Hair says.

I pack up my things long after everyone else is gone, savoring 140 the last of the quiet. As I leave, I stop at the dry-erase board with the "Closed Loop Process" flowchart. I add my initials, RMR, box them, and draw an arrow to the box. I will live on in the office as an acronym, forever. Well, for two weeks, at least, until someone takes down the board. That's as close as you get to forever in this office.

Guiding Questions

1. This essay was published during a broad economic expansion—a time when jobs were plentiful but transient. Would the workplace anonymity that Rothman describes be possible in the moment in which you are reading? Why or why not?
2. What does Rothman have to say about work—the kinds of work we do, where we do it, and what counts as "real" work? What economic changes does he document?
3. In this piece, Rothman is an outsider to a place but poses as an insider. What ethical issues arise when an outsider masquerades as an insider? What unique perspective does it offer?
4. This is a piece of creative nonfiction. However, after the *New Yorker* published this essay, it came to light that Rothman made up the incident of getting a massage and never mentioned that his mother worked at the company where the story takes place. The *New Yorker* issued an apology in the next issue, noting, "The magazine does not disguise details or mix fact and fiction without informing the reader (not even in a comic piece like this one), and we sincerely regret the error." His agent defended him by arguing that he had not set out to write a piece of investigative journalism, and Rothman himself admitted to changing details of the office in order to disguise the identity of the company. Do you feel differently about the essay or Rothman now that you know these facts?

Paths for Further Exploration

1. Write an essay that describes how an unexpected job change affected you or your family.
2. Write a researched essay that examines a job or field that interests you. How did you get interested in it? How is this type of job changing? What are the prospects for those attempting to find work in this field? By the end of your research, reflect on whether or not you think you will pursue this kind of employment.
3. Write an essay in which you describe the culture of a previous or current workplace. Describe your colleagues, the physical space, what kind of work you did, and your place within that community. Think about keeping the kind of day-to-day journal Rothman did as one possible way to write this essay. Think about how the workplace communicates what it values most: the employees? The furniture? The technology? Something else?
4. As a student, do you have a "work space" for your academic pursuits? Analyze and describe what this space reveals about your work as a student, how you value it, and how the community around you values it (or doesn't).

Border/Borderama/Detroit: Part 1

JERRY HERRON

Jerry Herron is the dean of the Irvin D. Reid Honors College at Wayne State University. He was born in Abilene, Texas, and received his B.A. from the University of Texas at Austin and his M.A. and Ph.D. from Indiana University. He has written two books: Universities and the Myth of Cultural Decline *and* AfterCulture: Detroit and the Humiliation of History. *The following is the first installment in his three-part series "Borderland/Borderama/Detroit," which first appeared on the site Design Observer (www.designobserver.com).*

──────────── ✦ ────────────

Detroit Looks Just Like a City . . .

. . . Especially at night, from my apartment downtown, with its floor-to-ceiling glass: that's when Detroit really *does* look like a city; friends have come over to dinner, 28 floors up, sitting around my table, and inevitably someone turns toward a window and remarks, as if arriving at an original insight, which of course it is for the person making the observation, who has just now noticed the altogether astonishing fact that despite what you might expect, what people know about this place, and what the person about to be delivered of the insight also thought up until this very instant: "Detroit looks just like a city!" The conversation stops, maybe, for a few seconds, while the other guests glance toward the windows, the vast grid of lights arrayed across the night-time landscape out toward the dark, invisible horizon. And it's not the first time you've been witness to such a discovery, not if you have lived here any time at all. The other guests nod polite agreement: Yes, Detroit *does* look just like a city. And then they go back to eating their dessert.

But it's *not* a city, not when the sun comes up and you can see the place. It *was* a city once, that's clear, or at least Detroit seems to have been a city, given the physical evidence left behind in maybe the most moved-out-of metropolis ever settled and then evacuated by Americans—houses and factories, theaters and schools, streets and whole neighborhoods now walked away from on so spectacular a scale that you can't fault other people when they register amazement. "It is a remarkable city," Rebeca Solnit wrote in *Harper's*, "one in which the clock seems to be running backward as its buildings disappear and its population and economy decline." Her wonderment is precisely rendered, if not precisely news:

> This continent has not seen a transformation like Detroit's since the last days of the Maya. The city, once the fourth largest in the country, is now so depopulated that some stretches resemble the outlying farmland and others are altogether wild. . . . Between the half-erased neighborhoods are ruined factories, boarded-up warehouses, rows of storefronts bearing the traces of failed enterprise, and occasional solid blocks of new town houses that look as though they had been dropped in by helicopter. [1]

Detroit looks just like a city, except it's not one any more. But instead of vanishing, like those Mayan cities of Mesoamerica, it persists in a death-in-life existence, and that is what lends the place an uncanny relevance and makes it so persistent an object for journalistic last words, none of them, of course, ever being the last word. Detroit may be emptied out, but it is hardly over, nor will it be any time soon, precisely because of the questions that this city/not raises. What could have happened here? Does it have anything to do with the rest of America? Such questions are particularly pressing just now, as the world's population—at some point in 2008—crossed a border never yet traversed by humans, with the majority of us becoming urban for the first time in history.

And that is just where Detroit's relevance lies. It is not only the busiest border crossing in the United States—literally—thanks to the volume of Canadian–American trade that passes through by water and rail and highway, but the busiest border in another, perhaps more crucial sense. Detroit sits precisely at the border of city and not-city; its condition renders the conflict between the natural world and the built environment in a especially forceful way, as Solnit points out. Here, the fearful energy released by a city in decay raises questions not only about the economic and governmental systems that produced Detroit (and America), but also about the humanity of citizens so transformed by urbanism that they can visit upon each other all the miseries and cruelty locally deployed. It's enough to make a person wonder, and especially to make Americans wonder, and maybe the rest of the world wonder too, as we all verge on a global urbanism and the city/not opposition achieves universal relevance. We wonder how so much that is valuable, in both material and human terms, could be so quickly and violently squandered. And we wonder at the cost—the waste and cruelty, and what the city has to do with it all, and what this place might portend.

Border and Borderama

So the dispatches keep arriving from the border of city and not-city. But unlike the Mesoamerican parallel that Solnit points to, Detroit's vanishing is not some distant historic event; it is an ongoing condition, compounded in its spectacular oddity by the simultaneous rebirth of certain parts of town. Here, the border is always shifting and redefining itself. On one side, the entropy and violence that un-build the city and return it to some pre-urban state—the ruined neighborhoods and inner-city prairie that writers and tourists never fail to be struck by, "an urban void nearly the size of San Francisco" as Solnit puts it. [2] And on the other side, the energy and capital investment that define the parts of town that never went away, and what is more baffling still, the parts of the city that are growing and redeveloping.

"It's remarkable, really," according to Mary Kramer, publisher of *Crain's Detroit Business*. "Despite the political turmoil in Detroit and the economic turmoil throughout Southeast Michigan, our reporters found new angles for this third annual 'Living and Investing in the D' supplement." Kramer goes on to enumerate the good-news items—urban gardens, revitalized neighborhoods, downtown comeback, plans for light rail, etc.—all played out against the backdrop of corruption and political bungling. [3] Her piece is aptly titled "Optimism amid Turmoil," and that is surely the story of "the D," and the two cities that occupy this historically conflicted real estate. That the two—city and not-city, life and death—should be so obviously linked is a discomfiting prospect, with the resulting metropolis being apparently like no other, although maybe the border between Detroit and everything else is not so fixed as it is made to appear in popular representations.

And here is a truly chilling possibility: that Detroit is linked causally somehow to the rest of America, that this mix of rot and revival, violence and reinvigoration, is a condition inherent to ourselves that the city only exacerbates. Maybe Detroit is the cost

Americans pay for being who we are. Consider the facts, which is what the *Wall Street Journal* invited:

> Detroit is 81% black and, according to the Census Bureau, one-third of its residents live below the poverty line. The nuclear family is all but non-existent in the city. In 1960, 25% of black residents were born to single mothers. By 1980, that number had climbed to 48%. Today, over 80% of Detroit's black children are born to single-parent households. Just one in nine black boys is raised with a father. According to academic research, over 50% of black men in Detroit are high-school dropouts. In 2004, 72% of those dropouts were jobless. By their mid-30s, 60% have done prison time. Among black dropouts in their late 20s, according to a University of California, Berkeley, study, more are in prison (34%) than are working (30%). [4]

The article refers—inevitably—to violence and murder as well, noting that a Congressional Quarterly report (based on FBI statistics) rates Detroit "America's most dangerous city." "Some have said that Detroit is in the throes of committing cultural suicide," the writer, Henry Payne, concludes. "It may be more accurate to call it a cultural homicide." Not that any of this isn't true about the city, and there is no reason to doubt the facts being reported. The question is how those facts are being applied to construct a border that will separate Detroit from everything else in this country. Is this really a singular case—the case of a city committing cultural suicide or homicide? Or is it a case of something broader and more generally shared—a city being done in by the racialization of poverty and crime in America, with this place only making more visible things that exist—homicidally—across our culture? In this context, it's not the actual border that counts, but the way the border gets represented, as a means of separating things we want to believe from things we want to believe aren't relevant because they apply to somebody else.

Think of it this way, then. Detroit is not so much a border as it is a "borderama," a spectacle contrived to perform culturally relevant work. I am poaching here on the performance-art term of Guillermo Gómez-Peña, and his staged interventions, the point of which are to make conscious the otherwise unconscious functioning of the borders we construct. And Detroit is surely like that—not the place, but the things done with the place, in the name of entertainment or news, or both, from broadcast television to Hollywood films to the *Wall Street Journal*. The borderama spectacle of America's city/not is never far from the public consciousness.

I am using the term spectacle, of course, in the sense suggested by Guy Debord, who remains an unimpeachable guide when it comes to borderama:

> Understood in its totality, the spectacle is both the result and the project of the dominant mode of production. It is not a mere decoration added to the real world. It is the very heart of this real society's unreality. In all of its particular manifestations—news, propaganda, advertising, entertainment—the spectacle represents the dominant *model* of life. It is the omnipresent affirmation of the choices that have *already been made* in the sphere of production and in the consumption implied by that production. In both form and content the spectacle serves as a total justification of the conditions and goals of the existing system. The spectacle also represents the *constant presence* of this justification since it monopolizes the majority of the time spent outside the production process. [5]

The spectacle buys us into where and who we already are. The actual borders here are ones potentially dangerous to cross, as the statistics make clear—borders between "good" and "bad" parts of town, neighborhoods that are safe, and those where things go violently wrong. And those borders implicate problems that Americans may generally share, or at least share the fear of, problems that result from "choices that have *already been made* in the sphere of production and in the consumption implied by that production," as Debord says. So if Detroit represents choices we have already made, then how to live with the results? How to understand ourselves in relation to real and troubling things which are unavoidable? We spectacularize our visits to the city/not site of our anxieties, which is the reason Detroit is so consistently in the news, which is not really news at all. Who needs to be told that this place is old and poor, black and dangerous, depopulated and scary? Nobody. But who needs reassurance? All the rest of us, of course, who make periodic borderama excursions, the point of which is to afford us the comforting assurance that Detroit is what the rest of America is in recovery from, and that such recovery is available as elective choice. We want to believe that where you are is all a matter of choice, and that everybody is free to choose, so that stupid and destructive choices are all the fault of the person doing the choosing. This may be a lie, but it is no less powerful for that.

The Paris of Southeastern Lower Michigan

I have a t-shirt with that phrase imprinted on it: "Detroit, the Paris of Southeastern Lower Michigan." It was a gift from a friend, who left town several years ago, fed up with his most recent home invasion—after the alarm went off in the middle of the night, the police arriving, checking things out, with nothing taken but a TV set, and the post-traumatic family gone back to bed, when they hear something downstairs because the burglar has come back to finish the job, figuring correctly that the alarms would now be disabled and the family duly chastened so they'd keep out of the way. So the thief finished his work, the police returned, and next morning my friend decided it was time to go, leaving me the t-shirt as a kind of legacy. It's like other shirts that people here wear occasionally, imprinted with various city/not slogans advertising a certain stubborn pride in our various negative claims to fame, such as being the sometime murder capital of the United States. We indemnify our catastrophes with an in-your-face self-captioning. "Beware," goes the admonition, per a recent t-shirt sighting, "I have friends in Detroit." We're already partying at the borderama even before the news crews and reporters arrive to "discover" our most recent calamity.

But we were not always that way, which is important to keep in mind. For a long time, Detroit really was America's great success story, as an article in *Fortune* magazine explained in 1956: "The community's great $4.5-billion auto industry makes and sells a product that every American loves; the industry's 400,000 workers are among the highest paid in the world; and all in all, U.S. capitalism seems to stand out in its finest colors and in its greatest genius in the manufacturing area around Detroit. [6]

"It is a company that helped lift hundreds of thousands of American workers into the middle class," the *New York Times* wrote, 53 years later, on the day GM declared bankruptcy. "It transformed Detroit into the Silicon Valley of its day, a symbol of America's talent for innovation." [7] That transformation was spectacular in its dimensions. In 1890, Detroit was the 14th largest city in the United States, with a population of 205,876 and an area of 22.19 square miles. It was a prosperous if modest place, with a diversified economy based on timber and railroad cars, cigar manufacturing and stoves, locomotives, pharmaceuticals, and marine engines. By the 1920 census, following the birth of the assembly line and the Model T, Detroit had become the fourth largest city in the country, with a one-industry economy and a population of 993,675—over four times what it had been only 30 years before—and an area of 79.62 square miles. The city population peaked around the 1950 census, at just under two million, almost twice what it had been in 1920, by which point Detroit had achieved its present size of 140 square miles. And then, just as the city reached its historic high of population and prosperity, people began to leave, as the rush to suburbia began, with the population today estimated at less than 900,000, the lowest it's been for almost 100 years.

The interesting thing about this demographic rocket ride, with an ascent and descent perhaps more rapid than that of any other U.S. city, is that it suggests a kind of one-off urbanism inherent to this place, certainly, and perhaps to American city-making generally. The city—*this* city—was never meant to be like other cities, especially European cities, with a population achieving a certain size and density and then remaining there, for generations; Detroit was always on the way to becoming something else, with a population that no sooner peaked than it began immediately to shrink. The riot of 1967 was still almost two decades off when this ex-migration began, so that wasn't the reason. Not that there's a single or a simple explanation. But one thing is clear. The people who came here never intended to stay. And it is this prospect of improbable—but indicative—human behavior that has been making Detroit significant almost from the beginning.

We were one of the stops on the tour of Alexis de Tocqueville, the young French aristocrat, sent by his government in 1831, along with Gustave de Beaumont, to investigate the penitentiaries of the new United States, on the assumption that the French might learn something from our supposedly more rational and humane system of incarceration. There's an easy irony here, in the fact that America is still the world's leading jailor, with more of our citizens living behind bars than in any other country; but it's an open question whether anybody would still consider us to be a model. It's not the study of prisons that made Tocqueville's fame, of course, but his two-volume investigation, *Democracy in America* (1835, 1840). He landed in this country at a rambunctious time, as Jacksonian democracy was in full sway, with its populist enfranchisements and expansionist bravado. We presented a good test case, in other words, for a cultivated European whose own country was in the midst of revolutionary transformation, and who found himself—like many others—wondering if a people could really govern themselves democratically.

To that end, Detroit presented an interesting case. The population when Tocqueville arrived was just over 2,000. The city at that point was more than 100 years old, having been founded in 1701 by a French entrepreneur, Antoine Laumet (1658–1730), who preferred the self-invented title, sieur Antoine de Lamothe-Cadillac. Nothing much had been produced in Detroit during a century and more of existence, except for the periodically bloody conflicts between French and English troops and their Native American surrogates. But the place held a special significance for Tocqueville, much as it does for tourists today. "We were curious to see entirely savage country," his partner Beaumont wrote, "to reach the farthest limits of civilization." [8] What the men found, however, was more contradiction than pure manifestation. As they approached Detroit by river on the afternoon of July 22, 1831, they were greeted with a paradigmatic sight. On the Canadian side of the strait where Detroit is located, a Scottish Highlander in full uniform; on the American side, two Indians in a canoe, naked, with painted bodies and rings through their noses. [9] That symbolic opposition still rules, 200 years later, over the city and city/not spectacle of Detroit.

But it's not metaphors I'm after. And here Tocqueville's report has come honestly by its enduring interest to Americans. He recognized early on an exceptional feature of our national character—one that he thought bore the potential to become our undoing; that feature is *individualism*, a new word that Tocqueville did not invent, but applied skillfully, to describe us:

> Individualism is a reflective and peaceable sentiment that disposes each citizen to isolate himself from the mass of those like him and to withdraw to one side with his family and his friends, so that after having thus created a little society for his own use, he willingly abandons society at large to itself. Selfishness is born of a blind instinct; individualism proceeds from an erroneous judgment rather than a depraved sentiment. It has its source in the defects of the mind as much as in the vices of the heart. Selfishness withers the seed of all the virtues; individualism at first dries up only the source of public virtues; but in the long term it attacks and destroys all the others and will finally be absorbed in selfishness. Selfishness is a vice as old as the world. It scarcely belongs more to one form of society than to another. Individualism is of democratic origin, and it threatens to develop as conditions become equal. [10]

Associations, Tocqueville thought—our collective belonging to other than individual causes—would save us from the dangers inherent in individualist democracy. Otherwise, there could be little hope for the American experiment:

> Thus not only does democracy make each man forget his ancestors, but it hides his descendants from him and separates him from his contemporaries; it constantly leads him back toward himself alone and threatens finally to confine him wholly in the solitude of his own heart. [11]

This dangerous tendency that Tocqueville noted, almost 180 years ago, is surely no less an explanation of Detroit and the bafflement that visitors register, when confronted with the catastrophic results of a people accustomed to dwelling in the solitude of our own hearts.

As to the urbanism that results, there's a wonderful passage in a letter Beaumont wrote, following his visit to Detroit. In it, he recounts an experience he and Tocqueville had when they entered the shop of a Mme. de Moderl to buy some mosquito netting:

> While she was giving us what we asked, my eyes happened to encounter a little print posted in her store. This print represents a very well dressed lady and at the bottom is written: *Mode de Longchamps 1831.* How do you find the inhabitants of Michigan who give themselves the styles of Paris? It's a fact that in the last village of America the French mode is followed, and all the fashions are supposed to come from Paris. [12]

City and not-city were alive here, then, in that shop, in "the last village of America," which also contained news of the latest Paris fashions—presumably because citizens needed such information to maintain an appropriate sense of who they were here in the Paris of southeastern lower Michigan.

That exceptional, American condition is what sets our cities apart, like the people in them, as Witold Rybczynski points out in his study *City Life*; it's what Beaumont noted in that Detroit shop, the distinctive way in which our individualism deployed itself:

> The United States is the first example of a society in which the process of urbanization began, paradoxically, not by building towns, but by spreading an urban culture. Here is an important distinction, and perhaps also another reason for the ambivalence that marks American attitudes toward the city: there never was a sense of cities as precious repositories of civilization. Because urban culture spread so rapidly, it lost its tie to the city, at least in the public's perception. [13]

And that, Rybczynski says, is why our cities are not like Paris—not because Americans are a society of bunglers who can't imitate correctly, but because we were never trying to build Paris in the first place: "[I]f our cities are different—and they clearly are—it may be not only because we build them differently and use them differently but also because we imagine them in a different way." [14] And there is surely no more different-seeming city than Detroit—America's greatest city/not.

But all of our cities are—to a greater or lesser degree—cities/ not, in the terms Rybczynski suggests; they are not places where most of us want to live. As the Associated Press reports, "Without immigrants pouring into the nation's big metro areas, places such as New York, Los Angeles and Boston would be shrinking as native-born Americans move farther out." [15] We are metropolitan but not urban.

When *Money* magazine posts its yearly list of "best places to live," they are not cities, typically, but small towns, such as Middleton, Wisconsin, with a population of 17,400. [16] Served by transportation and communication networks, Americans don't need cities the way other people seem to, any more than those residents of Detroit in 1831 needed Paris in order to keep up with the latest styles. We proceed by spectacular means toward the fulfillment of our exceptional individuality. And most of the time, it seems—both to ourselves and to others—as if we were all along intending something entirely different, something unrelated to actual conditions on the ground, which are not our doing, really, but somehow self-generating. That kind of forgetting is perhaps comforting, even necessary. But it comes at an extraordinary cost.

Credits

"Borderland/Borderama" is excerpted from *Distributed Urbanism: Cities After Google Earth*, an anthology just published by Routledge, and appears here with the permission of the publisher.

Exploring the decentralized systems through which cities are increasingly organized and produced, *Distributed Urbanism* highlights architectural practices that are emerging in response. Unlike early forms of urbanism, in which production, communication and governance entities were sited within a central business district, contemporary urbanism is shaped by distributed mechanisms such as information technologies (i.e. SatNav or Google Earth), cooperative economic models and environmental networks, many of which are physically remote from the cities they shape.

Distributed Urbanism presents a series of case studies highlighting the architectural implications of these remote design agencies on 21st-century cities. Edited by Gretchen Wilkins, Senior Lecturer at RMIT in Melbourne, it features work, both imagined and real, by leading architects and theorists worldwide, including projects in Rotterdam, Tokyo, Barcelona, Detroit, Hong Kong, Dubai, Beijing and Mumbai.

Notes

1. Rebecca Solnit, "Detroit Arcadia: Exploring the Post-American Landscape," *Harper's Magazine*, July 2007, 66.
2. Ibid., p. 67.
3. Mary Kramer, "Optimism and Turmoil," *Crain's Detroit Business: Living and Investing in the D*, 24, no. 32a, 2.
4. Henry Payne, "Cross Country: Murder City," *Wall Street Journal*, December 8, 2007: A10.
5. Guy Debord, Statement 6, *The Society of the Spectacle*.
6. M. Holli, *Detroit* (New York: St. Martin's, 1976).
7. Micheline Maynard, "After Many Stumbles, the Fall of an American Giant," *New York Times*, June 1, 2009, sec. A: 1, 12.
8. H. Brogan, *Alexis de Tocqueville: A Life* (New Haven: Yale University Press, 2006): 170.
9. Ibid., 169.
10. Alexis de Tocqueville, *Democracy in America*, ed. and trans. Harvey C. Mansfield and Delba Winthrop (Chicago: University of Chicago Press, 2002), 482–483.
11. Ibid., 484.
12. Gustave Beaumont, in G. Pierson, *Tocqueville in America* (Baltimore: Hopkins, 1996), 284.
13. Witold Rybczynski, *City Life: Urban Expectations in a New World* (New York: Scribner, 1995), 114.
14. Ibid., 27.
15. "Without Immigrants, Metro Areas Would Shrink," Associated Press, MSNBC, April 5, 2007.
16. "Best Places to Live," *Money*, 2007.

Guiding Questions

1. What is the purpose of Herron's essay? Does it have more than one?
2. How does Herron define "border" in this essay? And what does he mean to accomplish by coining the term "borderama"?
3. How would you define "city"? What makes a place "city," and what makes it "not city"?

4. Do you know other cities that resemble Detroit in terms of the poverty, crime, and neglect? If so, are there any efforts to revitalize those cities?

5. How effective is Herron's use of other voices and quotes from other authors in discussing Detroit and its possible meanings? Are any of these more or less effective for you? Why?

Paths for Further Exploration

1. This piece is the first of a three-part series Herron wrote on Detroit. Read the other two installments (available at http://places.designob-server.com/feature/borderland-borderama-detroit-part-2/13808/and http://places.designobserver.com/feature/borderland-borderama-detroit-part-3/13818/) as Herron develops his depiction of Detroit and its future. Use his series as a model for writing your own history and analysis of a city/not city that you know.

2. Herron references the performance art of Guillermo Gomez-Pena and his "staged interventions" that "make conscious the otherwise unconscious functioning of the borders we construct." Go online to look at some of some of Gomez-Pena's work and write an analysis piece: www.pochanostra.com/

3. Herron's piece seems to suggest that we as Americans may "need" a place like Detroit in order to be able to process our complicated feelings about cities, industry, nature, race, the environment, and a whole host of other complex issues. Are there myths of Detroit that seem to you to be doing important work for the culture? How does Chrysler's relatively recent "Imported from Detroit" ad campaign (which debuted during the 2011 Super Bowl), featuring Detroit-native rapper Eminem, make use of these myths or attempt to comment on them? Does this campaign depend upon people knowing other versions of Detroit (such as the film *8 Mile*)?

Scientific Applications

SONNY FABBRI

Sonny Fabbri is from Long Island, New York. He graduated from Boston College in 2007 with a major in biology. The following excerpt is from a longer essay in which he discusses what steps led him to college and what vocation he is considering pursuing. As part of the assignment, students observed a class in a field of their interest, discussed their observations, and imagined themselves joining this community. Asked also to consider the role of writing and the language and style used in a particular community, Fabbri responds by invoking the language used in the scientific world.

———————— ✦ ————————

L *ist your possible area(s) of academic concentration/major.*

Filling out my college applications, I pause at this deceptively simple command. I recognize the college's attempt to categorize me, but I also recognize the question behind the question: What do you want to do with your life? My counselor has advised me to write something in the spaces, so I declare biology as my major. Life processes have always intrigued me, and biology seems like a logical choice.

With this decision made, I begin my own life processes experiment.

Every experiment includes a system, the environment under study. Similar to the way ecologists search for the proper area for field research, I search for the right college in which to conduct my experiment. My search begins at the end of my junior year when I acquire and assemble my college applications. Although the process requires considerable energy, my family acts as catalysts, speeding up the process and lowering the work needed for me to complete the job. My mother even types the personal information sections of the applications to increase the rate of the process.

After extensive proofreading, each package leaves my home 5 and enters the processing center known as the college placement office. The office adjusts each application and transports them into the college environment. What happens in the next step, I can only hypothesize.

From ten applications, only three applications will survive the process. With three schools to choose from, I make another crucial decision: to enroll at Boston College as a biology major.

Once I am integrated into the BC community, I pursue my interest in biology when I register for the required introductory science courses. Although I have conducted my initial experiments in biology, I remain uncertain about the results of my future trials.

Now, at the end of my first semester, I have given more serious thought toward my major. I realize choosing a major involves experimentation across a variety of studies.

Observation: I remain uncertain about my interests and my major.

Question: How do I ease my uncertainty?

Hypothesis: By taking advantage of the variety of courses at college, will focus my interests into a major and career.

Experiment: I will explore the possibilities in biology and also test different areas of study.

Predicted Result: I will find an interesting subject to pursue that may lead to a possible vocation.

Anatomy and Physiology, Genetics, Bacteriology, Molecular Biology, Evolution, Molecular Immunobiology. I have considered categories within the biology department, as my writing instructor requires that for our final writing assignment we investigate classes within a discipline of our choice to observe and research. With uncertainty, I pick a course from the list in the Course Offering Schedule:

BI55401 8734 3 three Physiology MW3 Higgins 265 Balkema

10   Phy . . . si . . . ology. What? My pre-med advisor recommends I choose Dr. Grant Balkema's physiology class to visit. Remembering his advice, I click on the BI55401 link and open up into a world of . . . confusion. Well, it's not that I'm confused, but what exactly is phiseoligee? According to Dr. Balkema's course description, "This is a study of the fundamental principles and physicochemical mechanisms underlying cellular and organismal function" (BI). OK, but Dr. Balkema defines physiology too specifically, so I consult my dictionary to better understand the basic meaning of the subject. The topic appears interesting—at least to someone like me interested in "organismal function." Besides, I have only four days to finish the first draft, so Biology 554 it is.

Minutes later, I send an e-mail to Dr. Balkema, asking for permission to sit in on his class for a writing assignment. That night, I receive a reply: "Sure." My initial excitement at his prompt response fades into a feeling of nervousness as I consider sitting in on a class filled with upperclassmen.

On Wednesday, I walk through Higgins and eventually find room 265. Escaping notice by most of the students, I slip into an empty chair. As I blend into the environment, I notice the hum of the air-conditioning vent above me and the receding peach walls of the room. The instructor enters, and I walk toward him. After I stutter my name and restate the reason for my appearance, I sit down again, and Dr. Balkema begins his lecture, tugging down the screen and powering up the projector. The words "Regulation of Ions" stand out in black letters against the green background of the projection screen. As I stare at the screen, I catch the occasional familiar word: glucose, potassium, renal vein. But as the material accumulates, I lose focus. I try following the red dot of his laser pointer as it skirts across the projection screen, but instead I study Dr. Balkema's shorthand writing style. He presents the information with small arrows, black-and-white diagrams, and enough sentence fragments to exhaust the grammar check of a word processor. I imagine myself learning in the future how to communicate in this punctuated writing style, one so different from the language I use in the other communities in my life.

Although his projections organize the material, Dr. Balkema's teaching techniques are what make the information accessible. He relates his lecture to everyday life. For example, in his discussion of absorption in the kidney, Dr. Balkema explains the dangers associated with overuse of pain killers. He states that high concentrations of Ibuprofen in the blood can damage components of the kidneys. The students nod—everyone can relate to this example. Dr. Balkema informs his students but also engages them with questions and jokes. The atmosphere of the physiology class transforms me from visitor to student. I leave the class feeling comfortable in this community.

The following week I begin the next phase of the experiment: my interview with Dr. Balkema. Several minutes into the conversation, I pitch him the deeper questions: "Wh . . . uh . . . what advice would you give to a student considering biology as a major, but only considering?"

Dr. Balkema thinks and then replies, "Continue in the intro courses, and see what happens. Take electives, and look to see which courses are exciting."

I sit back down in front of my computer to type the next draft of this experiment. "See which . . . courses . . . are exciting. . . ." I remember the fascinating information I learned from his lecture. I remember the reasons that led me to choose biology as a major. Writing about the physiology class has allowed me to revisit my interest in biology. However, visiting Dr. Balkema's class is only

15

one part of one experiment. His advice proves I still have more tests to complete.

That next step of the experiment includes locating other sources of information in the biology world. I decide to read the 2003 *BC BioNews* and find an article within it. A title captures my attention: "What is Postdoc? An Expanding Trend in Biomedical Science" (Roche 14). The article profiles a postdoctoral student who has earned a Ph.D. but has chosen to pursue training under the leadership of a scientist (Roche 14). The program he has joined allows scientists increased independence in the lab but also the opportunity to study under a recognized scientist. While studying biology, I have imagined a similar scenario for myself: earning a degree and then researching in a laboratory. Ultimately, I envision myself working at a cancer research center. The article makes me wonder about opportunities available to me to gain experience as a researcher.

In addition to observing a class, I have collected samples for my experiment—an interview and an article. I need one more sample from the biology world before I can complete my report. I search the Biology department web page. As I click through the department, I notice a reference to Dr. Clare O'Connor's research in protein methylation. I read the abstract: "The goal of this research is to understand [. . .] the reactions catalyzed by a protein carboxyl methyltransferase. [. . .] oocytes are microinjected with isoaspartyl substrates." Although I am confused by the language, I connect with the words "microinjected with isoaspartyl substrates." In my current biology course, I read about genetic engineers who injected foreign DNA into cells. The work of those scientists has thus far appeared remote, but reading about the work of Dr. O'Connor changes my perspective. I realize professors at Boston College perform the processes that seemed so removed in my textbook. I might even perform those experiments someday. Although I am years away from achieving the expertise of Dr. O'Connor, I connect to her study and obtain meaningful results from this Internet research.

20   Although I have completed the procedures of the writing experiment, focusing my studies into a major requires further testing. Part of the continuous process involves learning from previous procedures. While the writing experiment has strengthened my interest in biology, my conclusions serve only as a background. I have learned to test new areas to discover my interests. These future trials will provide the final results. With new experiments, I will test my hypothesis and reach those results.

Works Cited

Balkema, Grant. *BI 554 Physiology* (Fall: 3). 29 April 2003. Boston College WebCT. 20 Nov. 2003. Web. <'http://www.bc.edu/student-services/acd/courses/BI/bi55400.html', '700','300', 'csdesc')>.

_____. Personal Interview. 24 Nov. 2003. Print.

O'Connor, Clare. "Field of Interest: Protein methylation and the repair of age-damaged proteins." 27 Aug. 2003. The Trustees of Boston College. 2 Dec. 2003. Print. <http://www.bc.edu/schools/cas/biology/facadmin/oconnor/>.

Reynolds, Glenn H., "Nanotechnology Research Must Be Supported." 31 Oct. 2002. Fox News. 4 Dec. 2003. Web. <http://www.foxnews.com/story/0,2933,67119,00.html>.

Roche, John, P. "What Is a Postdoc? An Expanding Trend in Biomedical Science." *BC BioNews 2003*.14. Print.

Guiding Questions

1. The dominant metaphor of Fabbri's essay is that of scientific experimentation. How does this metaphor help shape the essay? Do you think it is effective?
2. In this piece, Fabbri does primary research on a topic that interests him. What counts as research and evidence in his essay?
3. What form does he decide to use to present his results? Why is it important for Fabbri to narrate the essay the way he does?
4. Fabbri finds himself disoriented in the midst of a new discourse, the unfamiliar language of biology. How does he deal with this new discourse? How does he represent the process of getting oriented?

Paths for Further Exploration

1. Why are you in college? Why did you select the college you currently attend? How does college fit into your plans for the future?
2. What major or career are you considering? Select a class in a field of your interest and contact the instructor to ask if you can observe. Once you are in the classroom, note the culture of the community: How many students are present? How big is the classroom? Does the teacher lecture, guide discussion, or both? Collect handouts, take notes, and schedule a time to interview the instructor about the class and possible career options. What other questions might you ask? Can you picture yourself participating in this classroom or vocational community?
3. Fabbri acquires the language of a particular academic discourse. Describe the language of a particular academic community you observe, such as an economics department, a sociology class, or student

art studio. What kind of writing might students need to do in this community?

4. Design and describe the ideal college classroom for any kind of course you want to select, or a room that would work well for several kinds of courses. What physical details should be in the room? What technology should the students and teacher have access to and why? What kind of lighting, sound, and textures should be there? Should it have food? Plants? Places to nap? Be creative. (Consider supplementing your written description with visual aids such as a sketches, photo manipulations, and/or even computer-generated graphics.)

On the Range
ERIC SCHLOSSER

In the following chapter from his bestselling book, Fast Food Nation, *which was on the* New York Times *bestseller list for over a year and which he helped adapt into a 2006 film version, award-winning journalist Eric Schlosser examines how the forces of food production and suburban sprawl combine to affect the life of one Colorado rancher and his family. Schlosser is a correspondent for the* Atlantic Monthly, *and his most recent book,* Chew on This: Everything You Don't Want to Know about Fast Food *(with Charles Wilson), was published in 2006 and aimed at young adult readers.*

———————— ✦ ————————

Hank was the first person I met in Colorado Springs. He was a prominent local rancher, and I'd called him to learn how development pressures and the dictates of the fast food industry were affecting the area's cattle business. In July of 1997, he offered to give me a tour of the new subdivisions that were rising on land where cattle once roamed. We met in the lobby of my hotel. Hank was forty-two years old and handsome enough to be a Hollywood cowboy, tall and rugged, wearing blue jeans, old boots, and a big white hat. But the Dodge minivan he drove didn't quite go with that image, and he was too smart to fit any stereotype. Hank proved to be good company from the first handshake. He had strong opinions, but didn't take himself too seriously. We spent hours driving around Colorado Springs, looking at how the New West was burying the Old.

As we drove through neighborhoods like Broadmoor Oaks and Broadmoor Bluffs, amid the foothills of Cheyenne Mountain, Hank pointed out that all these big new houses on small lots sat on land that every few generations burned. The houses were surrounded by lovely pale brown grasses, tumbleweed, and scrub oak—ideal kindling. As in southern California, these hillsides could erupt in flames with the slightest spark, a cigarette tossed from a car window. The homes looked solid and prosperous, gave no hint of their vulnerability, and had wonderful views.

Hank's ranch was about twenty miles south of town. As we headed there, the landscape opened up and began to show glimpses of the true West—the wide-open countryside that draws its beauty from the absence of people, attracts people, and then slowly loses its appeal. Through leadership positions in a variety of local and statewide groups, Hank was trying to bridge the gap between ranchers and environmentalists, to establish some common ground between longtime enemies. He was not a wealthy, New Age type playing at being a cowboy. His income came from the roughly four hundred head of cattle on his ranch. He didn't care what was politically correct and had little patience for urban environmentalists who vilified the cattle industry. In his view, good ranchers did far less damage to the land than city-dwellers. "Nature isn't an abstraction for me," he said. "My family lives with it every day."

When we got to the ranch, Hank's wife, Susan, was leading her horse out of a ring. She was blond and attractive, but no pushover: tall, fit, and strong. Their daughters, Allie and Kris, aged six and eight, ran over to greet us, full of excitement that their dad was home and had brought a visitor. They scrambled into the minivan and joined us for a drive around the property. Hank wanted me to see the difference between his form of ranching and "raping the land." As we took off onto a dirt road, I looked back at his house and thought about how small it looked amid this landscape. On acreage hundreds if not thousands of times larger than the front lawns and back yards surrounding the mansions of Colorado Springs, the family lived in a modest log cabin.

Hank was practicing a form of range management inspired by the grazing patterns of elk and buffalo herds, animals who'd lived for millennia on this short-grass prairie. His ranch was divided into thirty-five separate pastures. His cattle spent ten or eleven days in one pasture, then were moved to the next, allowing the native plants, the blue grama and buffalo grass, time to recover. Hank stopped the minivan to show me a nearby stream. On land

5

that has been overgrazed, the stream banks are usually destroyed first, as cattle gather in the cool shade beside the water, eating everything in sight. Hank's stream was fenced off with barbed wire, and the banks were lush and green. Then he took me to see Fountain Creek, which ran straight through the ranch, and I realized that he'd given other guests the same tour. It had a proper sequence and a point.

Fountain Creek was a long, ugly gash about twenty yards wide and fifteen feet deep. The banks were collapsing from erosion, fallen trees and branches littered the creek bed, and a small trickle of water ran down the middle. "This was done by storm runoff from Colorado Springs," Hank said. The contrast between his impact on the land and the city's impact was hard to miss. The rapid growth of Colorado Springs had occurred without much official planning, zoning, or spending on drainage projects. As more pavement covered land within the city limits, more water flowed straight into Fountain Creek instead of being absorbed into the ground. The runoff from Colorado Springs eroded the land beside the creek, carrying silt and debris downstream all the way to Kansas. Hank literally lost part of his ranch every year. It got washed away by the city's rainwater. A nearby rancher once lost ten acres of land in a single day, thanks to runoff from a fierce storm in Colorado Springs. While Hank stood on the crumbling bank, giving an impassioned speech about the watershed protection group that he'd helped to organize, telling me about holding ponds, landscaped greenways, and the virtues of permeable parking lots covered in gravel, I lost track of his words. And I thought: "This guy's going to be governor of Colorado someday."

Toward sunset we spotted a herd of antelope and roared after them. That damn minivan bounced over the prairie like a horse at full gallop, Hank wild behind the wheel, Allie and Kris squealing in the back seat. We had a Chrysler engine, power steering, and disk brakes, but the antelope had a much superior grace, making sharp and unexpected turns, about two dozen of them, bounding effortlessly, butts held high. After a futile chase, Hank let the herd go on its way, then veered right and guided the minivan up a low hill. There was something else he wanted to show me. The girls looked intently out the window, faces flushed, searching for more wildlife. When we reached the crest of the hill, I looked down and saw an immense oval structure, shiny and brand-new. For an instant, I couldn't figure out what it was. It looked like a structure created by some alien civilization and plopped in the middle of nowhere. "Stock car racing," Hank said matter-of-factly.

The grandstands around the track were enormous, and so was the parking lot. Acres of black asphalt and white lines now spread across the prairie, thousands of empty spaces waiting for cars. The speedway was new, and races were being held there every weekend in the summer. You could hear the engines and the crowd from Hank's house. The races weren't the main problem, though. It was the practice runs that bothered Hank and Susan most. In the middle of the day, in one of America's most beautiful landscapes, they would suddenly hear the drone of stock cars going round and round. For a moment, we sat quietly on top of the hill, staring at the speedway bathed in twilight, at this oval strip of pavement, this unsettling omen. Hank stopped there long enough for me to ponder what it meant, the threat now coming his way, then drove back down the hill. The speedway was gone again, out of sight, and the girls were still happy in the back seat, chatting away, oblivious, as the sun dropped behind the mountains.

A New Trust

Ranchers and cowboys have long been the central icons of the American West. Traditionalists have revered them as symbols of freedom and self-reliance. Revisionists have condemned them as racists, economic parasites, and despoilers of the land. The powerful feelings evoked by cattlemen reflect opposing views of our national identity, attempts to sustain old myths or create new ones. There is one indisputable fact, however, about American ranchers: they are rapidly disappearing. Over the last twenty years, about half a million ranchers sold off their cattle and quit the business. Many of the nation's remaining eight hundred thousand ranchers are faring poorly. They're taking second jobs. They're selling cattle at break-even prices or at a loss. The ranchers who are faring the worst run three to four hundred head of cattle, manage the ranch themselves, and live solely off the proceeds. The sort of hardworking ranchers long idealized in cowboy myths are the ones most likely to go broke today. Without receiving a fraction of the public attention given to the northwestern spotted owl, America's independent cattlemen have truly become an endangered species.

Ranchers currently face a host of economic problems: rising land prices, stagnant beef prices, oversupplies of cattle, increased shipments of live cattle from Canada and Mexico, development pressures, inheritance taxes, health scares about beef. On top of all that, the growth of the fast food chains has encouraged consolidation in the meatpacking industry. McDonald's is the nation's largest purchaser of beef. In 1968, McDonald's bought ground beef from 175 local suppliers. A few years later, seeking to achieve greater product uniformity as it expanded, McDonald's reduced the number of beef suppliers to five. Much like the french fry industry, the meatpacking industry has been transformed by mergers and acquisitions over the last twenty years. Many ranchers now argue that a few large corporations have gained a stranglehold on the market, using unfair tactics to drive down the price of cattle. Anger toward the large meatpackers is growing, and a new range war threatens to erupt, one that will determine the social and economic structure of the rural West.

A century ago, American ranchers found themselves in a similar predicament. The leading sectors of the nation's economy were controlled by corporate alliances known as "trusts." There was a Sugar Trust, a Steel Trust, a Tobacco Trust—and a Beef Trust. It set the prices offered for cattle. Ranchers who spoke out against this monopoly power were often blackballed, unable to sell their cattle at any price. In 1917, at the height of the Beef Trust, the five largest meatpacking companies—Armour, Swift, Morris, Wilson, and Cudahy—controlled about 55 percent of the market. The early twentieth century had trusts, but it also had "trustbusters," progressive government officials who believed that concentrated economic power posed a grave threat to American democracy. The Sherman Antitrust Act had been passed in 1890 after a congressional investigation of price fixing in the meatpacking industry, and for the next two decades the federal government tried to break up the Beef Trust, with little success. In 1917 President Woodrow Wilson ordered the Federal Trade Commission to investigate the industry. The FTC inquiry concluded that the five major meatpacking firms had secretly fixed prices for years, had colluded to divide up markets, and had shared livestock information to guarantee that ranchers received the lowest possible price for their cattle. Afraid that an antitrust trial might end with an unfavorable verdict, the five meatpacking companies signed a consent decree in 1920 that forced them to sell off their stockyards, retail meat stores, railway interests, and livestock journals. A year later Congress created the Packers and Stockyards Administration (P&SA), a federal agency with a broad authority to prevent pricefixing and monopolistic behavior in the beef industry.

For the next fifty years, ranchers sold their cattle in a relatively competitive marketplace. The price of cattle was set through open bidding at auctions. The large meatpackers competed with hundreds of small regional firms. In 1970 the top four meatpacking firms slaughtered only 21 percent of the nation's cattle. A decade later, the Reagan administration allowed these firms to merge and combine without fear of antitrust enforcement. The Justice Department and the P&SA's successor, the Grain Inspection, Packers and Stockyards Administration (GIPSA), stood aside as the large meatpackers gained control of one local cattle market after another. Today the top four meatpacking firms—ConAgra, IBP, Excel, and National Beef—slaughter about 84 percent of the nation's cattle. Market concentration in the beef industry is now at the highest level since record-keeping began in the early twentieth century.

Today's unprecedented degree of meatpacking concentration has helped depress the prices that independent ranchers get for their cattle. Over the last twenty years, the rancher's share of every retail dollar spent on beef has fallen from 63 cents to 46 cents. The four major meatpacking companies now control about 20 percent of the live cattle in the United States through "captive supplies"— cattle that are either maintained in company-owned feedlots or purchased in advance through forward contracts. When cattle prices start to rise, the large meatpackers can flood the market with their own captive supplies, driving prices back down. They can also obtain cattle through confidential agreements with wealthy ranchers, never revealing the true price being paid. ConAgra and Excel operate their own gigantic feedlots, while IBP has private arrangements with some of America's biggest ranchers and feeders, including the Bass brothers, Paul Engler, and J. R. Simplot. Independent ranchers and feedlots now have a hard time figuring out what their cattle are actually worth, let alone finding a buyer for them at the right price. On any given day in the nation's regional cattle markets, as much as 80 percent of the cattle being exchanged are captive supplies. The prices being paid for these cattle are never disclosed.

To get a sense of what an independent rancher now faces, imagine how the New York Stock Exchange would function if large investors could keep the terms of all their stock trades secret. Ordinary investors would have no idea what their own stocks were really worth—a fact that wealthy traders could easily exploit. "A free market requires many buyers as well as many sellers, all with equal access to accurate information, all entitled to trade on the same terms, and none with a big enough share of the market to influence price," said a report by Nebraska's Center for Rural Affairs. "Nothing close to these conditions now exists in the cattle market."

15   The large meatpacking firms have thus far shown little interest in buying their own cattle ranches. "Why would they want the hassle?" Lee Pitts, the editor of *Livestock Market Digest*, told me. "Raising cattle is a business with a high overhead, and most of the capital's tied up in the land." Instead of buying their own ranches, the meatpacking companies have been financing a handful of large feedlot owners who lease ranches and run cattle for them. "It's just another way of controlling prices through captive supply," Pitts explained. "The packers now own some of these big feeders lock, stock, and barrel, and tell them exactly what to do."

The Breasts of Mr. Mcdonald

Many ranchers now fear that the beef industry is deliberately being restructured along the lines of the poultry industry. They do not want to wind up like chicken growers—who in recent years have become virtually powerless, trapped by debt and by onerous contracts written by the large processors. The poultry industry was also transformed by a wave of mergers in the 1980s. Eight chicken processors now control about two-thirds of the American market. These processors have shifted almost all of their production to the rural South, where the weather tends to be mild, the workforce is poor, unions are weak, and farmers are desperate to find some way of staying on their land. Alabama, Arkansas, Georgia, and Mississippi now produce more than half the chicken raised in the United States. Although many factors helped revolutionize the poultry industry and increase the power of the large processors, one innovation played an especially important role. The Chicken McNugget turned a bird that once had to be carved at a table into something that could easily be eaten behind the wheel of a car. It turned a bulk agricultural commodity into a manufactured, value-added product. And it encouraged a system of production that has turned many chicken farmers into little more than serfs.

"I have an idea," Fred Turner, the chairman of McDonald's, told one of his suppliers in 1979. "I want a chicken finger-food without bones, about the size of your thumb. Can you do it?" The supplier, an executive at Keystone Foods, ordered a group of technicians to get to work in the lab, where they were soon joined by food scientists from McDonald's. Poultry consumption in the United States was growing, a trend with alarming implications for a fast food chain that only sold hamburgers. The nation's chicken meat had traditionally been provided by hens that were too old to lay eggs; after World War II a new poultry industry based in Delaware and Virginia lowered the cost of raising chicken, while medical research touted the health benefits of eating it. Fred Turner wanted McDonald's to sell a chicken dish that wouldn't clash with the chain's sensibility. After six months of intensive research, the Keystone lab developed new technology for the manufacture of McNuggets—small pieces of reconstituted chicken, composed mainly of white meat, that were held together by stabilizers, breaded, fried, frozen, then reheated. The initial test-marketing of McNuggets was so successful that McDonald's enlisted another company, Tyson Foods, to guarantee an adequate supply. Based in Arkansas, Tyson was one of the nation's leading chicken processors, and it soon developed a new breed of chicken to facilitate the production of McNuggets. Dubbed "Mr. McDonald," the new breed had unusually large breasts.

Chicken McNuggets were introduced nationwide in 1983. Within one month of their launch, the McDonald's Corporation had become the second-largest purchaser of chicken in the United States, surpassed only by KFC. McNuggets tasted good, they were easy to chew, and they appeared to be healthier than other items on the menu at McDonald's. After all, they were made out of chicken. But their health benefits were illusory. A chemical analysis of McNuggets by a researcher at Harvard Medical School found that their "fatty acid profile" more closely resembled beef than poultry. They were cooked in beef tallow, like McDonald's fries. The chain soon switched to vegetable oil, adding "beef extract" to McNuggets during the manufacturing process in order to retain their familiar taste. Today Chicken McNuggets are wildly popular among young children—and contain twice as much fat per ounce as a hamburger.

The McNugget helped change not only the American diet but also its system for raising and processing poultry. "The impact of McNuggets was so huge that it changed the industry," the president of ConAgra Poultry, the nation's third-largest chicken processor, later acknowledged. Twenty years ago, most chicken was sold whole; today about 90 percent of the chicken sold in the United States has been cut into pieces, cutlets, or nuggets. In 1992 American consumption of chicken for the first time surpassed the consumption of beef. Gaining the McNugget contract helped turn Tyson Foods into the world's largest chicken processor. Tyson now manufactures about half of the nation's McNuggets and sells chicken to ninety of the one hundred largest restaurant chains.

It is a vertically integrated company that breeds, slaughters, and processes chicken. It does not, however, raise the birds. It leaves the capital expenditures and the financial risks of that task to thousands of "independent contractors."

20   A Tyson chicken grower never owns the birds in his or her poultry houses. Like most of the other leading processors, Tyson supplies its growers with one-day-old chicks. Between the day they are born and the day they are killed, the birds spend their entire lives on the grower's property. But they belong to Tyson. The company supplies the feed, veterinary services, and technical support. It determines feeding schedules, demands equipment upgrades, and employs "flock supervisors" to make sure that corporate directives are being followed. It hires the trucks that drop off the baby chicks and return seven weeks later to pick up fullgrown chickens ready for slaughter. At the processing plant, Tyson employees count and weigh the birds. A grower's income is determined by a formula based upon that count, that weight, and the amount of feed used.

The chicken grower provides the land, the labor, the poultry houses, and the fuel. Most growers must borrow money to build the houses, which cost about $150,000 each and hold about 25,000 birds. A 1995 survey by Louisiana Tech University found that the typical grower had been raising chicken for fifteen years, owned three poultry houses, remained deeply in debt, and earned perhaps $12,000 a year. About half of the nation's chicken growers leave the business after just three years, either selling out or losing everything. The back roads of rural Arkansas are now littered with abandoned poultry houses.

Most chicken growers cannot obtain a bank loan without already having a signed contract from a major processor. "We get the check first," a loan officer told the *Arkansas Democrat-Gazette*. A chicken grower who is unhappy with his or her processor has little power to do anything about it. Poultry contracts are short-term. Growers who complain may soon find themselves with empty poultry houses and debts that still need to be paid. Twenty-five years ago, when the United States had dozens of poultry firms, a grower stood a much better chance of finding a new processor and of striking a better deal. Today growers who are labeled "difficult" often have no choice but to find a new line of work. A processor can terminate a contract with a grower whenever it likes. It owns the birds. Short of that punishment, a processor can prolong the interval between the departure of one flock and the arrival of another. Every day that poultry houses sit empty, the grower loses money.

The large processors won't publicly disclose the terms of their contracts. In the past, such contracts have not only required that growers surrender all rights to file a lawsuit against the company, but have also forbidden them from joining any association that might link growers in a strong bargaining unit. The processors do not like the idea of chicken growers joining forces to protect their interests. "Our relationship with our growers is a one-on-one contractual relationship . . .," a Tyson executive told a reporter in 1998. "We want to see that it remains that way."

Captives

The four large meatpacking firms claim that an oversupply of beef, not any corporate behavior, is responsible for the low prices that American ranchers are paid for their cattle. A number of studies by the U.S. Department of Agriculture (USDA) have reached the same conclusion. Annual beef consumption in the United States peaked in 1976, at about ninety-four pounds per person. Today the typical American eats about sixty-eight pounds of beef every year. Although the nation's population has grown since the 1970s, it has not grown fast enough to compensate for the decline in beef consumption. Ranchers trying to stabilize their incomes fell victim to their own fallacy of composition. They followed the advice of agribusiness firms and gave their cattle growth hormones. As a result, cattle are much bigger today; fewer cattle are sold; and most American beef cannot be exported to the European Union, where the use of bovine growth hormones has been banned.

The meatpacking companies claim that captive supplies and 25 formula pricing systems are means of achieving greater efficiency, not of controlling cattle prices. Their slaughterhouses require a large and steady volume of cattle to operate profitably; captive supplies are one reliable way of sustaining that volume. The large meatpacking companies say that they've become a convenient scapegoat for ranchers, when the real problem is low poultry prices. A pound of chicken costs about half as much as a pound of beef. The long-term deals now being offered to cattlemen are portrayed as innovations that will save, not destroy, the beef industry. Responding in 1998 to a USDA investigation of captive supplies in Kansas, IBP defended such "alternative methods for selling fed cattle." The company argued that these practices were "similar to changes that have already occurred . . . for selling other agricultural commodities," such as poultry.

Many independent ranchers are convinced that captive supplies are used primarily to control the market, not to achieve greater slaughter-house efficiency. They do not oppose large-scale transactions or long-term contracts; they oppose cattle prices that are kept secret. Most of all, they do not trust the meatpacking giants. The belief that agribusiness executives secretly talk on the phone with their competitors, set prices, and divide up the worldwide market for commodities—a belief widely held among independent ranchers and farmers—may seem like a paranoid fantasy. But that is precisely what executives at Archer Daniels Midland, "supermarket to the world," did for years.

Three of Archer Daniels Midland's top officials, including Michael Andreas, its vice chairman, were sent to federal prison in 1999 for conspiring with foreign rivals to control the international market for lysine (an important feed additive). The Justice Department's investigation of this massive price-fixing scheme focused on the period between August of 1992 and December of 1995. Within that roughly three-and-a-half-year stretch, Archer Daniels Midland and its co-conspirators may have overcharged farmers by as much as $180 million. During the same period, Archer Daniels Midland executives also met with their overseas rivals to set the worldwide price for citric acid (a common food additive). At a meeting with Japanese executives that was secretly recorded, the president of Archer Daniels Midland preached the virtues of collaboration. "We have a saying at this company," he said. "Our competitors are our friends, and our customers are our enemies." Archer Daniels Midland remains the world's largest producer of lysine, as well as the world's largest processor of soybeans and corn. It is also one of the largest shareholders of IBP.

A 1996 USDA investigation of concentration in the beef industry found that many ranchers were afraid to testify against the large meatpacking companies, fearing retaliation and "economic ruin." That year Mike Callicrate, a cattleman from St. Francis, Kansas, decided to speak out against corporate behavior he thought was not just improper but criminal. "I was driving down the road one day," Callicrate told me, "and I kept thinking, when is someone going to do something about this? And I suddenly realized that maybe nobody's going to do it, and I had to give it a try." He claims that after his testimony before the USDA committee, the large meatpackers promptly stopped bidding on his cattle. "I couldn't sell my cattle," he said. "They'd drive right past my feed yard and buy cattle from a guy two hundred miles further away." His business has recovered somewhat; ConAgra and Excel now bid on his cattle. The experience has turned him into an activist. He refuses to "make the transition to slavery quietly." He has spoken at congressional hearings and has joined a dozen other cattlemen in a class-action lawsuit against IBP. The lawsuit claims that IBP has for many years violated the Packers and Stockyards Act through a wide variety of anticompetitive tactics. According to Callicrate, the suit will demonstrate that the company's purported efficiency in production is really "an efficiency in stealing." IBP denies the charges. "It makes no sense for us to do anything to hurt cattle producers," a top IBP executive told a reporter, "when we depend upon them to supply our plants."

The Threat of Wealthy Neighbors

The Colorado Cattlemen's Association filed an amicus brief in Mike Callicrate's lawsuit against IBP, demanding a competitive marketplace for cattle and a halt to any illegal buying practices being used by the large meatpacking firms. Ranchers in Colorado today, however, face threats to their livelihood that are unrelated to fluctuations in cattle prices. During the past twenty years, Colorado has lost roughly 1.5 million acres of ranchland to development. Population growth and the booming market for vacation homes have greatly driven up land costs. Some ranchland that sold for less than $200 an acre in the 1960s now sells for hundreds of times that amount. The new land prices make it impossible for ordinary ranchers to expand their operations. Each head of cattle needs about thirty acres of pasture for grazing, and until cattle start producing solid gold nuggets instead of sirloin, it's hard to sustain beef production on such expensive land. Ranching families in Colorado tend to be land-rich and cash-poor. Inheritance taxes can claim more than half of a cattle ranch's land value. Even if a family manages to operate its ranch profitably, handing it down to the next generation may require selling off large chunks of land, thereby diminishing its productive capacity.

Along with the ranches, Colorado is quickly losing its ranching culture. Among the students at Harrison High you see a variety of fashion statements: gangsta wannabes, skaters, stoners, goths, and punks. What you don't see—in the shadow of Pikes Peak, in the heart of the Rocky Mountain West—is anyone dressed even remotely like a cowboy. Nobody's wearing shirts with snaps or Justin boots. In 1959, eight of the nation's top ten TV shows were Westerns. The networks ran thirty-five Westerns in prime time every week, and places like Colorado, where real cowboys lived, were the stuff of youthful daydreams. That America now seems as dead and distant as the England of King Arthur. I saw hundreds of high school students in Colorado Springs, and only one of them wore a cowboy hat. His name was Philly Favorite, he played guitar in a band called the Deadites, and his cowboy hat was made out of fake zebra fur.

The median age of Colorado's ranchers and farmers is about fifty-five, and roughly half of the state's open land will change hands during the next two decades—a potential boon for real estate developers. A number of Colorado land trusts are now working to help ranchers obtain conservation easements. In return for donating future development rights to one of these trusts, a rancher receives an immediate tax break and the prospect of lower inheritance taxes. The land remains private property, but by law can never be turned into golf courses, shopping malls, or subdivisions. In 1995 the Colorado Cattlemen's Association formed the first land trust in the United States that is devoted solely to the preservation of ranchland. It has thus far protected almost 40,000 acres, a significant achievement. But ranchland in Colorado is now vanishing at the rate of about 90,000 acres a year.

Conservation easements are usually of greatest benefit to wealthy gentleman ranchers who earn large incomes from other sources. The doctors, lawyers, and stockbrokers now running cattle on some of Colorado's most beautiful land can own big ranches, preserve open space with easements, and enjoy the big tax deductions. Ranchers whose annual income comes entirely from selling cattle usually don't earn enough to benefit from that sort of tax break. And the value of their land, along with the pressure to sell it, often increases when a wealthy neighbor obtains a conservation easement, since the views in the area are more likely to remain unspoiled.

The Colorado ranchers who now face the greatest economic difficulty are the ones who run a few hundred head of cattle, who work their own land, who don't have any outside income, and who don't stand to gain anything from a big tax write-off. They have to compete with gentleman ranchers whose operations don't have to earn a profit and with part-time ranchers whose operations are kept afloat by second jobs. Indeed, the ranchers most likely to be in financial trouble today are the ones who live the life and embody the values supposedly at the heart of the American West. They are independent and self-sufficient, cherish their freedom, believe in hard work—and as a result are now paying the price.

A Broken Link

Hank died in 1998. He took his own life the week before Christmas. He was forty-three. When I heard the news, it made no sense to me, none at all. The man that I knew was full of fire and ready to go, the kind of person who seemed always to be throwing himself into the middle of things. He did not hide away. He got involved in the community, served on countless boards and committees. He had a fine sense of humor. He loved his family. The way he died seemed to contradict everything else about his life.

It would be wrong to say that Hank's death was caused by the consolidating and homogenizing influence of the fast food chains, by monopoly power in the meatpacking industry, by depressed prices in the cattle market, by the economic forces bankrupting independent ranchers, by the tax laws that favor wealthy ranchers, by the unrelenting push of Colorado's real estate developers. But it would not be entirely wrong. Hank was under enormous pressure at the time of his death. He was trying to find a way of gaining conservation easements that would protect his land but not sacrifice the financial security of his family. Cattle prices had fallen to their lowest point in more than a decade. And El Paso County was planning to build a new highway right through the heart of his ranch. The stress of these things and others led to sleepless nights, then to a depression that spiraled downward fast, and before long he was gone.

The suicide rate among ranchers and farmers in the United States is now about three times higher than the national average. The issue briefly received attention during the 1980s farm crisis, but has been pretty much ignored ever since. Meanwhile, across rural America, a slow and steady death toll mounts. As the rancher's traditional way of life is destroyed, so are many of the beliefs that go with it. The code of the rancher could hardly be more out of step with America's current state of mind. In Silicon Valley, entrepreneurs and venture capitalists regard failure as just a first step toward success. After three failed Internet start-ups, there's still a chance that the fourth one will succeed. What's being sold ultimately matters less than how well it sells. In ranching, a failure is much more likely to be final. The land that has been lost is not just a commodity. It has meaning that cannot be measured in dollars and cents. It is a tangible connection with the past, something that was meant to be handed down to children and never sold. As Osha Gray Davidson observes in his book *Broken Heartland*

35

(1996), "To fail several generations of relatives . . . to see yourself as the one weak link in a strong chain . . . is a terrible, and for some, an unbearable burden."

When Hank was eight years old, he was the subject of a children's book. It combined text with photographs and told the story of a boy's first roundup. Young Hank wears blue jeans and a black hat in the book, rides a white horse, tags along with real cowboys, stares down a herd of cattle in a corral. You can see in these pictures why Hank was chosen for the part. His face is lively and expressive; he can ride; he can lasso; and he looks game, willing to jump a fence or chase after a steer ten times his size. The boy in the story starts out afraid of animals on the ranch, but in the end conquers his fear of cattle, snakes, and coyotes. There's a happy ending, and the final image echoes the last scene of a classic Hollywood Western, affirming the spirit of freedom and independence. Accompanied by an older cowhand and surrounded by a herd of cattle, young Hank rides his white horse across a vast, wide-open prairie, heading toward the horizon.

In life he did not get that sort of ending. He was buried at his ranch, in a simple wooden coffin made by friends.

Guiding Questions

1. How does this essay zoom out from the particular example of Hank's struggles to broader cultural and economic issues? How does Schlosser connect the different kinds of information he includes in the essay?
2. This essay makes its argument through several different appeals— logical, ethical, and emotional. Do these various appeals work together to create a coherent argument? Which sections are the most persuasive?
3. This is a highly researched piece. How is it similar to or different from the standard "research paper"? In what contexts would this style of argument and research be appropriate?

Paths for Further Exploration

1. Is there someone you know whose job will become extinct in the next few years? Interview that person and then conduct some research on that particular field. Write an essay in which you include parts of the interview and a discussion of this vanishing field. Likewise, what new jobs have emerged in the last two decades? What jobs are they replacing? What lifestyles do they sustain?
2. Research some aspect of food production tied to land use in the United States. (You may want to consult the rest of Schlosser's *Fast Food*

Nation, the book this chapter is from, to help you get started.) Write a persuasive paper arguing your view of "best practices" for land use and food production relative to a specific location.

3. Investigate particular jobs or industries to see which of them have high rates of injury, illness, suicide, or death. What types of goods and services do these workers produce for the rest of us, and what do the conditions they work within say about what we value as a community?

Apocalypse: What Disasters Reveal

JUNOT DIAZ

Junot Diaz is a Dominican-American writer, and the immigrant experience is central to his fiction as well as his activism. In 2008, he received the Pulitzer Prize for Fiction for his novel, The Brief Wondrous Life of Oscar Wao. *He is the Rudge and Nancy Allen Professor of Writing at Massachusetts Institute of Technology and the fiction editor for* Boston Review. *This essay appeared in the May/ June 2011 issue of the* Boston Review.

＼ ──────── ✦ ────────

What Disasters Reveal

One

On January 12, 2010 an earthquake struck Haiti. The epicenter of the quake, which registered a moment magnitude of 7.0, was only fifteen miles from the capital, Port-au-Prince. By the time the initial shocks subsided, Port-au-Prince and surrounding urbanizations were in ruins. Schools, hospitals, clinics, prisons collapsed. The electrical and communication grids imploded. The Presidential Palace, the Cathedral, and the National Assembly building—historic symbols of the Haitian patrimony—were severely damaged or destroyed. The headquarters of the UN aid mission was reduced to rubble, killing peacekeepers, aid workers, and the mission chief, Hédi Annabi.

The figures vary, but an estimated 220,000 people were killed in the aftermath of the quake, with hundreds of thousands injured and at least a million—one-tenth of Haiti's population—rendered homeless. According to the Red Cross, three million Haitians were affected. It was the single greatest catastrophe in Haiti's modern history. It was for all intents and purposes an apocalypse.

Two

Apocalypse comes to us from the Greek *apocalypsis*, meaning to uncover and unveil. Now, as James Berger reminds us in *After the End*, apocalypse has three meanings. First, it is the actual imagined end of the world, whether in *Revelations* or in Hollywood blockbusters. Second, it comprises the catastrophes, personal or historical, that are said to resemble that imagined final ending— the Chernobyl meltdown or the Holocaust or the March 11 earthquake and tsunami in Japan that killed thousands and critically damaged a nuclear power plant in Fukushima. Finally, it is a disruptive event that provokes revelation. The apocalyptic event, Berger explains, in order to be truly apocalyptic, must in its disruptive moment clarify and illuminate "the true nature of what has been brought to end." It must be revelatory.

"The apocalypse, then," per Berger, "is the End, or resembles the end, or explains the end." Apocalypses of the first, second, and third kinds. The Haiti earthquake was certainly an apocalypse of the second kind, and to those who perished it may even have been an apocalypse of the first kind, but what interests me here is how the Haiti earthquake was also an apocalypse of the third kind, a revelation. This in brief is my intent: to peer into the ruins of Haiti in an attempt to describe what for me the earthquake revealed— about Haiti, our world, and even our future.

After all, if these types of apocalyptic catastrophes have any value it is that in the process of causing things to fall apart they also give us a chance to see the aspects of our world that we as a society seek to run from, that we hide behind veils of denials.

Apocalyptic catastrophes don't just raze cities and drown coastlines; these events, in David Brooks's words, "wash away the surface of society, the settled way things have been done. They expose the underlying power structures, the injustices, the patterns of corruption and the unacknowledged inequalities." And, equally important, they allow us insight into the conditions that led to the catastrophe, whether we are talking about Haiti or Japan. (I do believe the tsunami-earthquake that ravaged Sendai this past March will eventually reveal much about our irresponsible reliance on nuclear power and the sinister collusion between local and international actors that led to the Fukushima Daiichi catastrophe.)

If, as Roethke writes, "in a dark time, the eye begins to see," apocalypse is a darkness that gives us light. But this is not an easy thing to do, this peering into darkness, this ruin-reading. It requires nuance, practice, and no small amount of heart. I cannot, however, endorse it enough. Given the state of our world—in which the very forces that place us in harm's way often take advantage of the confusion brought by apocalyptic events to extend their power and in the process increase our vulnerability—becoming a ruin-reader might not be so bad a thing. It could in fact save your life.

Three

So the earthquake that devastated Haiti: what did it reveal?

Well I think it's safe to say that first and foremost it revealed Haiti.

This might strike some of you as jejune but considering the colossal denial energies (the veil) that keep most third-world countries (and their problems) out of global sightlines, this is no mean feat. For most people Haiti has never been more than a blip on a map, a faint disturbance in the force so far removed that what happened there might as well have been happening on another planet. The earthquake for a while changed that, tore the veil from before planet's eyes and put before us what we all saw firsthand or on the TV: a Haiti desperate beyond imagining.

If Katrina revealed America's third world, then the earthquake revealed the third world's third world. Haiti is by nearly every metric one of the poorest nations on the planet—a mind-blowing 80 percent of the population lives in poverty, and 54 percent lives in what is called "abject poverty." Two-thirds of the workforce has no regular employment, and, for those who do have jobs, wages hover around two dollars a day. We're talking about a country in which half the population lack access to clean water and 60 percent lack even the most basic health-care services, such as immunizations; where malnutrition is among the leading causes of death in children, and, according to UNICEF, 24 percent of five-year-olds suffer stunted growth. As the Haiti Children Project puts it:

> Lack of food, hygienic living conditions, clean water and basic healthcare combine with epidemic diarrhea, respiratory infections, malaria, tuberculosis and HIV/AIDS to give Haiti among the highest infant, under-five and maternal mortality rates in the western hemisphere.

In Haiti life expectancy hovers at around 60 years as compared to, say, 80 years, in Canada. Hunger, overpopulation, over-cultivation, and dependence on wood for fuel have strained Haiti's natural resources to the breaking point. Deforestation has rendered vast stretches of the Haitian landscape almost lunar in their desolation. Haiti is eating itself. Fly over my island—Hispaniola, home to Haiti and my native Dominican Republic—as I do two or three times a year, and what you will see will leave you speechless. Where forests covered 60 percent of Haiti in 1923, only two percent is now covered. This relentless deforestation has led to tremendous hardships; it is both caused by and causes poverty. Without forests, 6,000 hectares of arable land erode every year, and Haiti has grown more vulnerable to hurricane-induced mudslides that wipe out farms, roads, bridges, even entire communities. In 2008 four storms caused nearly a billion dollars in damage—15 percent of the gross domestic product—and killed close to a thousand people. The mudslides were so extensive and the cleanup so underfunded that much of that damage is still visible today.

In addition to resource pressures, Haiti struggles with poor infrastructure. Political and social institutions are almost nonexistent, and a deadly confluence of political instability, pervasive corruption, massive poverty, and predation from elites on down to armed drug gangs has unraveled civic society, leaving the majority of Haitians isolated and at risk. Even before the earthquake, Haiti was reeling—it would not have taken the slightest shove to send it into catastrophe.

All this the earthquake revealed.

Four

When confronted with a calamity of the magnitude of the Haitian earthquake, most of us resort to all manners of evasion—averting our eyes, blaming the victim, claiming the whole thing was an act of god—in order to avoid confronting what geographer Neil Smith calls the axiomatic truth of these events: "There's no such thing as a natural disaster." In every phase and aspect of a disaster, Smith reminds us, the difference between who lives and who dies is to a greater or lesser extent a social calculus.

In other words disasters don't just happen. They are always made possible by a series of often-invisible societal choices that implicate more than just those being drowned or buried in rubble.

This is why we call them social disasters.

The Asian tsunami of 2004 was a social disaster. The waves were so lethal because the coral reefs that might have protected the vulnerable coasts had been dynamited to facilitate shipping. And the regions that suffered most were those like Nagapattinam, in India, where hotel construction and industrial shrimp farming had already systematically devastated the natural mangrove forests, which are the world's best tsunami-protectors. Hurricane Katrina was a social disaster. Not only in the ruthless economic marginalization of poor African Americans and in the outright abandonment of same during the crisis, but in the Bush administration's decision to sell hundreds of square miles of wetlands to developers, destroying New Orleans's natural defenses. The same administration, according to Smith, gutted "the New Orleans Corps of Engineers budget by 80 percent, thus preventing pumping and levee improvements." As with the tsunami and Katrina, so too Haiti.

But Haiti is really exemplary in this regard. From the very beginning of its history, right up to the day of the earthquake, Haiti had a lot of help on its long road to ruination. The web of complicity for its engulfment in disaster extends in both time and space.

Whether it was Haiti's early history as a French colony, which artificially inflated the country's black population beyond what the natural bounty of the land could support and prevented any kind of material progress; whether it was Haiti's status as the first and only nation in the world to overthrow Western chattel slavery, for which it was blockaded (read, further impoverished) by Western powers (thank you Thomas Jefferson) and only really allowed to rejoin the world community by paying an indemnity to all whites who had lost their shirts due to the Haitian revolution, an indemnity Haiti had to borrow from French banks in order to pay, which locked the country in a cycle of debt that it never broke free from; whether it was that chronic indebtedness that left Haiti vulnerable to foreign capitalist interventions—first the French, then the Germans, and finally the Americans, who occupied the nation from 1915 until 1934, installing a puppet president and imposing upon poor Haiti a new constitution more favorable to foreign investment; whether it was the 40 percent of Haiti's income that U.S. officials siphoned away to repay French and U.S. debtors, or the string of diabolical despots who further drove Haiti into ruin and who often ruled with foreign assistance—for example, François "Papa Doc" Duvalier, who received U.S. support for his anti-communist policies; whether it was the 1994 UN embargo that whittled down Haiti's robust assembly workforce from more than 100,000 workers to 17,000, or the lifting of the embargo, which brought with it a poison-pill gift in the form of an IMF-engineered end to Haiti's protective tariffs, which conveniently enough made Haiti the least trade-restrictive nation in the Caribbean and opened the doors to a flood of U.S.-subsidized rice that accelerated the collapse of the farming sector and made a previously self-sufficient country overwhelmingly dependent on foreign rice and therefore vulnerable to increases in global food prices; whether it was the tens of thousands who lost their manufacturing jobs during the blockade and the hundreds of thousands who were thrown off the land by the rice invasion, many of whom ended up in the cities, in the marginal buildings and burgeoning slums that were hit hardest by the earthquake—the world has done its part in demolishing Haiti.

This too is important to remember, and this too the earthquake revealed.

Five

The earthquake revealed our world in other ways. Look closely into the apocalypse of Haiti and you will see that Haiti's problem is not that it is poor and vulnerable—Haiti's problem is that it is poor and vulnerable at a time in our capitalist experiment when the gap between those who got grub and those who don't is not only vast but also rapidly increasing. Said another way, Haiti's nightmarish vulnerability has to be understood as part of a larger trend of *global inequality*.

We are in the age of neoliberal economic integration, of globalization, the magic process that was to deliver the world's poor out of misery and bring untold prosperity to the rest of us. Globalization, of course, did nothing of the sort. Although the Big G was supposed to lift all boats, even a cursory glance at the stats shows that the swell of globalization has had a bad habit of favoring the yachts over rafts by a whole lot. The World Bank reports that in 1960 the per capita GDP of the twenty richest countries was eighteen times greater than that of the twenty poorest. By 1995 that number had reached 37.

In this current era of neoliberal madness, sociologist Jan Nederveen Pieterse explains, "The least developed countries lag more and more behind and within countries the number of the poor is growing; on the other side of the split screen is the explosive growth of wealth of the hyper-rich." It would be one thing if the rich were getting richer because they are just that much more awesome than we are, but the numbers suggest that the rich may be getting richer in part by squeezing the poor and, increasingly, the middle class. This is a worldwide phenomenon. It is happening at the bottom of the market—in Haiti, for example, where per capita GDP dropped from around $2,100 in 1980 to $1,045 in 2009 (2005 U.S. dollars)—and at the top. In the United States, the poorest have gained much less than the wealthy: between 1993 and 2008, the top one percent captured 52 percent of total income growth.

The world's goodies are basically getting gobbled up by a tiny group of gluttons while the rest of us—by which I mean billions of people—are being deprived of even the crumbs' crumbs. And yet in spite of these stark disparities, the economic powers-that-be continue to insist that what the world needs more of is—wait for it—economic freedom and market-friendly policies, which is to say more inequality!

Pieterse describes our economic moment best:

> Overall discrepancies in income and wealth are now vast to the point of being grotesque. The discrepancies in livelihoods across the world are so large that they are without historical precedent and without conceivable justification—economic, moral, or otherwise.

This is what Haiti is both victim and symbol of—this new, rapacious stage of capitalism. A cannibal stage where, in order to power the explosion of the super-rich and the ultra-rich, middle classes are being forced to fail, working classes are being re-proletarianized, and the poorest are being pushed beyond the grim limits of subsistence, into a kind of sepulchral half-life, perfect targets for any "natural disaster" that just happens to wander by. It is, I suspect, not simply an accident of history that the island that gave us the plantation big bang that put our world on the road to this moment in the capitalist project would also be the first to warn us of this zombie stage of capitalism, where entire nations are being rendered through economic alchemy into not-quite alive. In the old days, a zombie was a figure whose life and work had been captured by magical means. Old zombies were expected to work around the clock with no relief. The new zombie cannot expect work of any kind—the new zombie just waits around to die.

And this too the earthquake revealed.

Six

I cannot contemplate the apocalypse of Haiti without asking the question: where is this all leading? Where are the patterns and forces that we have set in motion in our world—the patterns and forces that made Haiti's devastation not only possible but inevitable—delivering us? To what end, to what future, to what fate?

The answer seems to me both obvious and chilling. I suspect that once we have finished ransacking our planet's resources, once we have pushed a couple thousand more species into extinction and exhausted the water table and poisoned everything in sight and exacerbated the atmospheric warming that will finish off the icecaps and drown out our coastlines, once our market operations have parsed the world into the extremes of ultra-rich and not-quite-dead, once the famished billions that our economic systems left behind have in their insatiable hunger finished stripping the biosphere clean, what we will be left with will be a stricken, forlorn desolation, a future out of a sci-fi fever dream where the super-rich will live in walled-up plantations of impossible privilege and the rest of us will wallow in unimaginable extremity, staggering around the waste and being picked off by the hundreds of thousands by "natural disasters"—by "acts of god."

Sounds familiar, don't it?

Isn't that after all the logical conclusion of what we are wreaking? The transformation of our planet into a Haiti? Haiti, you see, is not only the most visible victim of our civilization—Haiti is also a sign of what is to come.

And this too the earthquake revealed.

Seven

If I know anything it is this: we need the revelations that come from our apocalypses—and never so much as we do now. Without this knowledge how can we ever hope to take responsibility for the social practices that bring on our disasters? And how can we ever hope to take responsibility for the collective response that will be needed to alleviate the misery?

How can we ever hope to change?

Because we must change, we also must refuse the temptation to look away when confronted with disasters. We must refuse the old stories that tell us to interpret social disasters as natural disasters. We must refuse the familiar scripts of victims and rescuers that focus our energies solely on charity instead of systemic change. We must refuse the recovery measures that seek always to further polarize the people and the places they claim to mend. And we must, in all circumstances and with all our strength, resist the attempts of those who helped bring the disaster to use the chaos to their advantage—to tighten their hold on our futures.

We must stare into the ruins—bravely, resolutely—and we must see.

And then we must act.

Our very lives depend on it.

Will it happen? Will we, despite all our limitations and cruelties, really heed our ruins and pull ourselves out of our descent into apocalypse? Truth be told, I'm not very optimistic. I mean, just look at us. No, I'm not optimistic—but that doesn't mean I don't have hope. Do I contradict myself? Then I contradict myself. I'm from New Jersey: as a writer from out that way once said, "I am large, I contain multitudes."

Yes, I have hope. We humans are a fractious lot, flawed and often diabolical. But, for all our deficiencies, we are still capable of great deeds. Consider the legendary, divinely inspired endurance of the Haitian people. Consider how they have managed to survive everything the world has thrown at them—from slavery to Sarah Palin, who visited last December. Consider the Haitian people's superhuman solidarity in the weeks after the quake. Consider the outpouring of support from Haitians across the planet. Consider the impossible sacrifices the Haitian community has made and continues to make to care for those who were shattered on January 12, 2010.

Consider also my people, the Dominicans. In the modern period, few Caribbean populations have been more hostile to Haitians. We are of course neighbors, but what neighbors! In 1937 the dictator Rafael Trujillo launched a genocidal campaign against Haitians and Haitian Dominicans. Tens of thousands were massacred; tens of thousands more were wounded and driven into Haiti, and in the aftermath of that genocide the relationship between the two countries has never thawed. Contemporary Dominican society in many respects strikes me as profoundly anti-Haitian, and Haitian immigrants to my country experience widespread discrimination, abysmal labor conditions, constant harassment, mob violence, and summary deportation without due process.

No one, and I mean no one, expected anything from Dominicans after the quake; yet look at what happened: Dominican rescue workers were the first to enter Haiti. They arrived within hours of the quake, and in the crucial first days of the crisis, while the international community was getting its act together, Dominicans shifted into Haiti vital resources that were the difference between life and death for thousands of victims.

In a shocking reversal of decades of toxic enmity, it seemed as if the entire Dominican society mobilized for the relief effort. Dominican hospitals were emptied to receive the wounded, and all elective surgeries were canceled for months. (Imagine if the United States canceled all elective surgeries for a single month in order to help Haiti, what a different that would have made.) Schools across the political and economic spectrums organized relief drives, and individual citizens delivered caravans of essential materials and personnel in their own vehicles, even as international organizations were claiming that the roads to Port-au-Prince were impassable. The Dominican government transported generators and mobile kitchens and established a field hospital. The Dominican Red Cross was up and running long before anyone else. Dominican communities in New York City, Boston, Providence, and Miami sent supplies and money. This historic shift must have Trujillo rolling in his grave. Sonia Marmolejos, a humble Dominican woman, left her own infant babies at home in order to breastfeed more than twenty Haitian babies whose mothers had either been seriously injured or killed in the earthquake.

Consider Sonia Marmolejos and understand why, despite everything, I still have hope.

Eight

"These are dark times, there is no denying." Thus spake Bill Nighy's character in the penultimate Harry Potter movie. Sometimes we have to look in our entertainment for truths. And sometimes we have to look in the ruins for hope.

More than a year has passed since the earthquake toppled Haiti, and little on the material front has changed. Port-au-Prince is still in ruins, rubble has not been cleared, and the port is still crippled. More than a million people are still in tent cities, vulnerable to the elements and disease and predatory gangs, and there is no sign that they will be moving out soon. The rebuilding has made many U.S. companies buckets of cash, but so far has done very little for Haitian contractors or laborers. Cholera is spreading through the relief camps, killing more than 4,500 so far, according to the United Nations. In December 2010 Paul Farmer reported that nearly a year after the disaster Haiti had received only 38 percent, or $732.5 million, of promised donations, excluding debt relief. In the Dominican Republic, threats of violence caused thousands of Haitian immigrants to abandon the Santiago area just weeks before the earthquake's first anniversary.

More than a year later, we can say safely that the world has looked away. It has failed to learn the lesson of the apocalypse of Haiti. Never fear though—if anything is certain it is this: there will be more Haitis. Some new catastrophe will strike our poor planet. And for a short while the Eye of Sauron that is the globe's fickle attention span will fall upon this novel misery. More hand wringing will ensue, more obfuscatory narratives will be trotted out, more people will die. Those of us who are committed will help all we can, but most people will turn away. There will be a few, however, who, steeling themselves, will peer into the ruins for the news that we will all eventually need.

After all, apocalypses like the Haitian earthquake are not only catastrophes; they are also opportunities: chances for us to see ourselves, to take responsibility for what we see, to change. One day somewhere in the world something terrible will happen, and for once we won't look away. We will reject what Jane Anna and Lewis R. Gordon have described in *Of Divine Warning* as that strange moment following a catastrophe where "in our aversion to addressing disasters as signs" we refuse "to interpret and take responsibility for the kinds of collective responses that may be needed to alleviate human misery." One day somewhere in the world something terrible will happen and for once we will heed the ruins. We will begin collectively to take responsibility for the world we're creating. Call me foolishly utopian, but I sincerely believe this will happen. I do. I just wonder how many millions of people will perish before it does.

Postscript

March 15: As I revise this essay, I am watching the harrowing images being beamed in from post-earthquake-post-tsunami Japan. Another apocalypse beyond the imagination—but one that might affect us all. The news is reporting that a third explosion has rocked the Fukushima Daiichi nuclear power plant and that there might be a fire in the fourth reactor. The worst nuclear accident since Chernobyl, a nicely combed man is saying. Even if the reactor cores do not melt down, radioactive "releases" into the environment will continue for weeks, perhaps even months. My friends in Tokyo report that the convenience stores that I so love have been emptied and that there are signs that the radiation has already begun to reach that metropolis of 13 million. And finally this, a perfunctory statement from the U.S. Nuclear Regulatory

Commission: "NRC's rigorous safety regulations ensure that U.S. nuclear facilities are designed to withstand tsunamis, earthquakes and other hazards." When pressed for details, NRC spokesman David McIntyre was reported to have said that the commission is not taking reporters' questions at this point.

Guiding Questions

1. Diaz writes that for something to be an apocalypse, it must not only be a disruptive event, it must also through its destruction be revelatory in some way. What does he want us to understand about places and our relationship to them in this essay?
2. Diaz wants to use the term "social disaster" to characterize the destruction in Haiti rather than "natural disaster." What difference does it make to consider something a "social disaster"? What decisions that people made contributed to this disaster? What role does poverty play in this and other disasters?
3. Diaz writes that "Becoming a ruin-reader might not be such a bad thing. It could in fact save your life." How so? Can you give examples of how the skills of being a ruin-reader can be helpful with regard to Haiti? Japan? Katrina?

Paths for Further Exploration

1. Has a "natural disaster" affected your home place recently or in the distant past? Is there a way you can become a "ruin-reader" of this incident and explore the role that human decisions and perhaps short-sightedness played in contributing to it? What do you learn if you try to write about it as a "social disaster"?
2. Think of a place—such as New Orleans, Japan, Sumatra, parts of Alabama—that were radically changed due to a weather event like a hurricane, tsunami, or tornado. What can you learn if you research the place, not as the victim of a natural disaster, but to uncover its apocalyptic revelation: what does this place tell us about place and sustainability? Poverty and wealth? Short-sighted versus long-term decisions? How can we make better decisions to avoid another disaster like this one?
3. Think big: What disasters might be unfolding on national, international, or even global scales? Who stands to suffer most from climate change? What about deforestation? The loss of biodiversity? Do the dynamics that Diaz points to make these things "social disasters" as well?
4. Disasters and apocalypses are staples of fantasy and science-fiction novels, movies, TV shows, video games, comic books, and a wide range

of other media. Perform a critical analysis of the way a particular disaster or apocalypse is portrayed in a text, film, game, or other piece of media and demonstrate what anxieties it may reveal about where we're going.

How Urban Planning Can Improve Public Health
JONATHAN LERNER

Jonathan Lerner writes on architecture, urbanism, art, design, and travel for national magazines and is a communications consultant for clients in the design industries. His work has appeared in The Wall Street Journal, The Washington Post, *and* Salon.com, *and he is the author of* Alex Underground *and* Caught in a Still Place. *He lives in New York City and is a volunteer with the Congress for the New Urbanism. This essay ran in the April 28, 2010 issue of* Miller-McCune.

———————— ✦ ————————

You hardly need scientific research to pinpoint objectionable aspects of suburban sprawl. The big-box commercial jumble, the lifeless cul-de-sac subdivision, the traffic, the sameness—all are plain to see. Disagreeable qualities of half-empty downtowns and deteriorated city neighborhoods are equally visible. Still, people don't usually think that the things they find aesthetically objectionable about their neighborhoods might literally be making them sick.

Yet a growing mass of scientific evidence does indicate that how places are designed and built can cause and complicate grave health problems for individuals and whole populations. Depression—the clinical kind, not the aesthetic and cultural malaise that sends people vacationing to, say, Barcelona—is one. Studies show that depression correlates with the lack of access to green space, a plight of many inner-city residents; the physical isolation of suburbanites; and the immobility enforced on those who cannot drive but have no transportation alternative.

As for cars, they don't just spew pollution and trap people alone for wasted hours. They cause accident injuries and deaths.

Moreover, unwalkable distances and the culture of automobility encourage sedentary habits, contributing to obesity and diabetes and other illnesses. Plowing up farmland for new subdivisions at the metropolitan edge not only diminishes local food supplies and reinforces industrial agriculture—with negative implications for nutrition and resource conservation—it also forces those who must "drive till they qualify" for housing to need a car for almost every household member. Those automobile costs, usually overlooked, have exacerbated soaring rates of foreclosure and suburban poverty, with unhealthful knock-on effects like stress, displacement and homelessness.

Many examples beyond these lead to a conclusion: The crucial questions about how we build focus less on aesthetics—important as that is to our well-being—than on public health, in its broadest sense.

City planning originated, around the turn of the last century, out of concerns over health problems created by filthy slums and industries. Then the fields of public health and planning came uncoupled. Public health took on a mainly biomedical focus on individual genetics, biology and behavior and how clinicians could affect those, and on a narrowly biological approach to epidemiology and evidence. Meanwhile the planning of built environments was hijacked by the car.

Now the fields of city planning and public health—pushed by economic crisis, climate change and green technology, among other factors—are converging again. This month, the Congress for the New Urbanism was set to hold its national convention in Atlanta; it was organized with help from the Centers for Disease Control and Prevention under the theme "New Urbanism: Rx for Healthy Places."

The convention is hardly the first effort to address the relationships between urban form and health. The World Health Organization's Healthy Cities movement was initiated in 1988; among other things, it encourages attention to health inequalities, participatory governance and the health considerations of economic and urban development. Some 1,200 European cities and many in Canada and Australia participate.

Back in the U.S., the Local Government Commission, an organization of elected and community leaders, government staff and planners and architects, adopted the Ahwahnee Principles for Resource-Efficient Communities in 1991. (The principles were named for the Yosemite National Park lodge where they were agreed to.) The principles targeted the dysfunctional qualities of sprawl-pattern development; these ideas came to underlie the New Urbanism and Smart Growth movements. Meanwhile, The Robert Wood Johnson Foundation's Active Living Research program supports extensive research into the urban form/public health nexus. The CDC's Healthy Community Design initiative does the same. Dr. Howard Frumkin, special assistant to the CDC director for climate change and health and co-author of Urban Sprawl and Public Health: *Designing, Planning, and Building for Healthy Communities*, actually calls the Congress for the New Urbanism "a public health group. By promoting walkability, mixed use, connectivity and civic space within communities, we know more and more, based on emerging evidence, that CNU is promoting public health."

To anyone who thinks the New Urbanism makes sense, research conclusions on how built environments affect health can seem self-evident. For example, studies have demonstrated that neighborhoods with shops, schools, libraries, workplaces and homes within easy walking distance tend to support higher levels of physical activity and have lower rates of obesity. Public transit use has a similar effect on activity and fatness. Research has indicated that exposure to nature may improve attention deficit hyperactivity disorder in children, and that people with access to parks exercise more.

Like, duh. "So much research is proving the obvious," says Ellen Dunham-Jones, associate professor of architecture and urban design at Georgia Tech and co-author of Retrofitting Suburbia: *Urban Design Solutions for Redesigning Suburbs*. "But once you get the numbers, you can hopefully get policy changes."

Research into the connection between urban life and public health is, however, also creating surprises. As an example, Dunham-Jones points to studies showing that compact communities reduce overall vehicular emissions—but that people who live next to highways and heavily trafficked arterial roads breathe in more emissions. "It may be healthy for the community at large but not for you," she says.

Pinning down the implications of such research subtleties remains a challenge. Frumkin identifies two still-poorly understood correlatives of built environment: "We have reason to believe that community design and building design have impacts both on mental health and on social capital. Social capital in turn is a very important determinant of overall health."

The plans for New Urbanism towns sometimes depict circles centered on retail areas, with radii labeled as the distance of a five- or 10-minute walk. But landscape architect Dee Merriam, a CDC community planner, says that even walkability, a seemingly unambiguous value, needs scrutiny. "The basic metric we've been using for urban design has been the automobile scale, and the walking scale is a totally different metric," she says. "What is the distance of a five-minute walk? It's probably very different for a young athlete than for an elderly woman or someone with toddlers."

Merriam says more investigation is also needed into green space, despite its known health connections; Dunham-Jones agrees, saying that research has raised complex questions about trade-offs. "Cities would prefer to have one big central park to maintain, than to have a whole lot of little parks. To really get people jogging, you need a big park. But to get little kids to go play, it's much better to have a lot of little parks," she says. "We can improve health by doing all sorts of things, but we're not at the point where we're maximizing dollar investment."

Some new efforts to find design solutions for health challenges involve food. Ideas range from turning abandoned space in declining neighborhoods into urban farms—projects like this are already under way in Detroit and elsewhere—and allotting space for community gardens in new developments. There is even a vision of "agriburbia," where entire neighborhoods are landscaped with orchards and cropland that could feed people in and beyond the development while providing local employment opportunities.

A recent design workshop addressed another piece of the healthy living puzzle: multigenerational or "lifelong" communities, where people can continue to live actively as they grow old. Specialists on aging, developers, planners and architects tried to envision the transformation of parts of metro Atlanta, reiterating the "must-haves" of New Urbanism—transit and walkability, mixed uses, multiple housing types—but describing how such elements could better accommodate the aging with, for example, shorter walking distances and shuttles to transit stops and shopping areas.

So the Congress for the New Urbanism, the CDC and others are taking important steps to address the cause-and-effect relationships of built environment and public health. But for towns and cities to be less damaging to health, those connections must become more universally acknowledged by health professionals, designers, planners and the decision-makers and developers for whom they work. Moreover, for the environment to support better health, public consciousness has to change. Individual choices will have to sustain healthier patterns of development, and political support will be needed, too, because some of the proposed changes in development demand big cultural shifts, particularly around auto use.

Many advocates say what's needed is a holistic view that considers health, the environment, social relations, political processes and the economy as part of the development process. Jason Corburn, associate professor of city and regional planning at University of California, Berkeley, and author of Toward the Healthy City: *People, Places, and the Politics of Urban Planning*, insists that architects and planners "need to recognize that they're part of governance," since a healthy city should invite open participation in its political processes, planning included. "This is not to say that design is not important," he says, "but that it should be just one piece of thinking relationally about multiple influences upon health."

One tool that helps government officials identify such influences is the health impact assessment, an evaluation process similar to the environmental impact statement. Such health assessments are a relatively new phenomenon in the U.S., but several dozen have already been conducted, and the CDC is actively promoting their use. While there is a legal basis under environmental protection laws for evaluating health impacts of proposed projects, the officials responsible are often unfamiliar with the HIA concept, or can feel that it deals in types of evidence not traditionally considered valid in making development decisions.

But traditional thinking has produced the sickening built environments most Americans now inhabit. Even "progressive" ideas won't necessarily change them. For example, if everybody owned a car that drove 100 miles on a gallon of gas, the country would burn less oil—but sprawl would still be encouraged, and the population would continue to grow fatter, sicker and more isolated. It may be possible to influence the public to choose transit over cars; entrenched attitudes toward tobacco were changed after all. But to change transport habits, America needs to provide transit systems and walkable destinations as practical options, and that's where the architects and planners come in.

Guiding Questions

1. Lerner argues that urban planning is not just an issue of aesthetics but also one of public health. What is some of the evidence he raises for this? What aspects contribute to the health or sickness of a neighborhood?

2. Lerner complicates the idea of a healthy or well-planned city by listing several trade-offs: for jogging, one big park is useful; for kids, several

small parks are better. Discuss this or other trade-offs. How would you recommend cities or towns decide what is the best way to allocate limited space and resources?

3. In terms of planning and public health, how would your home place rate? Can you walk many places? What about access to parks? Clean air?

4. Lerner confronts a problem that many writers about place-based issues have to confront: Readers who are interested in these issues enough to read this piece probably already know at least some of what he's going to say; readers who aren't already interested need to be brought up to speed without being bored to death. How does he approach this problem? Do aspects of his tone (such as starting one paragraph after citing an expert's findings with "Like, duh") strike you as helpful in reaching the broadest range of readers?

Paths for Future Exploration

1. Lerner references several resources for planning healthier cities, such as the Ahwahnee Principles for Resource-Efficient Communities, the CDC Healthy Community Design Initiative, and the Robert Woods Johnson Foundation Active Living Research Program. Learn more about one or more of these resources and what the initiative plans and hopes for. Is it achieving its goals?

2. Use any one of the references in Question One to do a study of your home place or where you live now. How well does it fare it terms of its resource efficiency or healthy community design? What changes would benefit your community most?

3. Write a persuasive, researched essay that recommends a specific change to make a community healthier. Use Lerner's essay—and consider as well Alayne Brown's essay on obesity in the Caribbean—and some references he cites to help make your argument.

An Examination of Living through Enjoyment: Live-Action Role-Play
AMANDA ODOM

Amanda Odom writes an essay based in Mobile, Alabama, exploring the phenomenon of live-action role-play (LARP) games. This essay was originally published in the journal Transformative Works and Culture, *which publishes "articles about popular media, fan communities, and transformative works, broadly conceived." The journal aims to "provide a publishing outlet that welcomes fan-related topics, and to promote dialogue between the academic community and the fan community."*

———————— ✦ ————————

1. The woods are warm tonight in Mississippi, and I have bite marks on top of bite marks from the mosquitoes. My group has assembled for the final hours of a 3-day campaign in "Call of Cthulhu," a nihilistic horror game set in the 1920s and steeped in the arcane. We look scruffy, in T-shirts and wifebeaters, wearing sandals or barefoot. The landscape is scattered with lawn chairs and discarded Coke cans.

2. For our characters, things are rather different. A chilling wind cuts across us as we stand at the top of a bluff overlooking a small town just a few miles outside the luxurious winter retreat where select faculty and graduate students of Miskatonic University have assembled for a holiday. Wool and fur and leather do little to warm us; we've been out here too long and the fact that nothing stirs at the bottom of the hill, nothing wanders in the town in the standard way, is enough to freeze the blood in our veins. In just 3 days, the quaint little place has become a ghost town—worse, actually, because we have seen the frostbitten come to our door, black and cold and unaware of their condition, too far gone to save. Something has happened here.

3. As a player, I know what has happened. Well, not exactly. I don't know which great elder god has been unleashed to destroy our party. I do know that I'm playing Call of Cthulhu, and quite often campaigns end badly; characters die, towns are destroyed, evil is unleashed . . . that sort of thing.

4. My character, Edmund, knows nothing about it. It's his lodge the characters are at, and if he is unhappy to be tramping about in the snow, it has more to do with the warm brandy and cozy armchairs back home than with fear of the dark unknown. He is here because he has to be. It's his home, these are his guests, and the people down there have been attached to his family, in the form of retainers and otherwise, for some time.

5. I know what is down there. The townspeople have become monstrous. People running naked in the snow, forfeiting skin and muscle and tendon in their frantic whim, still moving on bone, stilts that keep them inexplicably upright, their bodies somehow alive in a terrible ecstasy that propels them through the snow in search of . . . well, that part I don't know yet. I do know that when my group goes into this area of the game, we will set off the final

events of the campaign. I also know that my character will probably die. He's an idiot, a skeptic, and a dilettante. Practically speaking, this means he doesn't know what is going on, and he won't believe it when he does see it. His skill with a hunting rifle is more perfunctory than not. But as a player, I have to let my character do what he is going to do. After all, that's part of the fun.

6. So Edmund does the worst possible thing. He musters up his voice and he calls down, "Hello?" This triggers several events. The packhorse startles forward just a foot. The guide, who had so carefully explained to us the importance of watching where you step in the snow, moves forward to take the reins. A look of alarm and then, swiftly, resignation comes over him as the snow bank shifts and breaks and takes him down to the bottom, a broken doll. Down in the village, something moves.

7. In game play, we pantomime. I say, "Hello." The game leader explains that when the player to my right stepped forward, he shifted the snow, so the player hurls himself forward a few feet and crumples, and someone throws a rock into the woods to make noise so we can say "Look over there" with a reason. Someone asks how many supplies our characters lost with the guide. We start figuring out who among our group has characters that can shoot guns with any accuracy.

8. In a role-playing game (RPG), characters assume fictional personas and enact previously determined behaviors. The more common forms of role-play include sexual play, interactive gaming, and computer and video game system gaming. For each, there are specific and distinctive aspects that uniquely identify them as separate, though all fall under a general umbrella of gaming in character (IC). That is, players create or utilize previously rendered personas in play.

9. Live-action role-play (LARP) is a particular type of interactive role-playing in which players perform the actions of their characters in a physical setting, physically interacting with the other players to a greater or lesser degree, rather than interacting through mere verbal discourse or electronic interface. Falk and Davenport (2004:127) argue that "These post-desktop games inhabit our physical surrounding and objects within it, employing human senses" and that they "take on ubiquitous and tangible forms—properties that contribute to the blurring of the lines between player and game character, game world and real world." Thus, LARPs offer more immersive experiences for the players than standard RPGs because LARPing communities enable realistic interactive socialization.

10. In everyday society, people must act based on the explicit and implied manifold nuances of the layperson and the skilled worker, the parent and child, the citizen or soldier, and so on. We are taught that action in society is best enacted by feigning the appropriate knowledge, attitudes, and roles. The general notion is that via practice, people will eventually produce the actual. Just as people attempt random simulations of inferior quality while learning to play an instrument, so too will they playact until they learn to *be*.

11. In life, socializing practices are learned by cues, many visual, situational, and theoretical. The practical application of socializing is engaged, however, not by memorizing rules or by attempting to reiterate the rhetoric attached to them—rhetoric steeped in the rich cultural traditions of religion and culture—but by acting. The term *acting* brings to mind a twofold usage—that is, to act as a state of doing something and to act as a state of feigning some other thing. In "The Impact of Relationships on Games," Gordon Olmstead Dean (2007:195) acknowledges, "The principal antecedent of larp is certainly drama." He adds, "It has been posited that larp is essentially interactive theatre—a form of drama where there is no distinction between presenter and audience." However, he very firmly advocates that the players "do not just watch, we are drawn into the drama in a very literal sense."

12. This is because, as shown in the example of a gaming night, the players interact with each other in a very real sense. Both standard RPG and LARP stories branch out on the basis of decisions made not in all times and places by the individuals but by the myriad players working on their own agendas, some forming groups and alliances, some conspiring under cloak and with dagger, others unknowing puppets of the game master's (GM) vision. Seasoned players are able to understand the rules and conform to the restrictions of the world in which the game occurs, of the game, of the group, and of their own roles in each. The players are not the characters; they are actors fulfilling their roles. Thus, the needs of the players may be in conflict with the needs of the characters, but the needs of either are secondary to the needs of the game. Players play for various reasons. In the games, characters must have reasons for acting. The reasons for the player playing and the character acting are not the same. For example, a Civil War re-enactor, or someone playing an alternate history version of the Civil War, may play with full knowledge that a character is going to fail in his or her mission. The player understands this, but the character would not. The player must then play IC to the hilt, pursuing the unattainable goal with a will, in spite of his or her knowledge out of character (OOC).

13. In such games, players choose characters on the basis of types (and types may be based on species, race, gender, class, tribe, or similarly pertinent signifiers). Just so, the world-building devices are based on generic concepts (whether the world is based in fantasy or horror, whether the setting is the present day or the Dark Ages, the 1920s or the far-flung future). In addition, players select a variety of general attributes to define their characters, including, but not limited to, height, weight, sexuality, education, speed, stamina, and charisma. They also specifically select defining criteria compatible with backstories preset or created by players. These feature strengths and weaknesses related to who their characters are. For example, a barbarian swordsman (like those traditionally found in the game *Dungeons & Dragons*) tends to focus on physical, martial exercises. Extensive academic education is not a probable character attribute for such an entity. Additionally, a character accustomed to utilizing brute strength as a problem-solving tactic may be brash or bullying. On the other hand, a hideously deformed and physically limited character (like the Nosferatu in the *World of Darkness* games) relies on stealth, manipulation, and strategic mental maneuvering to achieve his or her goals. Diplomacy would be a virtue in such a case, but such a character would rarely be a prominent social figure.

14. For LARPs, these ideas hold true as they hold true in RPGs. In addition, though, there are sensory layers available within the game mechanics in LARPs that are not available in video games, across tabletops, or on the written page. For example, touch is often a component to a greater or lesser degree. In some instances, players may act out their characters' impulses by indicating physical affection, wrath, or other feelings through symbolic or actual touch. That is, characters may actually touch in a realistic manner, hugging each other, striking each other (lightly), or pushing and pulling at each other. The player's level of comfort may impact the game play here. For example, when I am playing *Vampire* with strangers, players may demonstrate physical connectedness by simply holding someone's hand or standing close. Physical proximity will serve to indicate physical relationships. With long-term gaming groups, however, players may feel able to act more literally. For example, people may hang on each other. The dynamics are rather simple. Game intentions are discussed OOC, generally at the beginning of games, before they are acted out IC. The games tend to be more fun in these instances because players feel more comfortable, which allows them to get into their character. In some games, battles may be staged and peace-bonded weapons (created or altered to prevent any real harm) may be

utilized. In other instances, symbols are used to indicate touch. For example, small beanbags may be thrown in a player's general direction to indicate the damaging assault of magic, bullets, or arrows. In other cases, damage may be indicated through strips of paper lost as one is injured in the course of a game. Certain games utilize "rock, paper, scissors" or similar methods to determine the effect of attack, defense, and similar actions.

15. In a standard RPG, the details of the settings are explained verbally or they are sketched in a blueprint form (the classic graph paper dungeon comes to mind). The most basic LARP offers a more tactile, 3-D experience, and more advanced setups go even further. In a real setting, players may experience visual stimulation. Some LARPers carefully design massive and detailed play areas. They may build wooden or cardboard structures to represent the game world. Some draw chalk outlines and boundaries to roughly detail the landscape. Others may use very little in the way of stages, costumes, and related materials. Some play in the public sphere, which can lead to a variety of interesting consequences. For example, in the *World of Darkness* games, vampires live in secret among humans. Some LARPers will play in public and will be penalized for attracting the humans to the game. In this scenario, all and sundry become non-player characters.

16. In every instance, the narrative is just as relevant as it is in the standard RPG. However, facial expressions, tones, and cues aid in the overall effect to a larger degree in a LARP. IC, everything a player says, does, or depicts is attributed to the character being played. Therefore, subtle changes in voice or posture offer cues that the other players are expected to analyze and act upon. It is vital that players announce intentions to go OOC. In one game, a player may decide that her character has a nervous tic that becomes evident when it loses composure. In another, a character may have a habit at leering at women in a sinister and inappropriate manner. How the players react should reflect how their characters would react. Certainly the players should not be offended by what the characters do or say, and the characters should only react in ways befitting their characters. On the basis of the latter scenario, if a female character is naive, she may miss obvious insinuations. If she is lascivious, she may embrace them. If she is aware of them but unappreciative, she may respond accordingly. Similarly, the smallest of physical actions may have larger consequences. Kicking an idle stone in real time could create an avalanche in game time. Stepping on the smallest twig may attract undesired attention. Coughing at the inappropriate moment may condemn a character to a harsh fate. In standard RPGs, the

actions of the characters are painted with broader strokes. In LARPs, a player's activities become the character's movements. The game takes on a sharper focus and is infinitely more realistic.

17. In fact, interactive game play simulates life—not the everyday, probable world, but the archetypical one. Common gaming genres include military strategy or historical reenactment (such as the Colonial Living History Alliance), fantasy and science fiction (such as live-action *Dungeons & Dragons* or *Star Wars*), and gothic and horror (such as *World of Darkness* and *Call of Cthulhu*). Within each, one is expected to play roles, to conform to fixed rules (made by the GM, by the rule book, by the conventions of the players, and by the players' development of their characters) that define landscapes as surely as gravity, to adapt to a story as it unfolds and to change the story to alter or even redefine entirely the fate or the individual characters, the group, or the world (if one is clever enough) and to conform to the rigid certainties and absolutes of the plot devices.

18. It has been argued by many in the gaming community that video gaming has enhanced the RPG experience. Certainly, with each successive generation and video game system, the technology has allowed for an ever more immersive experience. From movies like *Tron, Lawnmower Man,* and *War Games* to cyberpunk games like *Chill,* players have imagined the future of gaming to be one of sensory appeal. The classic image of this is a person wearing a full body suit complete with a visor that allows total fixation on simulated reality. It is true that video games have come a long way; I felt validated when, the first time I picked up my Wii remote to play *Metroid,* I took the controller in hand, thrust it forward, and turned it sharply to open a door in the game. The only thing closer to opening a door . . . would be opening a door. That, in fact, is the point of LARPing. The live-action aspect of a LARP allows players to open and close such doors in real life through a virtual, socially interactive game played in real time in a physical setting. Thus, LARPing anticipated the movement toward virtual play that video games have worked to create. At this point, the LARP surpasses video games by offering a more realistic, alternative form of role-play.

Works Cited

Chaosium. Chaosium Incorporated. 2007. Web. 12 Nov. 2008.

Dean, Gordon Olmstead. "The Impact of Relationships on Games." *Lifelike.* Ed. Jesper Donnis et al. Copenhagen: Projektgruppen KP07, Landsforeningen, 2007. 194-209. Print.

Dungeons & Dragons. Wizards of the Coast, Inc. N.d. Web. 12 Nov. 2008.

Falk, Jennica, and Glorianna Davenport. "Live role-playing Games: Implications for Pervasive Gaming. *Lecture Notes in Computer Science Series*. Ed. Mathias Rauterberg. New York: Springer Berlin/Heidelberg, 2004. 127-38. Print.

World of Darkness. White Wolf Publishing. N.d. Web. 12 Nov. 2008.

Guiding Questions

1. Odom opens the essay by "dropping" us into the middle of an intense action scene. Do you find this opening effective? What about her use of names or terms (like "Cthulhu," or "Miskatonic University") that have meaning to those already in-the-know but not to other readers? If you've never participated in things like RPG or LARP, is Odom's essay an effective introduction to and explanation of these activities and their communities?

2. Odom writes, "In fact, interactive game play simulates life—not the everyday, probable world, but the archetypical one." Do you engage in RPG or LARP? If so, do you find Odom's description and analysis of these communities accurate?

3. The essay contains primary research from Odom's experience but is framed in an academic manor, with numbered topics and paragraphs. Discuss this choice of organization and approach. What does it allow the writer to do? How does it affect you as a reader? Does it allow for a discussion between academic communities and fan communities that the journal aims to promote?

4. Odom argues that live-action role play currently surpasses video games by offering a more realistic, alternative form of role-play. Do you have any experience with both LARP and video games? Do you agree with Odom's assessment? Why or why not?

5. In what ways do role-playing video games and LARP create an awareness and sense of place? And to what extent do they erase or take players away from place? Does online participation erode a sense of place awareness, or can it add to it?

Paths for Further Exploration

1. Conduct an ethnographic study of one of your online communities in which you:
   • Describe the history and purpose of the community
   • List the rules for participation
   • Define some of the shared vocabulary

- Offer descriptions of members of the community (being mindful not to expose anyone who does not want to be exposed)
- Conduct interviews with members
- Analyze a sample text from the community (again, with permission) to illustrate communication among members
2. *The Guild* is a comical web series that profiles the relationships and antics of a guild of video gamers. If you're a video gamer, watch an episode or season of *The Guild* and analyze its relationship to actual video-gaming communities. To what extent does it work from existing stereotypes and cultural norms, and to what extent does it exaggerate or create them for comic effect?
3. Consider how communities based around specific shared activities or interests interact with the various places they encounter. That is: How do they shape, use, or alter any real physical spaces they use? How do they shape virtual or online spaces? Do they include or exclude others in these places, and by what criteria? Can you discover their "markings" in any particular place (online or off) once they've used it?

Social Movements in the Age of Social Media: Participatory Politics in Egypt
S. Craig Watkins

S. Craig Watkins has been researching young people's media behaviors for more than ten years. He teaches in the departments of Radio-Television-Film and Sociology and the Center for African and African American Studies at the University of Texas at Austin. His 2009 book, The Young and the Digital: What the Migration to Social Network Sites, Games, and Anytime, Anywhere Media Means for Our Future *(Beacon Press), is based on survey research, in-depth interviews, and fieldwork with teens, young twenty-somethings, teachers, parents, and technology advocates. He blogs at www.theyoungandthedigital.com, where this post originally appeared on February 18, 2011.*

✦

In the wake of the uprising that shook up Egypt and ended the thirty year regime of Hosni Mubarak a growing debate around the role of social media has ensued. The press, looking for catchy headlines, characterized the uprising as "the first Twitter revolution," or "Facebook revolution." Conversely, a number of critics and academics cry foul, proclaiming that people, not technology, conducted the revolution.

Anyone who has even a pedestrian understanding of social movements knows that they are often caused by the convergence of social, economic, cultural, and political factors. And this is certainly true in the Arab world. Decades of government corruption, elite economic self-interest, the arrogance of power, and historic economic inequalities were the primary catalyst for what Newsweek magazine called, "a youthquake that is rocking the Arab world." A recent tweet by former U.S. Secretary of Labor Robert Reich is subtle but profound: "We cannot in good conscience continue to reward the rich, penalize the poor, and ignore the middle. There will be a day of reckoning." While Reich was referring to the current political and economic climate in the U.S., the tweet speaks to the wider global condition. While social media was not the catalyst of the Egyptian protest, it was certainly a tool for mobilizing protest.

The five million Facebook accounts in Egypt make it the second most popular site in the country. YouTube is the third most visited site. Whereas protestors used Facebook to organize, set dates, and "peercast," that is, share mobile pictures and video with peers, Twitter became the social media backbone of the movement's day-to-day machinations.

I recently had a chance to speak with a young man who made Tahrir Square his home during parts of the uprising.

Karim (this is a pseudonym) studies social media and told me that he felt like he was participating in history. On February 5 he sent me a number of pictures from his Facebook album that captured various aspects of the massive demonstrations in Egypt. The pictures, of course, had an ethnographic aesthetic about them and offer a much more intimate perspective of the movement than did the highly selected images most people viewed on television. The Facebook album included pictures of people protesting, confronting the police, nurturing the wounded, laughing, celebrating, and, most important, bonding together in a common cause to transform their country. In many of the pictures I also noticed people capturing the protest with their mobile devices.

In literally thousands of instances they streamed pictures, videos, tweets, and Facebook updates for their comrades around Egypt and the world. This kind of media production is a hallmark feature of the digital media age. Egyptian protestors were not only consuming images of their efforts, they were also producing and sharing those images with the world and giving new meaning to the notion of participatory politics.

Karim explained the popularity of photos this way. "As you might know, sometimes these demonstrations are not safe; so, as soon as we reach Tahrir Square, we take photos of the demonstration and upload them to our Facebook profiles to tell our friends that we are participating and encourage them to come over."

Curious about the adoption of technology in the uprisings, I asked Karim how did social media influence the events in Egypt. Karim replied that, "the demonstration started on January 25 and the call for it was done mainly through Facebook." Facebook emerged, in part, as an efficient way to coordinate and organize protestors. The first Facebook post related directly to the events in February was made on January 14 at 11:18 pm, eleven days before the first massive protests in Tahrir Square. The main tag simply read: ‏رسالة إلى شعب مصر 25 رسالة إلى شعب مصر: ليكن‎. (Rough) Translation: "Message to the people of Egypt: Let the January 25 is the torch of change in Egypt."

According to Karim, social media was crucial from the outset of the movement because it gave people on the ground an information technology that they could control. "Because of the government's heavy control over all the traditional media," he explained, "the Internet is the only available option for all opposition parties and movements." That is also why after two days of protest the government shut down the internet and mobile phone service. Determined to keep the momentum people used everything from dial-up modems to proxy-servers.

The first and what will likely go down in history as one of the most famous Twitter hashtags in the Egyptian revolution was "#jan25," created by a twenty-one year-old woman named, who goes by the Twitter name, @alya1989262. Follow the "#jan25" feed (created January 15, one day after the above Facebook announcement) and one of the most striking features is the range and complexity of communication that took place via Twitter. In many ways, Twitter became the mediated eyes, ears, and voice of the day-to-day life of the protest.

#jan25 is, in essence, a transcript of history, a log not merely of what people were tweeting, but what they were thinking and, most important, doing. Twitter was used in a variety of ways during the protest. At times it was used as a tool for real time communication between protesters, informing each other about the location of police, where protestors should go, and what media around the world were saying about the events on the ground. According to @alya1989262, Twitter, "most importantly, allow[ed] us to share on the ground info like police brutality, things to watch out for, activists getting arrested, etc."

Twitter was also used to rally, recruit, and encourage people to come out and show their solidarity with the protestors. In other instances it was used as a broadcast medium, a technology that allowed the protesters to tell their side of the story, their side of history. In societies were freedom of the press is severely constrained and the press is often the mouthpiece of the government, social media emerges as an alternative broadcasting platform, a way to communicate and connect with the world. There is historical precedence for this.

In the 1960s leaders of the U.S. civil rights movement came to understand the power of television and how the images of police brutality turned the tide against the state sanctioned southern hostility toward freedom fighters and their demands for political equality. In the student led movement against the Vietnam War in chants like "the whole world is watching" was an effort to leverage the power of television to mobilize widespread support for their social movement. By staying connected to Twitter the protestors in Egypt were also able to track how well their efforts were trending beyond home. What did they see? The whole world really was watching them but this time on YouTube, Facebook, Twitter, and other social media platforms in addition to television. @alya1989262 acknowledged this, "Twitter trends also help us gauge how visible we are to the international community." What makes social movements in the age of social media so distinct is the real time nature of communication in the execution of protest as well as the ability to share perspectives, narratives, and experiences that establish an ambient connection to the outside world.

As we gain a better understanding of what happened in Egypt and other parts of the Arab world we will also learn more about who used mobile devices and social media to energize their efforts to create democratic freedoms. Karim contends that "the youth who called for the first demonstration on January 25 belong to upper middle class in Egypt and most of them, if not all, have Internet access." @alya1989262's account is similar. "A certain class of activists are armed with smartphones, which allow them to live-tweet the protests." Does this suggest that the movement was ignited by a generation of tech savvy and college educated citizens? Not necessarily. But the idea of this segment rising up to confront power is not all that surprising when you consider their condition. Roughly a third of the population in the Middle East is under thirty and a noteworthy percentage of them have college degrees. The young and the digital in the Middle East are connected to the world in a way that previous generations could not even have imagined. And yet, the unemployment rate of young college educated persons in the Middle East is staggeringly high. A recent report from NPR notes that 40% of young persons with college degrees in Saudi Arabia, for example, are unemployed. Faced with the prospects of a life with few if any meaningful opportunities to utilize their cultural capital—education—many young people realized that they had nothing to lose by confronting the Mubarak regime.

What happened in Egypt is yet another confirmation of what our research has consistently demonstrated regarding young people's engagement with social media: young people use social media not as a substitute for face-to-face interactions with their peers and the world but rather as a complement. Young people in Egypt did not use social media to avoid gathering with each other or to passively participate in their country's revolution. They used it to encourage gathering with each other for the expressed purpose of actively participating in the revolution. Twitter and Facebook did not start the revolution but they did help generations of Egyptians realize a world that not that long ago would have been impossible to imagine.

Guiding Questions

1. Watkins writes, "While social media was not the catalyst of the Egyptian protest, it was certainly a tool for mobilizing protest." Do you agree? In what ways do you see social media effecting change in the United States and abroad?

2. Watkins joins other media analysts who argue that "young people use social media not as a substitute for face-to-face interactions with their peers and the world but rather as a complement." Do you agree? What social media do you use? For what purposes do you use (or not use) social media? If you do not use social media, why? Does social media ever act as a substitute for face-to-face or other, more immediate interactions for you? Is that a good thing or not?

3. Watkins writes that "Twitter and Facebook did not start the revolution but they did help generations of Egyptians realize a world that not that long ago would have been impossible to imagine." In what ways did

that media help Egyptian youth imagine a different kind of society? In what ways does writing or sharing messages via social media help you imagine a different kind of world? What kind of world change would you most like to imagine?

4. How did the Egyptians' use of social media seem to connect them to particular places (specifically Tahrir Square) in addition to political, cultural, and youth movements? Does your use of social media connect you to—or distance you from—any particular places?

Paths for Further Exploration

1. Like Egypt, China also enforces restrictions on citizens' use of social media. What kinds of effects do you see these restrictions having on not only on Egypt and China but also other countries? Has your own use of social media been restricted by schools, parents, or other authorities? What has this done to your sense of place or sense of community?

2. Throughout the fall of 2011, as we prepared this edition of *Writing Places*, the Occupy Movement (which "started" as "Occupy: Wall Street") spread to cities across the United States, Europe, and beyond. Based on your research, how does the Occupy (or #OWS) Movement's use of various social media technologies compare to what Watkins describes in the Egyptian revolution? In what ways are/were Zuccotti Park (or other Occupy places) similar to or different from Tahrir Square as places that were defined and deployed by and across social media? What media is being used? How has this media been useful to the movement or protest? How has it been harmful?

3. In the civil rights, women's rights, gay rights, and anti-war movements in the United States in the 1960s and 1970s, many public places and private institutions were "occupied," or otherwise became deeply significant as places to these movements. Research some of these movements and their significant places, and write about how social media may have changed the definition of what it means to occupy a place, to use it for a cause.

The Flavor of Hope
Chiori Santiago

Chiori Santiago was a freelance writer and editor who covered visual art, performance, music, and environmental topics in the San Francisco Bay area for twenty years. She wrote a children's novel, Home to Medicine Mountain, *and edited two books,* Voices of Latin Rock: Music from the Streets *and* Reminiscing in Swingtime: Japanese Americans in American Popular Music 1925–1960. *In "Flavor of Hope," which first appeared in the September/October 2003 issue of* Orion *magazine, she highlights efforts of a local organization to improve the health of an urban community by offering organic produce to local residents at affordable prices. In 2007, Santiago died of complications from cancer.*

———————— ✦ ————————

1 Every Tuesday, Farm Fresh Choice makes buying vegetables a main event in west Berkeley, California. Today, with typical flourish, Caroline Loomis, Antonio Rosano, and Karina Serna unfurl bright tablecloths, lay them over folding tables, and fill baskets with organic produce, setting up a miniature market just outside the front door of a childcare center operated by Bay Area Hispano Institute for Advancement (BAHIA). As parents arrive to pick up their children, they stop to buy yams, avocados, and eggs plucked from nests that morning.

2 "¿Puedo cambiarlas?" a woman asks, hoping to trade a few bruised strawberries in the basket she's selected.

3 "Sí, sí, señora," Rosano replies, cheerily offering plump substitutes. "You have to get good ones; the children love them," he adds, shaking the fruit into a plastic bag. "Adios, que te vayas bien," he says in farewell.

4 Rosano is doing more than selling a sweet treat; he may be ensuring a child's future. By bringing organic produce to neighborhoods where it's easier to buy a bottle of malt liquor than a ripe peach, the nonprofit enterprise Farm Fresh Choice encourages residents to replace fast food with the "five a day" servings of fruits and vegetables promoted by a U.S. Department of Agriculture (USDA) campaign. The three-year-old program also provides a market for local farmers of color and boosts the regional economy. And by teaching young workers to manage the business, it is planting the seeds of long-term change.

5 "The basic tenet that drives us is that every person has a right to share the bounty of the Earth equally," says Farm Fresh Choice co-founder Joy Moore. "You can't just go to a child that's homeless and say, 'I'll feed you.' You have to empower people to help themselves; and not just that, but to share themselves."

6 The west and south Berkeley "flatlands" where the BAHIA center is located are less than two miles from the "gourmet

ghetto" where chef Alice Waters taught America to love baby veggies. But the organic bounty hadn't spilled over into this neighborhood. In one eleven-block stretch, according to Moore, liquor stores outnumber produce markets nine to one. A 1999 Berkeley Department of Health report found that residents, predominantly African-American and Latino families, were more prone to nutrition-related ailments than people living in Berkeley's wealthier areas.

"Basically, the study showed that my grandson was likely to die sooner than a white child living in the hills," says Moore, pointing out that obesity, hypertension, and diabetes are statistically higher among African-American families that have little access to fresh, nonprocessed foods.

"American culture was eating us up," adds Martha Cueva, site supervisor of the BAHIA childcare center. "Latin people in their home countries were surrounded by fresh food, but over here we're living in apartments with no plots to farm. Everyone's working, so it's easier to grab fast food when there's no time to go to the store."

The Health Department report jolted Cueva and Moore into action. As members of the Food Policy Council, a loose coalition of local, food-related nonprofits, they were determined to improve food delivery to their neighborhoods and change eating habits in the process.

But first, the council had to identify the barriers that stood   10
between residents and healthier food. A community survey identified three main reasons locals chose Big Macs over baby beets: convenience, cost, and availability. Convenience was the biggest obstacle. Organic food generally wasn't sold in flatlands neighborhoods, and so was inaccessible to seniors or anyone without a car. Community supported agriculture farms (CSAs) could deliver preboxed organic produce to subscribers, but "you can end up with a week's worth of rutabagas you don't know how to cook," says Moore. And that's not convenient either.

Then Moore learned of a USDA grant to fund programs that spread the "five a day" message. What better place to spread that message—and offer a wide choice of fixin's—than a produce stand in front of a childcare center? The parents, Cueva reasoned, would be a captive audience, stopping by routinely with their minds on dinner. "We married our idea to [the USDA's] and came up with Farm Fresh Choice," says Moore.

The four-year grant offered seed money in increasing increments, from $37,000 in 2000 to $45,000 this past year. Local environmental institutions and Alice Waters's Chez Panisse Foundation pitched in as well. Once the BAHIA stand was established, two more produce stands were added: at the Berkeley Youth Association (BYA) and the Young Adult Project. A fourth stand is planned near a south Berkeley senior center.

The grant also removed the cost barrier. The group used the money to subsidize produce sales, offering organic veggies to the public at wholesale prices. A week's worth of "five a day" averages just seven dollars per person through Farm Fresh Choice. And shoppers can use food stamps or a Farm Fresh Choice discount punch card, issued to members in seven dollar increments. About 150 families currently have Farm Fresh Choice memberships, which are offered free of charge. Nonmembers can participate, too, but they're encouraged to sign on as members. Thirty to fifty percent of business comes from nonmember walk-up shopping, Moore estimates.

The issue of supply was resolved when Farm Fresh Choice discovered growers practically in its own backyard. Moore contracted with six farms—all operated by people of color—to provide eggs, juice, and seasonal produce. These items are picked up from the local Tuesday farmers' market in the Farm Fresh Choice van and driven to the neighborhood stands.

15 One of the program's farmers, Richard Firme, grows organic greens and beans on land worked by his Filipino father. Raised on his Mexican mother's home cooking, he believes healthy eating should be a right, not a privilege. To Firme, Farm Fresh Choice seems a good deal all around: "They help me make extra income, they get to give good food to lots of people, and they're showing young kids one way to pull away from the environment they're in, and do something else."

Farm Fresh Choice hires Berkeley Youth Association teens at twelve dollars an hour, trains them, then puts them to work for three months at the BYA stand. When their stint is up, some stay on as regular employees. Moore sees the youthful workers as the key to the project's sustainability. "We use [them] as a sounding board; as a way to come up with fresh ideas to market the program."

The young workers keep journals and attend weekly meetings, where they join in opinionated discussions about global food policy and brainstorm ways to raise the $75,000 a year needed to keep the program going after the grants expire. At the moment, they're deciding whether to charge an annual fee for membership;

they decide instead to try increasing participation through a colorful brochure and door-to-door canvassing.

"You guys are doing work that goes on in corporate board, rooms," Moore says, listening and nodding as a team debates the issues.

Creativity has been key to the program's success. Martha Cueva recalls how they originally had trouble selling greens, which are a staple for many African Americans, but not as common in Latino cooking. "We started cooking classes, and now the Latinos are buying more greens," she says.

Moore, who seems to run on optimism, thinks, Farm Fresh   20 Choice is a stone cast in the middle of a pond: its influence will ripple outward to change the habits of the next generation. "I'll do whatever it takes to plant the seed in their minds," she says. "I'll use guilt, I'll cajole, I'll badger people—if that's what it takes to get them to eat real food."

Guiding Questions

1. How does the introductory paragraph quickly set the scene for the piece?
2. What kinds of research do you think this piece required?
3. How does Santiago imagine an alternate future? What kind of argument does she make?

Paths for Further Exploration

1. Is there a particular community or organization that you would want to research? What is interesting about this community? What is your connection to the community—are you an insider or an outsider?
2. Consider Santiago's essay as well as Alayne Brown's essay "The Effects of Fast Food Restaurants on the Caribbean People." Write an essay that views a place through its food. You might describe a neighborhood, a restaurant, or a cafeteria. What does the food reveal about this place, about this particular community?
3. Santiago offers a hopeful view of the future. Are there other organizations that you know of contributing to a more positive vision of the future?

Tools for Getting Places

This section offers a toolkit of exercises and resources to guide your exploration of places, including brainstorming exercises, tips for interviewing, observation techniques, and helpful online resources.

TECHNIQUES

Getting Oriented

The following brainstorming exercises will help you start thinking about places and hone your descriptive and analytical skills.

1. Find a photograph of a place important to you. Study the image and then begin writing about it:

    - What place is captured in the picture? Where is it? Why is it important?
    - Describe the physical aspects of the place.
    - Describe your emotions, both during the time the photograph was taken and as you study it.
    - Who took the photograph? Who, if anyone, is in the photograph?

    Are there specific answers from this list that you can develop into an essay? As you begin writing about this photograph, remember to concentrate on the details and try to contextualize—not merely retell—a story of this place.

2. Explore your campus and select a persuasive text—a flyer, email petition, party invitation, advertisement, editorial, "roommate wanted" ad, etc. Where did you find the text? What kind of persuasive methods does it use to appeal to its

audience? Think about the community that generated this text and the community that received it—are they the same? What does this text indicate about this particular place and its communities?

3. Find a copy of the campus catalog/application package and study the pictures, statistics, and student testimonies. Determine how your college is "selling" itself; think about its persuasive techniques and its audience. Then visit your campus's website and compare the information, format, audience, and so forth. Do you feel the institution's representation of itself resonates with your understanding of this place?

4. Choose a restaurant and "read" it: Start with the specific by considering its location, interior, music, arrangement of tables, and other details. Then step back and analyze why this place exists, and what it reflects about society. Reread Julia Corbett's "Robotic Iguanas" and think about how the function and purpose of restaurants has changed in the last few decades and what those changes reflect about society.

5. Tear out a sheet of paper and draw a map of your hometown, current location, or where you imagine you'll be in the future. Draw the places that are most significant to you: your house, your friends' houses, a favorite hang-out, your high school, and so forth. Spend ten minutes or so drawing. Then take one of the places on your map and write about it. Describe it in as much detail as you can, from the physical description of the place to the emotional attachment you have to it. Why is this place on your map? How does it connect to the other places? If you were to write a research paper about this place, what angle might you take? Whom do you associate with this place?

INTERVIEWING

Locating Interview Subjects

- People you already know (parents, neighbors, roommates, coworkers) can be great sources of information. Consider the place you're writing about and what kind of information you seek. If you're experiencing a new place, can you interview an "insider," someone who knows the place, its culture, and its patterns well? If you are an insider, perhaps you'd like to interview a newcomer, someone who can notice customs and details that have become commonplace to you.

- Discuss: If you're hoping to interview someone you don't know well, what should you consider about asking permission and requesting the person's time? What does it require to be a good and respectful questioner and listener?

What Kind of Questions to Ask?

- **"Tell me about . . .":** the broadest question. Might prompt your interviewee to talk widely and explore aspects of a place you wouldn't consider. Good opener.
- **"Who, What, When, Where, Why?":** More directed questions but still open-ended. Good for getting specific but broad information.
- **Yes/No:** Narrow questions function to clarify a point, to obtain specific information. Good for follow-ups or seeking out specific information.

Recording an Interview

There is no right way to record an interview; decide the advantages and disadvantages for yourself:

- *Tape or Digital Recorder:* Allows you to focus on the discussion without struggling to write it all down. Requires transcribing later, which can be time consuming, but you'll have exact words. Some people feel inhibited when being recorded, and you'll need to have and be able to use the technology.
- *Taking Notes:* Many of the world's best interviewers don't record but listen and converse, scribbling down important words or phrases as the person talks. Immediately after, they add to those notes to make up a transcript.
- *Email:* Email and instant messaging (IM) technology allow for text-based interviews, which can be useful if interviewing someone at a distance; plus, the transcript comes ready-made. It's more work for the interviewees, however, and you don't get to hear their tone or sense their emotions and physical presence from working solely in print.
- *Online Video Chat:* If you want or need to interview someone not physically close to you and have the technology, consider conducting an interview over a live video chat. Be sure to think through how the format of an interview may affect the results you get *before* you start conducting it. Some video chat

programs will let you record the video so you can refer to it later; as with any recording, always be sure to get your subject's permission and to be clear about how you will—and will not—use the recorded video.

What to Do with Interview Information?

There are several possibilities . . .

1. *Summarize* (with no quoting): Best used to convey information that might not be all that interesting to read in a quote.
   - *Example:* Kaitlin told me about how working here has helped her meet more people around town and understand how the community works together. Certain town organizations want tickets to their upcoming events to be available at the Gourmet because of the large volume of people passing through. Currently, the PTA asked the shop to sell the Annual Wine Tasting tickets to customers.
2. *Quote a Key Word or Phrase:* Best used to capture the flavor or uniqueness of the speaker's tone.
   - *Example:* Dennis asserted that the weekdays were filled with "businesspeople and school teachers" quickly bustling to get to work.
3. *Integrate a Quote into Part of a Sentence:* Best used to grammatically fit in the speaker's words as the subject or predicate of a sentence.
   - *Example:* Martha quickly asserted, "this place wouldn't work as a chain." Too many people feel this atmosphere is better than an "impersonal store like a CVS."
4. *Quote Complete Sentences:*
   - *Example:* "Walmarts and Starbucks replacing mom-and-pop stores is a reality," I said. "Could those sweeps affect the Gourmet?" "Definitely not," he said with no hesitation. "There exists a certain ritualism here. Everyone has their own niche."
5. *Quote a Longer Block of Text:*
   - *Example:* Tom remembers the early days of the Gourmet:

When this place opened, you could buy a coffee for 59 cents. A bagel was 75. Everyone knew everyone. The postman, boy, he was a crabby man, but he always took his break here and sat in that corner warming up on cold mornings. There were no Starbucks back then.

Exercise: Working with an Interview Transcript

Questions to Consider

1. What kind of angle or approach to this place might one draw from the following interview transcript—what is the most interesting idea or aspect of this place, according to the interviewee?
2. Underline the five best or most useful phrases or sentences in this piece.
3. Write one sentence incorporating some part of this transcript in a way that you might do so in your essay.

Paula Mathieu, November 2, 2011:

What I like about Old Cambridge Baptist Church is that its looks are deceiving. From the outside, it seems like a stately, old and maybe even stodgy New England Church. I mean, it's right next door to the Harvard Inn. But then when you step inside, you see a whole different world, way more eclectic and funky, way more connected to the world, you know? I mean, step in the vestibule and you might see ballet dancers from the Jose Matteo Dance Company preparing for their evening performance. Kids from the neighborhood can take dance lessons there too. But the ballet company shares space with Irv's Sunday morning Church service. It's not a stodgy, high-church place at all. It's worn looking—could use good paint job.

And then the basement, wow, it's like a beehive of activity. I remember the first day I walked down the stairs there. Had to duck my head so I wouldn't hit it on the hanging pipes. The place was so dark, with narrow passages. I didn't think too much at the time, I dunno, it's funny how things change when you've been going for a while and then you look back and boy they were different than before, do you know what I'm saying? Anyhow, the basement houses so many different charity and activist organizations—*Spare Change News*, which is a newspaper sold by homeless people as a positive alternative to begging; Bread and Jams, a homeless day shelter; Solutions at Work, a jobs program and furniture bank. Those are the groups I know the most about. But then there's also the Gay and Lesbian Task Force and the Ethiopian Women's Group. But the whole place is a network of important activity, of real life, where people can go and get help if they need it. To me that's what makes OCBC a great Church—it really is of its community and plays an active role in it. Homeless people, dancers, churchgoers, gays and lesbians, Ethiopian women all can find a home there. It's not just a Sunday operation, but it caters to its "flock" seven days a week in a variety of ways.

How to List Interviews in Your Works Cited

Mathieu, Paula. Personal Interview. 2 November 2011.

OBSERVING A PLACE AND TAKING NOTES

Evenly divide a sheet of paper vertically. In the right column, perhaps using bullets to denote each observation, write down everything you observe: the smells of a place, the people around you, and so on. Be as observant of your surroundings as possible, even if the place is familiar to you. Write down everything you can, but also take time to pause and look around.

You may want to use your smartphone, digital camera, or other photo or video recording device to help you capture the place you're observing, but be sure to experience and observe the place primarily through your own senses, not filtered by technology or distracted by managing a recording. It might be a good idea just to take some brief supplemental video or photos only to help jog your memory later, and to keep most of your detailed observations to your eyes and note-taking.

Later, when you return to your room, sit down with these pages of observations and carefully review each item. As you read them, you'll likely begin to make some connections and analytical observations and ask some questions. In the left column, begin writing down these connections. For instance, here are some observations and conclusions about a student athletic complex:

Some students describe the complex as one of the most intimidating places on campus.	It's 12:00 and the place is very crowded
	Many female students using the Stairmaster
Women who constantly exercise on these machines are called Elliptical Nazis.	
	Instructors work out early in the morning

	Athletes use the facility throughout the day
How much does this place contribute to the eating disorders epidemic on campus?	Mostly women using the facility
What other campus spaces do faculty and students inhabit outside of the classroom?	
Are these facilities safe?	Some of the equipment looks dated
I wish I had noticed the number of females versus males; I'll notice this detail the next time I visit.	
Whom can I talk to about plans for renovating the complex?	

Some of the connections in the left column could lead to a number of interesting essays. As you review your observations, continue making connections and thinking in broader terms about your place. The left column will help you determine what details you can enhance, summarize, or leave out completely. You will want your descriptive essays to be a balance of concrete observations and abstract connections and conclusions—in other words, a balance of information from both columns.

RESPONDING TO CLASSMATES' ESSAYS ON PLACE

The following questions can help you respond to classmates' place writing. Write at least a few sentences addressing each of the following topic areas.

Angle

Has the writer crafted a clear angle or interesting hook that interests the reader in the piece? What is the angle? What could the writer do to engage the audience right from the beginning?

Observational Writing Skills

Has the writer clearly evoked the place or culture he or she wants to write about? Is the place clearly described, with interesting details that point to significant things or help to say something significant about it? Does this writing appeal to your senses as a reader? Is there enough description? Too much? What could help you understand and experience the place more fully?

Inside versus Outside Knowledge and Audience Awareness

How is the writer's status as insider, outsider, or both, treated? If the writer is an insider, does he or she provide enough background and set-up for readers who are outsiders? What further information would be useful? If the writer is an outsider, does he or she convey enthusiasm and curiosity about the topic? What further information would be useful? As a reader, is there anything (terms, concepts, places) you don't fully understand or want to know more about? What additional research or information would you find useful?

Interviews

What role does the interview(s) play? Has the writer interviewed one or more interesting informants about the place or culture? Would more questions for that informant or questions of other informants help clarify or expand the piece? What central questions have been answered through the use of the interviews? What questions do you wish the writer might have asked? Is enough material quoted directly from the interviews? Too much? Do you get a vivid sense of the interviewees? What could the writer do to give a clearer sense of the informant(s)?

Tone and Writing Style

Does the piece have any humor in it? At what points in the paper do you think humor might be appropriate? Are the overall tone and writing style concise, engaging, and a pleasure to read? What revisions should the writer consider regarding writing style and tone?

For the Reader

What aspects of this paper might be useful to you in revising your own paper?

TOOLS FOR EXPLORING

Location-based Applications

The explosive growth of mobile applications such as smartphones in recent years means it is more and more common for us to have access to information about a place while in that place (or even before getting there), creating a virtual lens through which we now view and experience locations. Here are just three examples of these types of applications and some popular application names.

- **Local review sites** like Yelp (www.yelp.com) offer a crowd-sourced collection of people's opinions regarding the businesses and services they frequent.
- **Augmented reality** applications add a digital layer of information over physical places. Many smartphone applications now allow users to look through their phone's viewfinder and see links to reviews floating on top of the actual places they see around them.
- **Location-based social networks** like foursquare (www.foursquare.com), Facebook Places (www.facebook.com), and Twitter location listings (www.twitter.com) allow users to "check in" to the physical places where they are and let the people in their networks know where they are and have been.

Accessing these applications while exploring a physical location can provide insights into the subjective experience of places people have while going about their daily lives.

Networked Scavenger Hunts

Geocaching and Letterboxing are variations on the age-old scavenger hunt, now augmented with online maps and mobile devices, and they offer a fun framework for finding new places and exploring familiar places in new ways.

- Geocaching: www.geocaching.com
- Letterboxing: www.letterboxing.org

BIOREGIONAL QUIZZES

Bioregional quizzes help you evaluate how much you know about the environment around you, and can be prompts for further research and discovery. "Where You At?" is one of the best-known bioregional quizzes and has been in use since 1981. It's currently archived in pdf form here: www.drs.wisc.edu/documents/ies112/ Where%20You%20At%20Quiz.pdf.

Don't be too discouraged if you don't know many of the answers at first, or even after a little research. Students from rural areas (or some countries other than the United States) are likely to have an easier time with it, but even they will be challenged. Very few people other than full-time scientists and/or totally committed and engaged environmentalists know the answers to all of these questions. But part of the point of a quiz like this is that fifty or 100 years ago, many more people would have had a much easier time answering these questions.

Where You At? A Bioregional Quiz

Developed by Leonard Charles, Jim Dodge, Lynn Milliman, and Victoria Stockley.
First appeared in *Coevolution Quarterly* 32 (Winter 1981): 1.

1. Trace the water you drink from precipitation to tap.
2. How many days until the moon is full? (Slack of 2 days allowed.)
3. What soil series are you standing on?
4. What was the total rainfall in your area last year (July–June)? (Slack: 1 inch for every 20 inches.)
5. When was the last time a fire burned in your area?
6. What were the primary subsistence techniques of the culture that lived in your area before you?
7. Name 5 edible plants in your region and their season(s) of availability.
8. From what direction do winter storms generally come in your region?
9. Where does your garbage go?
10. How long is the growing season where you live?
11. On what day of the year are the shadows the shortest where you live?
12. When do the deer rut in your region, and when are the young born?
13. Name five grasses in your area. Are any of them native?
14. Name five resident and five migratory birds in your area.

15. What is the land use history of where you live?
16. What primary ecological event/process influenced the land-form where you live? (Bonus special: what's the evidence?)
17. What species have become extinct in your area?
18. What are the major plant associations in your region?
19. From where you're reading this, point north.
20. What spring wildflower is consistently among the first to bloom where you live?

Scoring

0–3: You have your head up your ass.

4–7: It's hard to be in two places at once when you're not anywhere at all.

8–12: A firm grasp of the obvious.

13-16: You're paying attention.

17–19: You know where you're at.

20: You not only know where you're at, you know where it's at.

Here are some supplemental bioregional activities and questions:

1. Trace the flow of water (especially run-off from storms and watering lawns) from your home to an ocean or a large underground aquifer.
2. Choose a favorite meal and trace the ingredients backward as far as you can go, noting how many states or countries are involved.
3. Trace the path of the energy that powers your home or residence hall from its source to you. What pollutants are released along this pathway and by what processes?
4. What are three environmental issues facing your home area and/or your school's area?
5. What is the elevation above sea level where you live now?
6. Name seven trees common in your area.
7. Name seven mammals common in your area.
8. Name seven birds common in your area. Which are year-round residents? Which are summer residents, and where do they migrate to in the winter?
9. Name the three major waterways or bodies of water in your region.
10. How many full constellations can you see on moonless nights in your area?

LOCAL KNOWLEDGE

Local Organizations

Local chambers of commerce and historical societies (most have websites) can be good resources (along with the reference materials in your campus library) for research into local places. Architectural records, zoning laws, historical development statistics, land use histories and much, much more can be found through these organizations. Most colleges and universities also have archive collections of materials deemed important to the history of your school (and often of the surrounding areas). These collections often include amazing and valuable records of the physical and cultural history of your school, and college and university archivists are usually thrilled to talk to students and help them with research projects. Talk to your professor and/or a reference librarian about getting access to these materials.

Neighborhood Writing Groups

Groups like the Chicago Neighborhood Writing Alliance (www .jot.org/index.html), sponsors of the *Journal of Ordinary Thought*, and others like them around the country encourage writers from all walks of life to write about what's important to them. Often, these authors engage concepts of place in provocative ways, coming from perspectives not always found on colleges and universities. Check community websites in your own area to find similar writing communities.

Hyperlocal News and Blogging

It has become common for people to use blogs and other user-driven websites to share news and other information about local places. Sometimes this fills the gap created by the loss of local news outlets, but it also takes advantage of the opportunities web technologies provide to create and share information easily.

Place-based blogs and sites that aggregate local news can be useful sources of information if you are researching a locale that might not be covered by traditional news sources. So-called "micro-blog" functions like Twitter or foursquare's comments can be useful for tracking what's happening in a place *as* it happens, and for tracking people's reactions to that place and its events as people discover them. You'll need to evaluate sources to decide whether they are credible and what biases might inform their writing, but these can often provide a rich ground-level perspective on what's happening in a particular place and what it's like to live there.

Some examples:

- Patch: www.patch.com
- Everyblock: www.everyblock.com
- Placeblogger: http://placeblogger.com
- GlobalTweets: http:/globaltweets.com

Citizen Science

We often think of science as something that gets done only by highly trained professionals in universities or research labs. But there is a long tradition of projects that invite ordinary citizens to contribute to scientific knowledge without having to be formally trained in science. With the rise of the Internet and sophisticated mobile devices, new tools allow a wide variety of people to contribute to tree inventories, track radiation, record temperatures, document wildlife, and perform many other research and data-gathering tasks wherever they live, with little to no training. Examples:

1. Galaxy Zoo: www.galaxyzoo.org
2. Cornell Lab of Ornithology: www.birds.cornell.edu/citsci
3. Audubon Society Christmas Bird Count: http://birds.audubon.org/cbc
4. The WildLab: www.thewildlab.org
5. Project Noah: www.projectnoah.org

Maps and Geographic Data

Maps have long been a resource for representing places, both as sources of information and as rhetorical tools for making arguments about the meaning of place and, through borders and names, the meaning(s) and identities of those who live in various places. In recent years, maps have also become ways of visualizing data related to place, often referred to as Geographic Information Systems (GIS).

In your writing, maps can be useful for supporting your arguments about place, or they can themselves be subjects of rhetorical analysis.

College and University Libraries

A great place to start in looking for maps and geographic data is to check with the library at your university or college. Often librarians will specialize in GIS and/or map resources and can offer valuable assistance in finding information related to your interests.

Interactive Maps and Aerial Views

- Google Maps (http://maps.google.com) and Bing Maps (www .bing.com/maps)
- Google Earth: www.google.com/earth

Historical Maps

- David Rumsey Map Collection: www.davidrumsey.com

Public Geographic Data

- USA.gov: www.usa.gov/Topics/Maps.shtml
- U.S. government map data: http://geo.data.gov/
- EPA Enviromapper: www.epa.gov/emefdata/em4ef.home

CREDITS

Arrieta, Rose. "A Nation Divided," from *Orion* (Vol. 22, No. 4, July/Aug. 2003, pp. 34–41). Reprinted by permission of George Washington Williams Fellowship.

Brown, Alyne. "The Effects of Fast Food Restaurants on the Caribbean People." By permission of the author.

Carey, Katherine. "Say yah to da U.P., eh?" By permission of the author.

Casassa, Andrea J. "The Coffee Shop." By permission of the author.

Corbett, Julia. "Robotic Iguanus," from *Orion* (Sept./Oct. 2003). Reprinted by permission of Julia Corbett.

Diaz, Junot. "Apocalypse." Originally published in May/June 2011 *Boston Review*.

Dunn, Robin E. "King's Chapel and Burying Ground." By permission of the author.

Fabbri, Salvatore M. "Scientific Applications." By permission of the author.

Fletcher, Ron. "By Dawn's Early Light," 2003. *Boston Daily Globe*. Reproduced with permission of Ron Fletcher. Ron Fletcher writes and teaches in Boston, Massachusetts.

Harden, Blaine. "A History in Concrete," from *Preservation Magazine* (Nov./Dec. 1996). Courtesy of Blaine Harden.

Herron, Jerry. "Borderland/Borderama/Detroit." Originally published on July 6, 2010 on *Places: Forum of Design for the Public Realm* (www.designobserver.com) http://places.designobserver.com/feature/borderland-borderama-detroit-part-1/13778/.

Lerner, Jonathan. "How Urban Planning Can Improve Public Health." Originally published on April 28, 2010 on Miller-McCune.com

Lindgren, Tim. "On Being from Fargo." First appeared on author's website (http://www.whereproject.org/node/view/96), published on May 21, 2004, under a Creative Commons license (Attribution-NonCommercial_ShareAlike 2.0). Reprinted by permission of the author.

Madlock, Felicia. "Where I'm From" is reprinted with the permission of the author. Originally published by the Neighborhood Writing Alliance in the *Journal of Ordinary Thought* (Fall 2002).

Odom, Amanda. "An examination of living through enjoyment: Live-action role-play," 2009. *Transformative Works and Cultures*, no. 2.

Owens, Derek. "Where I'm Writing From." By permission of the author.

Rothman, Rodney. "My Fake Job." Reprinted by permission of Collins McCormick Literary Agency.

Savage, Kevin. "Elm City." By permission of the author.

Schlosser, Eric. "On the Range," from *Fast Food Nation: The Dark Side of the All-American Meal* by Eric Schlosser. Copyright © 2001 by Eric Schlosser. Reprinted by permission of Houghton Mifflin Company. All rights reserved.

Sedaris, David. "The Ship-Shape," from *Dress Your Family in Corduroy and Denim*. Copyright © 2004 by David Sedaris. Reprinted by permission of Little, Brown and Company, Inc.

Solnit, Rebecca. "The Most Radical Thing You Can Do," from *Orion Magazine* (Nov./Dec. 2008). Courtesy of Rebecca Solnit.

Solnit, Rebecca. "The Silence of the Lambswool Cardigans," from *Orion Magazine* (Jul./Aug. 2003). Courtesy of Rebecca Solnit.

St. John, Warren. "Refugees Find Hostility and Hope on Soccer Field," 2007. *The New York Times* (Jan. 21).

Watkins, Craig. *The Young and the Digital*. 2010. Beacon Press.

Wheaton, Kimberly. "Mom and the Kitchen." By permission of the author.